The

# EVERYTHING Parenting a Teenager Book

Dear Reader:

The myth persists that teens are more influenced by their peers than their parents. Nothing could be further from the truth! Although teens do heed friends' advice about clothes, hair, and music, research indicates that their basic value system remains closer to their parents'. Moreover, when it comes to questions about dating, sex, drugs, alcohol, work, and school, teens say that they prefer to talk to their parents. Unfortunately, they also say that they usually end up seeking advice from their friends. The big question is why?

The answer is that when teens express an interest in something that contains any kind of risk, the protective instincts of their parents kick in. They issue warnings, moralize, lecture, set limits, and threaten consequences. Such tactics may deter younger children from placing themselves in harm's way, but teens are more likely to tune out or rebel. If they do the latter, instead of avoiding whatever their parents consider dangerous, they leap into it.

The challenge of parenting a teen is relinquishing the familiar role of protector and becoming a thoughtful mentor and loving guide. That is easier said than done. Letting go of control is scary if not down-right terrifying. Unlearning old patterns of communicating and mastering new ways of relating require practice, practice, practice. The struggle, however, is worthwhile. Efforts to protect teens may keep them safe today, but with lots of mentoring and guidance they learn how to protect themselves. That keeps them safe for a lifetime.

Sincerely,

Dr. L Somm

## The EVERYTHING® Series

### Editorial

| | |
|---|---|
| Publishing Director | Gary M. Krebs |
| Managing Editor | Kate McBride |
| Copy Chief | Laura MacLaughlin |
| Acquisitions Editor | Bethany Brown |
| Production Editor | Jamie Wielgus |

### Production

| | |
|---|---|
| Production Director | Susan Beale |
| Production Manager | Michelle Roy Kelly |
| Series Designers | Daria Perreault<br>Colleen Cunningham |
| Cover Design | Paul Beatrice<br>Frank Rivera |
| Layout and Graphics | Colleen Cunningham<br>Rachael Eiben<br>Michelle Roy Kelly<br>John Paulhus<br>Daria Perreault<br>Erin Ring |
| Series Cover Artist | Barry Littmann |

# THE EVERYTHING® PARENTING A TEENAGER BOOK

A survival guide for parents!

Linda Sonna, Ph.D.

Adams Media
Avon, Massachusetts

An Everything® Series Book.


Published by Adams Media, an F+W Publications Company
57 Littlefield Street, Avon, MA 02322 U.S.A.
*www.adamsmedia.com*

ISBN: 1-59337-035-0
Printed in the United States of America.

J I H G F E D C B A

**Library of Congress Cataloging-in-Publication Data**
Sonna, Linda
The everything parenting a teenager book / Linda Sonna.
p. cm.
(An everything series book)
ISBN 1-59337-035-0
1. Parent and teenager. 2. Parenting. I. Title: Parenting a teenager book. II. Title. III. Series: Everything series.

HQ799.15.S675 2004
649'.125—dc22
2003020727

This publication is designed to provide accurate and authoritative information with regard to the subject matter covered. It is sold with the understanding that the publisher is not engaged in rendering legal, accounting, or other professional advice. If legal advice or other expert assistance is required, the services of a competent professional person should be sought.
—From a *Declaration of Principles* jointly adopted by a Committee of the American Bar Association and a Committee of Publishers and Associations

The information contained in this book is designed for educational purposes only and is not intended to provide medical advice or other professional services. The information should not be used for diagnosis, treatment, or as a substitute for professional care. If your child has a medical or behavioral problem or you suspect such a possibility, consult your health care provider. All case studies are composites designed to reflect common behaviors and situations. Information has been changed to protect parents' and children's identities.

Many of the designations used by manufacturers and sellers to distinguish their products are claimed as trademarks. Where those designations appear in this book and Adams Media was aware of a trademark claim, the designations have been printed with initial capital letters.

*This book is available at quantity discounts for bulk purchases.*
*For information, call 1-800-872-5627.*

# Contents

**Acknowledgments / ix**
**Top Ten Tips for Strengthening Teenagers to Withstand Peer Pressure / x**
**Introduction / xi**

1 **The Teen Scene / 1**
The Secret Life of Teens **2** • Meet the New Generation **3** • Teen Talk **4** • Teens' Other Family **4** • The New Morality **6** • Peer Power **8** • Teens and the Tube **10**

2 **Inside the Teen Mind / 13**
Teen Emotionality **14** • The Roller Coaster Years **14** • Emotions 101 **16** • Cheering Them Up **16** • Settling Them Down **18** • Teaching Anger Management **19** • Parents as Teachers **23**

3 **Teen Ages and Stages / 25**
Through the Years **26** • Surviving Junior High **26** • "Freaked-Out" Freshmen **27** • Sophomore Slump **28** • Jumping Juniors **30** • Senioritis **32** • Life after High School **33** • Finding Themselves **34**

4 **The Parenting Challenge / 37**
Letting Go **38** • The Parental Midlife Crisis **39** • Defining Your Goals **39** • Preparing Teens for Independence **41** • Teaching Life Skills **42** • Teaching Interpersonal Problem-Solving **44** • Teaching Conflict Resolution **45**

5 **Family Relationships / 49**
Sibling Relationships **50** • Girls and Moms **51** • Boys and Mothers **55** • Teens and Dads **57** • Family Solutions **61**

**Communicating with Teens / 63**

Reading Between the Lines **64** • Time to Talk **64** • Conversation Starters **66** • Responding to Teen Dramas **67** • Listening Skills **69** • Conversational Do's and Don'ts **70** • Responding to Teen Confessions **72**

**Disciplining Teens / 73**

Controlling Your Teen **74** • Teens as Individuals **74** • The Punishment Problem **76** • The Blame Game **78** • Teen Bullying of Parents **78** • Logical Consequences **79** • Respect! **81** • Protecting Your Teen **83** • Creative Problem-Solving **83**

**Teen Dating / 85**

Dating Dilemmas **86** • Young "Studs" and "Sirens" **89** • Dating Stages **91** • Teen Love Connections **92** • Dating Readiness **93** • Foolish Kids, Wise Choices **95**

**Teens on Wheels / 97**

A Parent's Nightmare **98** • Rights of Passage **98** • Experience as Teacher **101** • Dollars and Cents **104** • Accidents Happen **105** • Car Troubles **107** • Hard Lessons the Easy Way **109**

**School Daze / 111**

When Teens Won't Study **112** • Diagnosing School Problems **112** • School Conferences **114** • Instituting a Home Study Hall **115** • A Real Motivational Boost **117** • Overachievers **118** • Selecting Classes **120** • Solving Social Problems **120**

## 11 Extracurricular Fun / 125

Teen Boredom 126 • The Benefits of Extracurricular Involvements 126 • High School Sports 127 • Other School Activities 128 • Community Clubs and Organizations 129 • Private Lessons 132 • Something for Everyone 132 • Conquering the Summertime Blues 133 • Signs of Burnout 135 • Teen Hobbies 136

## 12 Teen Fashion / 137

Fashion Offenses 138 • Family Issues 140 • Separation Issues 141 • Peer Pressure 144 • Problematic Attire 145 • The Person Inside 146

## 13 On the Job / 147

Balancing Work and School 148 • Teen Employment 149 • Job Problems! 150 • The First "Real" Job 152 • Parents as Job Consultants 153 • Motivating Your Teen to Work 154 • The Best Summer Jobs 156 • Job Resources for Teens 158

## 14 Health and Wellness / 161

Teen Weight Watchers 162 • Teen Diets 163 • Vitamins and Minerals 166 • Teens and Sleep 167 • Sexual Health 169 • Teen Hygiene 171 • Immunizations for Adolescents 173 • Immune System Safeguards 173 • Happier Is Healthier 174

## 15 The College Maze / 175

College-Bound High School Students 176 • Early Planning 176 • College Entrance Tests 181 • Affording College 182 • Choosing a College 184 • Opportunity Unlimited 185

## 16 Family Problems / 187

Family Disruptions 188 • Parental Arguments 189 • Teens and Divorce 190 • Part-time Parenting 193 • Single Parenting 194 • Single Parents and Dating 196 • Solving Family Problems 197

17 **Juvenile Offenders / 199**
On the Wrong Path **200** • Boys Will Be Boys **201** • Delinquency Risk Factors **201** • The Parent Factor **205** • Solving Authority Problems **206** • Teaching Honesty **207** • Teaching Accountability **208** • A Potpourri of Solutions **210**

18 **Mental Health Issues / 213**
Teens and Depression **214** • Teen Suicide **216** • Schizophrenia **219** • Bipolar Disorder **221** • Self-Mutilation **222** • Attention Deficit Disorder **224**

19 **Teens, Drugs, and Alcohol / 227**
From Experimentation to Addiction **228** • Substance Use, Abuse, and Addiction **230** • Nicotine **232** • Alcohol and Teens **232** • The Marijuana Conundrum **233** • Heavy Hitting Drugs **236** • The Family Medicine Chest **238** • The Long Road Back **239**

20 **Beyond "Just Say No" / 241**
Peer Pressure **242** • Thoughts Versus Actions **244** • Responding to Teen Wildness **246** • When Logic Fails **248** • Parents in Charge! **251** • Teen Rebels **251** • Back on Track **253**

21 **The "Adult" / 255**
Home for the Holidays **256** • Neglected Parents **256** • Worldly-Wise Teens **257** • Boomerang Kids **259** • Tough Love **261** • Education for Independence **262** • A New Relationship **265**

**Appendix A** • Resources for Parents / **267**
**Appendix B** • Resources for Teens / **273**
**Appendix C** • Getting Teens to Do Chores in Seven Easy Steps / **277**
**Index / 283**

# Acknowledgments

Special thanks to Debi Guitierrez, Lois Mark, Jessica Quintana, Tanya Sonna, Bethany Brown, Michele Potter, Helen Dixon, Mary Gugino, Phaedra Greenwood, Ron Chavez, John Millerman, Jan Abeyta, Kathleen Knoth, Roy Mullins, Colleen and Tom Finley, Zion Gia Archuleta, Diane Gilliard, Margie Sipple, and Mark Sonna.

## Top Ten Tips for Strengthening Teenagers *to Withstand Peer Pressure*

1. Respect your teen's desire for friends and social acceptance so he will view you as a trustworthy confidante.
2. Discuss the costs and benefits of popularity, and let your teen know that true friends wouldn't encourage her to compromise her values.
3. Suggest that your teenager say, "I can't go—I'm grounded" whenever he needs to avoid a troublesome situation without losing face.
4. Encourage your teenager to stand up for people, causes, and ideas she believes in, and praise her for daring to be different.
5. Welcome your teen's friends into your home, including those you dislike, so you can supervise and get to know them.
6. Help your teen learn from your mistakes by relating your own struggles with peer pressure.
7. Give reasons for your decisions. Teaching your teen to obey without question will predispose her to conform to the dictates of her peers.
8. Teach your teenager how to disagree with you respectfully. If he knows that he can stand up to peers without alienating them, he may do it!
9. Strengthen your teen's ties to positive peers by encouraging participation in school, community, and religious activities.
10. Spend quality time with your teen. A warm parent/teen relationship is the best protection against peer pressure.

# *Introduction*

▶ WHILE THE TEENAGED YEARS are notoriously difficult for American children, in most cultures of the world, teenagers get along just fine. Even in the United States, this age group's problems are only a few generations old.

Before the 1930s, most American students began working full-time soon after their thirteenth birthday. Once they were contributing to the family via paychecks and housework, they were considered adults and treated accordingly. When the Great Depression sapped the nation of jobs, masses of students stayed in school. For young people, these years were considered the happiest time of life since they could postpone adult responsibilities. However, students soon discovered the downside. While other young adults were stalking dinner in the forests, tackling full-time jobs, or starting families of their own, students were still being told when to wash their hands, do their homework, and go to bed as if they were still kids.

Finding themselves trapped between two worlds, adolescents turned to one another for companionship and support. As they bonded around their common interests and problems in the 1940s, they created their own music, fashions, and dance. In the 1950s, Hollywood provided movies and stars for them to admire and emulate, and young people invented slang and nicknamed themselves "teenagers." Teen culture picked up speed, and by the mid-1960s young people had their own way of doing everything, from styling hair to chewing gum. They embraced a different set of values, too, and the generation gap was officially born.

In the 1970s and 1980s, the face of childhood changed as mothers flooded into the workforce and couples surged into the divorce courts. The day-care generation spent more time with peers than parents, and when these youngsters became teens, the generation gap widened to an abyss. In the 1980s, the abyss became a canyon as video games, VCRs, and the television increasingly isolated children. By the 1990s, children averaged less than two hours directly communicating with parents each week and thirty hours watching television. On it, they learned about the evils of parents, who the shows depicted as inept bunglers, and the glories of streetwise kids, who were typically cast as heroes. Regard for adults hit an all-time low, and by the time teens could "just say no," their parents couldn't get them to say yes to much of anything. At the dawn of the new millennium, pagers, cell phones, Internet chatlines, and instant messaging enabled teens to reach out and touch like-minded peers 24-7. The older generation's goal in life, it seemed to teens, was to squelch their fun.

The good news is that hormones and stress don't drive teen drama; history proves that adolescence doesn't have to be a difficult time of life. The secret to parenting members of this age group is to accept that they are adults and to treat them accordingly. That can be hard when your teenager isn't pulling his weight at home or contributing financially. It can seem impossible when her judgment, emotional control, and behavior are on a par with the average toddler. But it is possible. The first step is to trade the line, "Since you're acting like a two-year-old, I will treat you like one," for "Since you are a young adult, I will treat you like one regardless of how childishly you act." The second step is not to react to bouts of childish behavior by behaving childishly yourself.

Ironically, the headlong race to grow up usually ends once parents accept that their teenager has crossed the finish line into adulthood. The swagger and attitude disappear. Confessions of feeling young and uncertain follow, along with requests for advice, guidance, and limits. Most parents are amazed to see how quickly these young adults do what had previously seemed impossible: They act their age!

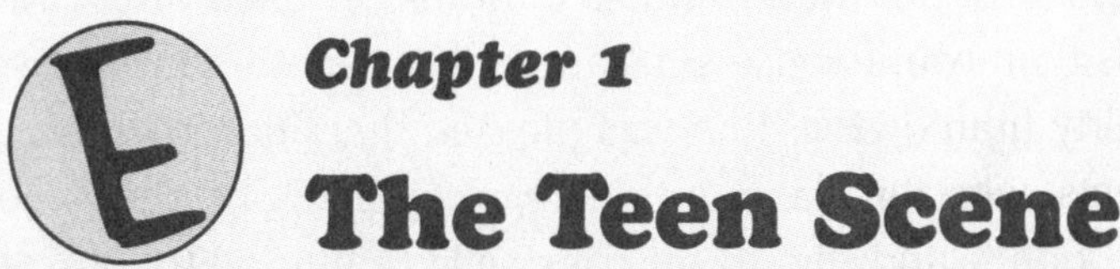

# Chapter 1
# The Teen Scene

Stand among a group of teens in a mammoth high school or large junior high, at a medium-sized party or at a small street corner gathering, and you are likely to be amazed at how different the clothes and conversations are from when you were that age. Much more has changed than fashion and slang. This generation grew up in a very different world and has its own take on life.

## The Secret Life of Teens

Rita's daughter hadn't been very happy in junior high but had since blossomed. Her mother was delighted that Sharon was turning into such a fine young woman and conscientious student. Her goal was to become a teacher. Since she belonged to Students Against Destructive Decision-Making and none of her friends smoked, drank, or used drugs, Rita didn't worry that Sharon would abuse substances. Now that she was a sophomore and had begun dating, Rita was pleased that Sharon chose polite, responsible boys. Sharon was not perfect, of course. She squabbled with her younger brother and had to be constantly reminded to turn down the volume on her music. Her room was a perpetual disaster area, and getting her to pick up after herself was a daily struggle. Still, Rita considered her daughter's problems minor.

While teen gang members who commit horrific crimes make the newspaper and television headlines, news about stunning teen accomplishments lie buried in the back pages or simply go unreported. Honor roll students, athletes, writers, artists, musicians, and community volunteers abound. Don't judge an entire generation by the horror stories that get most of the press.

One day Rita stacked up all of the books and papers that Sharon had left on the living room coffee table so she could dust. The stack toppled over and as Rita was picking everything up, she saw the F-word written in Sharon's handwriting in big letters on a piece of paper.

**Should I read the personal journal my son leaves around the house?**
Troubled teenagers sometimes leave clues for their parents, hoping they will intervene, but consider carefully before violating your teen's privacy. Once trust is broken, it's hard to regain.

The obscenity Sharon had written was on a note to a classmate. In it, Sharon called her English teacher an obscene name and made lewd comments about a classmate. Worst of all, she talked about rushes and dime bags like an addict. Her mother was trembling when she finished reading. Her daughter sounded like a promiscuous druggie! Was Sharon living a double life? It certainly looked that way.

## Meet the New Generation

As a conscientious parent, you have probably taught your child that drugs are dangerous and illegal, and that good kids who care about their health just say no. If so, you may be amazed to catch the lingering scents of marijuana and tobacco wafting from the clothes of clean-cut honor roll students. These days, class presidents and cheerleaders chat about ecstasy, speed, and LSD as easily as gang members. Fortunately, that doesn't mean that everyone is an addict or even a casual user.

Just as there is more talk than action when it comes to sex in teen circles, young people often exaggerate how much liquor they drink and inflate their drug use. While many teens do more than their parents know, they usually do less than their peers suppose.

If you have taught your teen that having sex outside of marriage is dangerous and morally wrong, you may be shocked to learn that being called a virgin is an insult. Walk through the halls at a high school or step onto a college campus, and you will find clean-cut couples pressed into passionate embraces, their limbs entwined. Neither they nor passersby will be concerned. Teens have witnessed people jumping in and out of bed on television virtually since birth and aren't shocked by sexual displays. The national discussions about President Clinton's affairs ended any remaining taboos surrounding discussions of sex. Ideas about what should be kept private and what is okay to do and talk about in public have definitely changed.

## Teen Talk

However your teen talks and behaves at home, you might still be shocked to hear what he says and how he says it when no adult is around. If you could be a fly on the wall during an unedited teen conversation, you might be convinced that the new generation has turned its back on all the old, time-honored values. Friendly exchanges are salted with sarcasm and peppered with obscenities. Many comments are so sexually explicit they would make a sailor blush—assuming the sailor had been born into a previous generation. When a teen feels mistreated, his ideas about how to get even are often violent enough to make a police detective's blood run cold.

Peers may regularly use slang and cuss when talking among themselves, but such language is not acceptable in formal settings. Your teen needs to be able to talk to people from different social groups and walks of life without alienating them. Disallow slang and obscenities at home so she learns to censor her speech.

In television sitcoms, actors exchange insults at the rate of about one per minute. Not surprisingly, dissing has become a national pastime among young people who have spent more time listening to television than teachers and parents combined. Insults that shock and offend most adults may strike teens as witty, funny, creative, or simply the normal way to communicate. Nevertheless, teens need to know their audience. Talk that peers take for granted may be highly offensive to adults. Insults that other teens find funny may upset siblings, who rarely like being teased.

## Teens' Other Family

If you think you are raising your child, think again. Modern youngsters are the products of two families. Their parents and siblings are one. Pop culture is the other. In the battle for children's minds and hearts, pop culture seems to be winning. Young people may be close to or alienated from their parents and siblings. They may be isolated at school and the community or actively involved in both. Nevertheless, most everyone has deep roots running into the global village.

## The Power of Pop Culture

Before today's teens learned to walk and talk, they were watching television shows and videos. The impact on them has been profound. They could recognize Big Bird before they knew all of their grandparents, uncles, and aunts by sight. When they reached school age, they received lessons in keyboarding in hardwired classrooms while learning their ABCs. Parents who held back from owning a television were in a better position to protect their children's minds, but their children still watched programs and movies and played video and computer games at friends' houses. Kids who weren't allowed to bicycle across town still traveled the world on the information highway.

FACT

You may have tried to teach your child that violence solves nothing and that sex outside of marriage is wrong. But by age thirteen, the average teen has witnessed 100,000 incidents of television violence and watched unwed couples hook up on dramas at the rate of twice per hour. It's hard to combat such powerful messages.

## Young Capitalists

While riding in a car, teens constantly see billboards and signs. On any public sidewalk the product names emblazoned on people's T-shirts, jeans, and hats expose them to a continuous stream of ads. When they step into a grocery or convenience store, an enticing array of brightly colored boxes and wrappers tell them why they should buy whatever is inside. It's not surprising that shopping and hanging out at the mall are such popular activities.

Few parents can compete with so many powerful media messages. No matter what kind of example they set, their child might prefer to shop until he drops than do most anything else. If you are concerned about your teen's values, one solution is to help him find a hobby or activity he can really get excited about. There are no guarantees, but having other fulfilling activities and passionate pursuits sometimes lessens the desire to accumulate baubles, trinkets, and toys.

Teenagers may not have seen a painting by a famous artist, attended a classical concert, or read a literary masterpiece. Yet, every one of them has seen, heard, and read millions of commercial images, jingles, and logos. If you want your teen to value the finer aspects of American culture, start exposing her to them now.

## The New Morality

Young people are always more willing to embrace new ideas than their elders, but the new generation is by far the most accepting. Perhaps they are less intimidated by new things because the pace of change has been so rapid throughout their lives. Certainly their experience with technology has taught them that old usually means obsolete and newer usually does mean better. Undoubtedly, all the school lessons about the importance of cultural differences and the need to honor diversity have had a profound impact.

The idea that everyone should be free to do his own thing isn't a new one, but it is now a deeply cherished teen value. Although peer pressures to dress, talk, and act like everyone else are as intense as ever in junior high, that changes dramatically by the sophomore year in high school. At that point, the generational motto could be "live and let live." Most teens have strong personal beliefs, but they don't think that entitles them to foist them on others. They talk about people behind their backs, but when caught and confronted, the standard response is, "Whatever. That's cool." Parents worry as much or more than ever about peer pressure, but modern teens aren't as likely to push one another into doing things as in the past. Teens who lack confidence may have a hard time just saying no. But when they do, their peers are more likely to respect them and accept their right to decline.

Experts have long urged parents to give their children reasons for their rules. Modern teens especially need to be told why. Your teen knows from watching television that older doesn't mean wiser. Pulling rank is a good way to undermine your credibility. Facts and logic are more likely to be convincing.

Modern teen culture holds that people should be free to have their own opinions, make their own decisions, and do their own thing. Teens don't take kindly to having others dictate to them. They view adults who try to control them as no better than the average schoolyard bully who tries to impose his will on others. When adults lay down the law and demand or forbid something their teen feels strongly about, many young people believe that dishonesty is probably the best policy. Doing what they want and then covering their tracks so their parents won't find out isn't necessarily viewed as betraying a trust. After all, who could blame someone for pretending to go along with a bully in order to avoid a nasty confrontation that the bully is certain to win? Teens also know that might doesn't make right.

After junior high, telling others how to live is taboo in most teen circles. Instead of feeling hurt from criticism, many teens feel a sense of righteous indignation. Controlling, critical adults are deemed unworthy of respect.

If teens are deceptive, it isn't because they enjoy pulling the wool over their parents' eyes. Often their motives are nobler. Once a teen has decided what she's going to do, she may feel there's no point in upsetting her parents by exposing them to information they couldn't handle. Most modern teens are quite protective of their parents, who they see as chronically stressed and easily overwhelmed. They don't want them flipping out, freaking out, wigging out, or needlessly upset. The old saying, "What they don't know won't hurt them" used to be said with a smirk. Now teens aren't smiling. Many young people feel obligated to protect their parents from potentially upsetting information.

## Peer Power

Many parents worry that their teen is drifting away from the safe harbor of family life and heading out into the vast sea of peers. Families complain that their child won't accompany them on outings, spends the evenings on the phone with friends, and is too busy to join them for dinner. Teens tell a different story, complaining that their parents are too busy and don't have time for them. And when there is time, conversations can quickly degenerate because parents are often uninformed about what their teen's life is really like.

Don't be surprised if your teen complains when you go out but ignores you when you are at home. Teens appreciate having the security of knowing that an adult is at hand if needed. That frees them to concentrate on themselves so they can do their own thing. Don't doubt that your presence is important.

### Divided Loyalties

There are a number of reasons why teens prefer to spend time with their peers than with parents. Lacking an identity of their own, many young teens believe that their companions reflect on them. They are too insecure to risk being seen with parents and siblings who don't measure up to the current version of cool. Teens would rather be having new experiences than accompanying their parents to the grocery store or washing dishes for the umpteenth time. Or they would rather process their experiences by talking to like-minded friends. Few parents enjoy spending two hours rehashing a two-minute conversation. Peers, however, find such conversations fascinating. Because teens have spent most of their lives in age-segregated groups, they are more able to relate to one another. They share more common experiences and interests with one another than with their parents.

When parents do manage to entice their teen to participate in a family activity, they may inadvertently make them so unpleasant that their child doesn't care to repeat the experience. Whether at the beach, movies, or dinner table, most parents continue to function as authority figures. They direct activities, telling teens what to do and how to do it. They correct behavior, pointing out when teens have done or said something wrong. They broach subjects teens prefer not to think about, such as their up-coming science project and needing to clean their room.

Your teen may want to join in family activities if she can count on being treated like an adult. Pursuing a hobby that is new to both of you can level the playing field. Try relating as a friend, and use extreme tact when correcting misbehavior.

Sibling rivalry usually continues through the teen years, and many teenagers don't want to participate in family activities that include brothers and sisters. If you want to spend more time with your teen, finding ways to exclude your other children may be all the incentive your teen needs to join you.

## Friends

However close you are to your teen, she still needs friends her own age. Friends fulfill needs that are hard to meet any other way. Through interacting with peers, your teen learns about different ideas and points of view, which helps her reconsider and clarify her own. Through listening to peers' problems, she learns compassion. Through sharing personal problems with friends who have first-hand experience with the same issues she is confronting, she receives good advice and sympathetic support. Friends can be harder to manipulate than parents, so they are often better at setting limits and enforcing consequences. By striving to reconcile differences that threaten valued friendships, your teen develops the skills she needs to sustain close, long-term relationships.

Your teenager needs to separate your dreams for him from his dreams for himself. Because peers aren't personally invested in your child's dreams, they can be more objective and focus on helping him sort out what he wants for himself.

## Forging an Identity

Your teen's central developmental task is to forge a unique identity. That's because in order to have a life of his own, your teen must expand his self-concept so that instead of merely viewing himself as your child, he thinks of himself as a person in his own right. Over the years he has received continuous feedback from you about his strengths and challenges. Now his friends' feedback helps him to understand how people outside of the family perceive him. Hence, friends help your teen to develop a more accurate and balanced sense of self. They are critical for helping him develop what he needs most: a personal identity. He needs that to be able to forge a future.

Avoid criticizing your teen's friends! She will take this as a personal slap in the face—which it is. After all, she chose them. To criticize them is to suggest that she has bad taste or has made foolish choices. Instead, suggest ways she can be with them without getting into trouble or being hurt by them.

It is easy for parents to blame their teen's friends for being bad influences. Remember that friendship is a two-way street. Your child may be influencing her peers rather than the other way around! If you are unhappy with her choice of companions, the first step is to find out what she sees in them. The next is to get to know them. If you remain convinced that your teens' friends do her more harm than good, try to interest her in an activity frequented by people you approve of. If you criticize your teen's friends, she will defend them—just as she would defend you if someone spoke disparagingly of you!

## Teens and the Tube

Sharon's mother contacted the school and set up an appointment with the school counselor to discuss the shockingly graphic letter her daughter had written. The counselor understood why Rita was so upset but was reassuring. He knew Sharon personally and was quite sure that she was doing well. Nevertheless, he offered to check around school to find out if Sharon was having problems he didn't know about. He explained that the kind of language Sharon used was normal these days. Respectful kids didn't expose parents to it if they thought it would upset them. Rita found that somewhat reassuring. On the way home, Rita decided to admit having read the letter. She would let her daughter know that she didn't approve of that kind of language even if her peers did.

When Rita returned home, Sharon was watching a sitcom on television. Rita heard a character say, "Soon you'll be turning tricks to buy a dime bag of that stuff." After the laugh track played, it turned out that the comment was about another character's overuse of nasal spray. Rita suddenly realized that Sharon's generation had spent years listening to television characters relate everything to sex and drugs. Getting rid of the television set probably wouldn't change anything now; but that might be a good way to make a statement. Rita decided to give that some serious thought. (E)

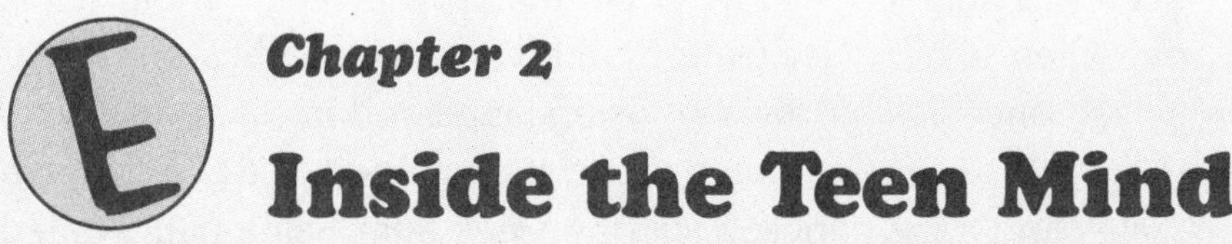

# Chapter 2
# Inside the Teen Mind

The teen years are a time of great emotional intensity. Not since your child's baby days—and most likely never again—will the emotional highs trigger such ecstasies of joy and the lows set off such depths of despair. Teens experience many new emotions, and most need help to identify and express their feelings appropriately. Schools don't offer this kind of emotional education, so you must be prepared to provide these critical lessons.

## Teen Emotionality

Keith's parents couldn't keep up with his ever-changing moods. One day he was on top of the world because he had made the hockey team. A week later he got mad at the coach and wanted to quit. His father offered to go to the school with him to talk to his coach, but Keith was adamant that he could handle the situation himself. The next day when his practice went well, his previous enthusiasm for hockey ignited once again. Hockey posters appeared in his room, and he rewrote his Christmas wish list so it contained just two items: new skates and a new hockey stick. A week after Santa had granted his very expensive wish, Keith announced that the practices were boring and he was going to quit the team. His parents objected and a big argument ensued. Keith was in a funk for two days but grudgingly continued playing at their insistence. A week later he was upbeat about hockey again, and went so far as to thank his mom for keeping him from giving up. What would tomorrow bring, his parents wondered. If it was hard for them to live with Keith, they imagined it must be even harder for him to live with himself.

## The Roller Coaster Years

If your teen's moods change dramatically from day to day or even hour to hour, you may suspect that hormones are responsible. While it does appear that estrogen can affect girls, science has not established that fluctuating testosterone levels are behind boys' mood swings. For both boys and girls, however, stress and social pressure are known culprits.

FACT

Change, even change for the better, is stressful, and teenagers experience many new emotions: unrequited love, crushes, yearning for emotional and sexual intimacy, uncertainty about the future, a desire for independence, fearfulness about growing up—to name just a few. Learning to cope takes time.

In the final analysis, the causes of your teen's emotionality don't really matter. Stress, pressure, and hormones will undoubtedly be facts of life for your teen for many decades to come. The challenge for him is to learn to manage intense feelings so they don't overwhelm him, and to use them to make his life better.

## Coping with Life's Ups and Downs

One reason that teens readily become overwhelmed by strong emotions is that they cannot fathom that their feelings will change. When in the grip of an all-encompassing emotion, they lack the experience to know that they won't always feel on top of the world, head-over-heels in love, grief-stricken over an excruciating loss, or furious over a perceived slight. It's important to help your teen understand that any pain she currently feels will eventually dissipate. Otherwise, she may see her future as little more than a dark cave and feel hopeless about ever glimpsing a ray of light. The idea that joyful feelings will diminish over time will undoubtedly be a disappointment, but it's equally important to recognize that whatever feels so very thrilling and wonderful today won't produce the same effect in a week.

When your teen does start to feel better after mourning a loss, comment that she seems more cheerful. Once she fully grasps that feelings really do change and can count on the fact that the pain from even the deepest wounds will lessen in time, she will be able to use this information to console herself. Circumstances may not change to our liking, but however dark life seems at the moment, people can count on the fact that eventually they will feel differently.

## Feelings Are Real, Too!

The fact that feelings change doesn't mean that they aren't real, however, and your reassurance on this point is important, too. After a love relationship ends or a friendship dissolves, teens often question the reality of what they felt and wonder if the other person ever really cared about them. The ensuing self-doubt and sense of betrayal can create a devastating crisis of confidence. It may help to explain that just because a roller coaster ride has ended doesn't mean it never happened!

## Emotions 101

Human emotions run the gamut from intensely pleasurable to totally miserable, but they are not good or bad—they just are. Actions, on the other hand, can be good or bad, appropriate or inappropriate, constructive or destructive. It is normal for babies to act instantly on all of their feelings. When they are hungry, they cry. When they are excited, they wave their arms and legs, grin, coo, and bounce. When they are angry, they scream and thrash about. With maturity comes the ability to choose whether or not to act on feelings. If the choice is to act, an emotionally mature person thinks about how best to proceed to obtain the most positive results for everyone concerned.

Your teen should take his feelings into account when making decisions. Still, he needs to understand the folly of basing his decisions solely on how he feels at the moment. Because feelings change so dramatically from day to day (and even moment to moment), rational thought and logic need to be involved, as well. And because it is virtually impossible to think clearly when emotions are running high, emotionally mature individuals don't act until they can consider the consequences more objectively. No matter how terrifying a roller coaster ride, indulging the urge to bail out would be disastrous. No matter how exciting the ride, letting go of the bar and standing up would be foolhardy, too; hence, the wisdom of not acting in the heat of the moment. The standard advice to "Sleep on it," "See how you feel in a day or two," and "If you still feel the same way in a month, go for it" is almost always sound.

## Cheering Them Up

The disappointments, betrayals, and losses that cause your teen to don the cloak of mourning may seem petty to you. You may be hard pressed to feel much sympathy for a grief-stricken youth reeling from a breakup with his latest girlfriend when you are at odds with your husband of twenty years. Upsets over a physical defect like unruly hair or pimples may seem like a joke when your father has been diagnosed with cancer. It's important to remember that problems are what we make of them, and the devastation your teen experiences when some small matter goes wrong can be as intense as your suffering over a major tragedy.

Discounting your teen's feelings won't make them go away, and trying to shame him out of feeling as he does will only deliver a blow to his self-esteem ("I'm bad for feeling as I do") or drive a wedge between you ("Dad doesn't understand what it's like to be a kid today"). Telling your teen to cheer up doesn't explain how to accomplish this feat. A better approach is to let him retreat to lick his wounds if that's what he feels like doing. If he can't recover on his own, some extra TLC and a joint search for ways to lighten his mood are in order. Here are a few things to consider when trying to bring him out of a funk:

- Rent a movie he wants to see, break out the popcorn, and hunker down together for a night at the movies.
- Keep younger siblings out of his hair so he can curl up in bed with a good book.
- Take over his chores for a day so he can relax and chill out.
- Go out to dinner at his favorite restaurant.
- Have him join you at the gym for a workout.

People who feel like victims have lower self-esteem than those who believe they can influence what happens to them, so if you think that your teen had a hand in bringing misery on herself, share your perceptions. That way, she can learn from her mistakes. Remember, though, to be gentle. Otherwise, she will feel like you're kicking her when she's down.

As you comfort your teen you are communicating to him that you understand he is suffering, that you care, and that you want to cheer him up. Knowing that someone cares when life seems overly difficult is the best antidote for emotional pain. As your son discovers what helps him to feel better—a cup of tea to soothe him, a game of cards to distract him, a sympathetic ear to console and reassure him, or some private time to regroup and recover—he'll learn what to do to help himself feel better when he's on his own and life has dealt him another blow. The coping skills you teach now will last him a lifetime.

Humor is often the best cure for the blues, but teasing your teen may backfire during periods of heightened self-doubt and sensitivity. If you're not a jokester by nature, save copies of jokes you receive via e-mail or cartoons from magazines and newspapers. Sit down together to go through them. Hopefully they'll spark some giggles, or at least some genuine smiles.

## Settling Them Down

Every parent wants their child to be happy, yet an amazing number are markedly uncomfortable when confronted with bubbling displays of teen exuberance. Many parents hope that by dampening their teen's excitement, they can protect her from disappointment down the road. To that end, they say things like, "I'm glad that you and Sherry are friends again, but who knows if it will last?" "You're happy about getting that job now. We'll see how you feel after you've spent eight hours flipping burgers." "Just because you made the team doesn't mean the coach will let you play. And how are you going to keep up with your schoolwork?"

Such subtle and not-so-subtle ways of throwing a wet blanket on your teen's excitement may dampen her joy. Worse, a negative response from you suggests that when she's got wonderful news, instead of sharing in it with her, you'll try to take it away. The best outcome of this unfortunate scenario is that your teen will turn to other people to share her good news. From being exposed to too much nay-saying, her feelings of pleasure when something good happens may be instantly replaced by thoughts about all of the things that could go wrong.

If you are worried that your teen's great news really heralds disaster, it is better not to rain on her parade. Wait to voice your concerns until some of the excitement has worn off. Even if you think it would be a disaster for your daughter to buy her boyfriend's aging car for an astronomical price, you can say, "Sounds like you're thrilled at the prospect of owning that car." Later you can initiate a more serious discussion: "I was thinking about John's car. You might want to check the blue book value to be sure it's as good of a bargain as it seems. It would be wise to have it checked out by a mechanic, too, to be sure there aren't any problems your friend isn't aware of."

## Teaching Anger Management

Youngsters who are prone to physical or verbal outbursts are at risk for having increasingly serious problems with aggression during the teen years. While some children are simply more sensitive and are more easily provoked than others, those who become verbally or physically aggressive need intensive help to develop anger management skills. The typical American child receives lots of lessons about how *not* to handle anger. "Don't hit." "Don't yell!" "Don't use that tone of voice!" "That's not nice to say." Unfortunately, being told what not to do doesn't answer the crucial question: What should I do when I'm angry?

Angry feelings run the gamut from mild crankiness to rage. In between are dislike, irritation, frustration, and fury. People often turn other feelings such as fear, jealousy, or sadness into anger, as well. Before helping your teen express his feelings, you need to help him to identify them correctly.

### Anger: What's It All About?

Anger is a normal human emotion. That doesn't mean it is a pleasant one, however. In fact, when your teen is stamping around the house and using each of your well-intentioned comments as grist for yet another argument, anger may seem to be the bane of your existence. Nevertheless, like every other emotion, anger is important because it signals a desire for some sort of change. Accordingly, it serves as an impetus for tackling problems, overcoming obstacles, striving to fulfill our needs, and moving *through* life's trials instead of backing away from them. Anger provides the motivational spark that drives people to try to right wrongs, bring about changes, and make the world a better place.

Before people can deal effectively with their anger, they must know what is causing them to feel as they do. Your teen may seem to be angry with you, but his crankiness may actually stem from a problem at school or with a sibling. Once the cause has been identified, the next issue is what to do about it. Whether your teen's anger is positive and constructive or negative and destructive depends on how he expresses it. Assertiveness often gets good results, while sarcasm and bullying usually backfire. Lashing out in a blind rage is virtually guaranteed to do much harm and little, if any, good.

If your teen is furious with someone, it is important to listen without judging. Having the chance to blow off steam by talking to a trusted confidante is often enough to reduce anger to a manageable level. Wait until he has cooled down before suggesting ways to address the problem.

If there is no way to fix whatever your teen thinks is wrong or to bring about the kind of change she wants, the challenge is to help her to come to terms with her feelings. This may entail accepting that a bad situation can't be changed and finding a positive way to cope with the situation.

## Calming Tactics

Many teens don't handle themselves well when they are angry. Because they can't think clearly, they do and say things they later regret. Since angry people are notoriously poor problem-solvers and decision-makers, the best recourse is a time out until some semblance of calm has been restored. Only then is it possible to evaluate the problem with some degree of objectivity.

For restoring calm, the old "count to 10" tactic is very effective—though some teens might need to count to 100! Deep breathing, meditating, taking a warm bath, reading a book, or watching television are good ways to relax, too. Vigorous exercise or involvement in an all-consuming activity such as cleaning the house or doing yard work can simultaneously serve as a mental distraction and help to release some of the energy driving the anger. Pounding a pillow, punching a punching bag, or ripping up phone books helps others. Confiding in someone can serve as an outlet, too. Writing a letter to the person your teen is angry with can also reduce tension. Discourage her from sending it until she's had a day or two to think about what she has written.

If you try to give your teen advice when she is angry, you may become the target of her anger. Instead of focusing on your desire to help, she may react as if you have insulted her. Be a good listener until she's calm enough to consider your advice more objectively.

## Parents as Role Models

Many parents believe they would be burdening their teen if they were to talk about things or people outside the family that they feel angry about. They avoid discussing this kind of unpleasantness in their child's presence. While this sounds caring and considerate, not sharing things that you're angry about negates your usefulness as a role model and undermines your credibility as a confidante. After all, it will be hard for your teen to accept advice about how to handle anger from someone who never gets angry. By sharing when you are angry about something, your teen gets to see first hand how an adult travels the course from "I am so mad I want to scream" to "I need to set up an appointment so we can try to work something out." The most powerful way to teach anger management is to serve as a good role model.

There is another, less direct way to serve as a role model. When your teen is having difficulty handling his anger, talk about a time you felt the same way. The actual situation you recount may be quite different; what matters is that your feelings were similar. Sharing a story from your own life is a powerful way to demonstrate that you understand what your teen is going through. At the same time, focusing on your experience can help him to distance himself from his own problem so that he can consider it more objectively. Your story doesn't have to have a happy ending—there's no need to suggest that everything worked out and you became a better person for the experience. In fact, by indicating that things never did work out to your satisfaction, you communicate an important message: feeling angry isn't the end of the world. Life is sometimes very unfair, but we can go on even if justice doesn't prevail.

FACT

If your teen threatens to even the score with someone he's mad at, help him formulate a productive response. Role-play together so he can consider his antagonist's point of view as well as his own. Win/lose solutions escalate conflicts. To resolve them, the outcome must be win/win.

Perhaps the most powerful lessons you will ever teach your teen about how to deal with anger take place when you are angry with your child. By expressing your own anger constructively, your teen experiences the process directly. To serve as a good role model, make it a practice to follow rules designed to make sure conflict is handled productively:

- Rather than ambushing your teen, briefly describe the issue you want to address and set up a mutually agreeable time to discuss it.
- Attack the problem, not the person. For example, say, "If you can't be truthful with me, I won't be able to trust you" instead of, "You're a liar."
- Discontinue the conversation if you feel yourself losing control. Name-calling, sarcasm, and delivering "low blows" solve nothing. The point of a "fair fight" is to work toward change, not to dump on someone.
- Stick to the topic. If your teen detours to another issue, say that you'll be glad to set up a time to discuss that concern later and quickly return to the subject at hand.
- Don't threaten consequences when you are angry. You may not want to carry them out once you are calm, and your teen will perceive your threats as a power play. Bullying is not an effective way to solve problems.
- Accept responsibility for your feelings by using "I-messages" rather than accusatory "you-messages"—for example, "I feel worried when I don't know where you are," not "You are supposed to call and tell me if you aren't where you said you would be."

- If you can't come up with a mutually acceptable solution, agree to disagree.
- End conversations that are going in circles and set up another time to continue the discussion.

It really does take two to argue, and as a parent you can stop an argument at any time. Just announce that you're not discussing the current subject any more today, and follow up your statement with absolute silence. If your teen continues to carry on for a bit, so be it. Without a response from you, he will soon give it up.

### Righting Past Wrongs

If you frequently lost your temper when dealing with your child in the past, during the teen years you may discover that small conflicts escalate rapidly. Younger children may feel too intimidated to stand up to out-of-control parents, but teens are likely to respond in kind. Indeed, some parents don't realize the kind of example they have been setting until their teen becomes verbally or physically abusive. In that case, the best recourse is to have a heart-to-heart about what has happened. Accept responsibility for your past mistakes, review the list of rules for fair fighting together, and agree to help one another follow them. Agree to call for a time out if either your teen—or you—breaks the rules.

## Parents as Teachers

Parents like Keith's are understandably fearful of their child's anger when it entails threats to act out. Would Keith have actually quit the hockey team? His parents were afraid he would, but sometimes when teens say, "I'm going to quit!" they mean, "Right now I'm so mad, I feel like quitting." Expressing themselves to a supportive person brings relief, and after they calm down clarity returns and they don't want to follow through with their threats.

Once Keith's parents understood the difference between feelings and actions, they didn't panic when he was angry or work so hard to try to settle him down. They realized that when they discounted his feelings or tried to control them, he escalated and turned his anger back on them. Not surprisingly, once they became good listeners, most of Keith's tirades ended as quickly as they had begun. They made it a practice to respond sympathetically and express confidence that when he calmed down and had time to consider seriously what to do, he would make the right decision. Sometimes he seemed to make the wrong one, but they resigned themselves to the fact that they couldn't teach him everything. Life would have to serve as his teacher, too.

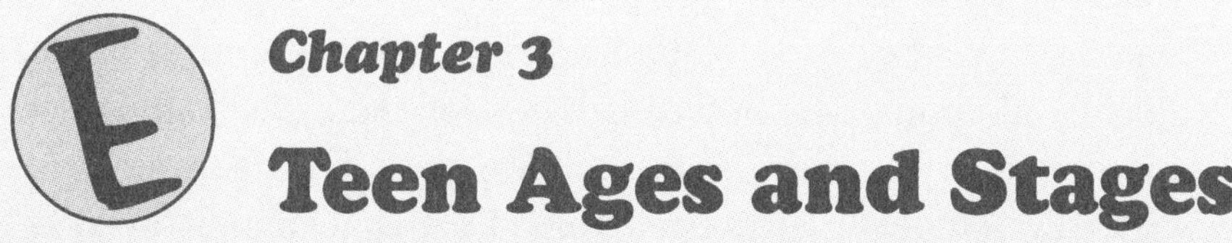

# Chapter 3
# Teen Ages and Stages

Between your child's thirteenth and twentieth birthday, you can count on life being a whirlwind. On the heels of puberty come high school, dating, driving, graduating, and moving away from home. In between your teen will make thousands of decisions. Even some of the seemingly small ones can have lifelong consequences. Hopefully, your child will turn to someone older and wiser for guidance when needed. Hopefully, that someone will be you.

## Through the Years

Tarah's parents had always supported her participation in a number of extracurricular activities, so they were surprised and dismayed when she quit piano, gymnastics, and the church choir in seventh grade. As best they could tell, the point was to free up time for her new hobbies: watching MTV; talking on the phone; and obsessing about her wardrobe, hair, and makeup. As a freshman she was so boy crazy, they feared she might end up married or pregnant before graduating. During her sophomore year, her problems with geometry and biology created an ongoing crisis. Even though her parents helped her study almost every school night, she had to go to summer school to make up a credit or give up hope of graduating with her class.

Tarah spent her junior year testing limits at home. During some nasty shouting matches, her parents delivered "shape up or ship out" ultimatums. Afterwards, they felt ashamed about having sunk to her level, but she did settle down—for a while. Tarah's senior year felt almost surreal. Things seemed fine in September and October, and then she came home drunk from her homecoming prom in November. She seemed to be on a good track through December and January, but in February she got two speeding tickets and totaled the car. She started dating a boy her parents approved of, then they caught her sneaking out of her room at night not once but twice. What would the future hold? Her parents were afraid to find out.

As teens mature, their interests often change and they abandon activities they have long enjoyed. Extracurricular involvements offer important opportunities to socialize and develop special skills. Teen boredom easily turns into teen trouble. Insist that your child participate in a club, sport, group, hobby, or lesson of his choosing.

## Surviving Junior High

Certainly some people must have liked seventh and eighth grades, but it's hard to find anyone who has fond memories of being a young teenager. During this infamously awkward stage, young children's rapid physical development makes them feel like strangers in their own bodies. Braces, glasses, pimples, perspiration, oily hair, and gangly bodies appear just as they are becoming interested in establishing relationships with members of the opposite sex. The result is excruciating self-consciousness and insecurity.

Your teen might not worry so much about what others think of him if he realized how rarely they do! But since his thoughts are mostly about himself, he assumes that everyone else is similarly preoccupied. It is normal for young teens to feel that they are always on stage and that the curtain is always up.

It is perhaps not surprising that when groups of insecure, self-conscious youths rub elbows at school all day long, they spend inordinate amounts of time making one another miserable. The common tactic young teens use to distract from their imagined defects is to criticize everyone else. Friendships serve as important ports in the storm by providing a reassuring sense of acceptance and belonging. Unfortunately, since young teens are extremely touchy, alliances are uneasy at best and constantly in flux. Two young teens may swear eternal friendship one day only to stop speaking the next because one made an off-handed comment that hurt the other teen's feelings. Couples flirt for a month, fall head-over-heels in love for a day, and part as arch enemies over an imagined slight a few days later.

Give your young teenager plenty of warm fuzzies; he is undoubtedly getting lots of cold pricklies at school and in the neighborhood. Supervise, set rules, and be consistent about enforcing consequences, but don't be angry when disciplining. Your son needs your emotional support like never before.

## "Freaked-Out" Freshmen

Change is always a bit scary, and starting high school is a huge step that most teens anticipate with a mixture of nervousness and excitement.

Hopefully your teen can attend a carefully designed, comprehensive orientation session before school starts so he has some idea about what to expect. If not, you can help relieve your child's anxieties about attending a new school by taking him for a tour so he can learn the campus layout. Call ahead to be sure that the school is in agreement, as the officials may want a staff member to accompany you. If you are exploring on your own, see if you can track down the cafeteria, nurse's office, restrooms, auditorium, gym, and locker room by yourselves. If your child already has his class schedule, locate each of his classrooms. Otherwise, find the sections of the building that house classrooms for the major subjects (English, science, math, art, music, history, foreign language, shop, etc.).

Hazing of freshmen ranges from mildly embarrassing to brutal. Headline-grabbing horror stories occasionally describe incidents in which students are badly injured because school officials don't realize the seriousness of the situation. Forbid your child to attend student-run initiation ceremonies. Alert the principal and/or police.

Make an effort to meet and introduce your son to the principal, a school counselor, or other administrator. Ask if the official can be a resource should your son need help with a problem. If not, ask the name of an appropriate contact person. Having someone to turn to if a problem arises goes a long way toward reassuring new students that they won't be left to sink or swim on their own. Find out what clubs and activities are available and encourage your teen to attend several to check them out. Even if the activity isn't particularly appealing, organized events provide social outlets and can help teenagers find a niche.

## Sophomore Slump

While teachers and parents complain that sophomores are difficult to deal with and to motivate, sophomores simply complain. They gripe about school being boring. They whine about home being boring. They claim that family outings are boring. Their old friends are boring. They expected the teenage years to be so great, but they are boring. Parenting a sophomore can be especially frustrating. You can try to help by thinking up some interesting pastimes to occupy your teenager's time and detail the chores that she simply must do. But anything you come up with will probably be too boring for her to consider.

QUESTION?

**My sophomore seems so unhappy. Might she be depressed?** About one in eight teens suffers from depression, so a psychological and/or medical evaluation may be in order. Otherwise, becoming actively involved in an activity or pursuing a hobby is often the best route to an attitude readjustment.

## Teen Boredom

Last year's nervousness about starting high school has long since subsided. Sophomores know the ropes and are in the groove. Now what are they supposed to do? Graduation is too far away to generate much concern about the future. They are stuck smack dab in the middle of the here and now—a place that most find very unpleasant.

The reason sophomores are so bored is clear enough: They have lots of energy and not enough outlets for it. They want go places and do things but few are able to drive. They want money, but aren't old enough to work. They want to date and party. But parents still control the car keys and cash, putting a serious damper on their children's social life.

## Sophomore Dangers

Just because most sophomores typically slump doesn't mean you should be complacent and assume this is just a phase. During this difficult period, many teenagers make poor decisions that can create long-term problems. A slide in grades may mean your teenager has decided to drop out when he turns sixteen and is merely biding his time until then. Some students begin failing classes to convince themselves and their parents that they might just as well withdraw at age sixteen. Because high school graduation seems a century away, even students with aspirations for higher education let their grades slide. They figure they can worry about their grades "later."

To combat boredom and generate some excitement, many sophomores join gangs, drag race, fight, and become involved in criminal activities. Too many discover that a chemical high is a guaranteed way to relieve boredom and combat stress.

You can't make your child study or do chores, but you can set limits: no transportation, allowance, or spending money unless he spends an hour a day on homework and does his chores. Don't argue, warn, threaten, or cajole. Don't even issue reminders, which is really nagging in disguise! Just hold firm.

Sophomores with passionate interests don't usually get into serious trouble. However, teenagers are at risk if they lack a solid educational or career goal and only care about playing video games, listening to music, and watching television. If your child falls into that category, devote as much time and money as you can muster to helping her find an activity she can become involved in. Has she always wanted to learn martial arts or how to pilot a plane? See Chapter 11 for suggestions.

If you can only afford a single flying lesson, that might be enough to spark your teenager's interest in becoming a pilot. That can spark some academic enthusiasm even if she never takes to the skies. If she didn't enjoy the lesson, at least she had a brief respite from the boredom.

## Jumping Juniors

Perhaps the energy surge that typically hits during junior year is because teenagers now have places to go, people to meet, and a way to get there since many of their friends are driving. In addition, most students have found a social niche. They enjoy the status and privilege of being upperclassmen.

It's easier for boys to find dates now that they are older than half of the girls. It's easier for girls to go on dates now that parents are more lenient about letting their daughters take off with a boy in a car. Being able to drive, date, and work expands their range of activities. As a result, teenagers' moods often lighten and brighten considerably. After years of standoffishness they sometimes feel moved to bless their parents with a spontaneous hug, kiss, or pat on the head. For many teens, this is the happiest year of high school.

**Before, everything was boring and your teenager couldn't be bothered to do more than eat, sleep, and relax. Now he probably won't be bothered with boring things like relaxing, eating, and sleeping. Encourage him to pay attention to his health.**

It could be that the junior year energy burst is partially the result of students feeling pressured to make lots of important life decisions in a very short time. Parents and teachers have spent many years urging their children to get with the program and *grow up.* The realization that independence is less than twenty-four months away seems to suddenly sink in.

Making important life decisions is harder for today's generation than previous ones because they have so many more options. Traditional life paths have gone the way of bobby socks and saddle shoes. Students can start college at age thirty, forty, fifty, or even later. They can have babies before getting married, never have babies, or never get married. About the only remaining tradition is moving out of the house after high school graduation. Even though large percentages of children later boomerang back home when financial problems overwhelm them, most juniors begin planning to go away to school or they begin thinking about how they will afford an apartment of their own.

Lacking other plans after high school, many girls decide that having a baby will give them meaning, purpose, and direction. Even if they don't snag a husband in the process, they anticipate that hugging and cuddling a little one will satisfy their need to give and receive affection.

If college is a possibility for your teenager, she should begin studying for or taking college boards during her junior year. She should also begin collecting college catalogues and thinking about a major. If she aspires to learning a trade, this is a good time to see if she can find part-time work in a related field and begin learning while she's earning.

FACT

**Students who still haven't fathomed a future for themselves are at risk of dropping out and drifting or heading toward a teen marriage and/or family. That means it's time for career counseling.**

## Senioritis

Senior year is an emotional time. As students continue to enjoy their friends, they begin preparing for their impending separation. That makes special high school activities bittersweet. At football and basketball games, most seniors are struck by the realization that next year they won't be sitting in the same bleachers listening to the same band and rooting for the same classmates. As they prepare for the high school Valentine's prom they realize they will never attend another. Whether picking up a course schedule, buying their books, or voting for a class president, they realize it is for the last time.

Senior year tends to be especially busy. Many students are busy finalizing their plans to attend college or a vocational school. Others are working at a job with a future or that can serve as a stepping stone to a career. Many are working to try to save money for a car, apartment, or tuition. Others devote long hours to studying and arranging school events so that their graduating class will have special memories to take with them when they leave. Having no plans for after high school makes seniors feel lost and afraid, although some hide behind a mask of false bravado and pretend not to care.

Events like homecoming take on a special significance now that the end of high school is drawing near. Building homecoming floats, having yearbook pictures taken, buying school rings, cheering sports teams, decorating gymnasiums for proms, and designing graduation invitations are among the activities seniors enjoy. It's easy for them to let schoolwork slide with so many distractions, especially if they've already been accepted to college or are unconcerned about their grades because they don't plan to attend higher education. Many students do the minimum needed to get by. However, what appears to be a typical downhill tumble sometimes turns out to be much more serious. Honor roll students fail a course required for graduation. Students who are barely passing drop out, ensuring they won't be able to get the kind of job that will enable them to become financially independent. Such senior year disasters often stem from fears of growing up and becoming independent. Parents are wise to watch carefully and seek help for a student who appears to be in the self-destruct mode.

FACT

At the same time students are excited about the future they are nervous about what it holds. The nail biting begins as college-bound students wait for admissions committees to decide their fate. Students without plans feel under the gun to make some decisions.

## Life after High School

Moving away from home is exciting, but adjusting to so many changes isn't easy. In fact, it is very stressful. Faced with new foods, new roommates, money worries, and lack of parental structure, most teens battle the occasional urge to toss in the towel and flee back to the comfort of the familiar. It takes at least a year to adjust to a new environment and turn new acquaintances into real friends, so some periods of feeling lonely and homesick are to be expected. Even if your teenager sounds confident and happy when she calls home, she may still have some doubts about her ability to make it on her own. Many young adults adopt a tone of false bravado so as not to worry their families. Your assurance that she can handle whatever challenges she confronts will mean a lot.

Young adults resent being told to dress warmly in winter and carry an umbrella when it rains. When they have only recently moved out of the house and are shaky about being able to make it on their own, they typically try to avoid people who undermine their confidence by treating them like they were five years old. Watch your words!

Most young adults very much look forward to returning home for the holidays, but many parents alienate their offspring shortly after they arrive. Father glances at the clock and asks the child who has lived on her own for several months, "Don't you think it's past your bedtime?" As their child is on her way out the door in the morning, mother quizzes her about where she is going, admonishes her for not first eating breakfast, and warns her to drive carefully. It is natural to revert to old patterns of relating, but it is important to avoid them if you hope for more visits.

Be supportive rather than critical when your teenager discusses problems and informs you about decisions she has made. "I just hope you know what you're doing" is negative. "I trust you'll make the right decision" is positive. Most teenagers then ponder the meaning of the word "right."

## Finding Themselves

After graduation Tarah enrolled in beauty school, dropped out a month later, got a job, moved into her own apartment, then got laid off and ended up back at home two months later. She watched soaps on television until her parents said she would have to pay rent if she wasn't in school. She grudgingly enrolled in a computer course, and suddenly found her niche. As if making up for lost time, she took heavy loads so she could finish an associate's degree early.

As Tarah walked onto the stage to receive her diploma, her parents were struck by how their daughter had changed from a gangly, self-conscious girl at the start of her teenaged years to a poised, confident young lady in just seven years. They were proud of her, but weren't sure that they deserved much credit. Often they had felt like very bad parents. They had never stopped loving her for a second, but there were some stretches when it had been very hard to be around her. Thankfully, they were now confident that the hard days were in the past. (E)

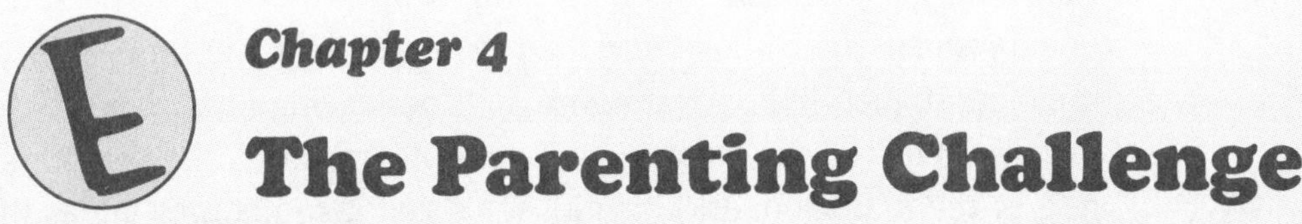

## Chapter 4

# The Parenting Challenge

You have labored long and hard to prepare your child for independence, and your most important job will soon end. You can expect the grieving process to begin long before your child moves out. Although your relationship with your teen will change dramatically, growing up doesn't have to mean growing away. Emotional closeness can endure through physical separations. In fact, you may find that you and your child are closer when you aren't living under the same roof.

## Letting Go

When Beatrice and Bruce came home from a hectic workday to four bickering kids, blasting stereos, a kitchen full of dirty dishes, and hampers overflowing with laundry, they sometimes longed for the end of this difficult stage of their childrens' lives. Occasionally they shared visions of how their life would be when the children were out of the nest and they could reclaim their house and their lives. At the same time, they dreaded the thought that their oldest son would be leaving in a matter of months. Actually, William was so busy with school, the band, the yearbook, the hockey team, his job, and his girlfriend that it sometimes felt as though he was already gone. At those moments, sadness washed over them in a wave. When they saw his empty chair at the table too many nights in a row, they wished they could turn back the hands of the clock, gather their firstborn into a family hug, and never let him go.

Preparing your child for independence is like helping the spouse you love get ready to divorce you. Don't be surprised if you push your teen away one minute and cling too tightly the next. Be gentle with yourself. Letting go isn't easy.

Beatrice and Bruce wanted William's last few months at home to be especially good ones. That should have been easy, since they had always been close to their son, but it seemed to them that William was going out of his way to irritate them. For instance, he left the milk out on the counter all night and it soured. He said he would run out to buy more, but Beatrice was furious that he had let food go to waste out of sheer carelessness. Later, she felt badly about having called him irresponsible, inconsiderate, and selfish.

In what had become a rare event, William joined the family for dinner. His parents were pleased, but during a conversation about the upcoming election, William praised the Green Party for wanting to protect the earth and accused the Republicans and Democrats of destroying it. In the ensuing argument, William said he would find another place to live if they wanted him gone. His parents were shocked. They tried to reassure him of their love by being extra nice to him, but when he overslept and was obviously going to be late for a hockey game, they both just lost it.

## The Parental Midlife Crisis

While much is made of teen mood swings and unpredictable behavior, many parents find themselves feeling and acting like adolescents themselves. They overreact to small problems, explode over minor difficulties, and become hypercritical nags. The stress of dealing with a young know-it-all can certainly explain these bouts of emotionality and losses of temper, but often there is more to it than that. It is common for parents to go through a midlife crisis just as their child is preparing in earnest to leave home.

FACT

Parents' involvement in personally rewarding activities can have unexpected benefits for their children. For instance, children's grades typically dip slightly, then improve dramatically when a parent goes back to school even though they spend less time together. The importance of parental role modeling cannot be overstated.

A typical response of women entering the early stages of menopause and of men nearing the peak of their careers is to review their accomplishments and rethink their long-term goals and priorities. Despite the stereotype, few middle-aged men actually trade the family sedan for a new red sports car or their wife for a younger model. Still, realizing that the years flew by so quickly can create a sense that time is running out. During their forties and fifties, many people feel an urgency to fulfill some of their dreams before old age saps their energy and health.

## Defining Your Goals

The demands of child-rearing are such that most parents sacrifice some of their own dreams during their long years of raising a family. Many work hard to provide their youngsters with special opportunities they wished their parents had given them. Unfortunately, there is no guarantee that your child will appreciate your efforts. Even if he does, you are likely to find that having someone else live your dreams isn't as fulfilling as you had hoped. Feelings of resentment on the part of you or your child provide a good clue that the gift you are trying to give your child is actually your gift to yourself. Trying to live through your child is unlikely to work out happily for either of you. It is better to try to fulfill some dreams of your own than to deny your child's individuality and saddle him with the burden of trying to live for both of you.

FACT

To make the transition from caretaker to friend, pause before giving advice to your teenager and ask yourself, "Would I say this to a friend? How would I feel if a friend said this to me?" To remain close to an adult child, you must observe the same boundaries and rules you would with someone outside of the family.

Focusing on your own life will help to free your teenager to take charge of his own. When your child enters high school, consider returning to the special hobby or cherished pastimes you put aside when family and job responsibilities usurped all of your time and energy. Alternatively, consider becoming involved in a new activity you always wanted to experience but never made time for. A great way to begin is by calling your local community college to request a catalogue. Besides offering regular credit courses, most provide a wide range of continuing education classes. Subjects include everything from jewelry making to Chinese cooking to guitar.

Raising children is so demanding that couples' life satisfaction as well as their satisfaction with their marriage typically decline shortly after the birth of their first baby. It remains relatively low until the children are grown. Most people find that after the children leave and before old age sets is an especially satisfying time of life. Nevertheless, anticipating your teen's departure is likely to be a time of heightened anxiety, and facing an emptying nest can precipitate a bout of grief and mourning. Besides devoting more time to activities that don't involve the children, another way to ease the transition is to focus your efforts on preparing your teen for independence. You'll spend less time worrying about your child now and after he leaves home if you are confident about his ability to meet the challenges of being on his own.

Are you "mothering" your teen or "smothering" him? If most of your energy goes into taking care of and worrying about your child, it's time to loosen the apron strings. Start shifting responsibilities to your child so he can learn to take care of himself. Teens don't need to worry about themselves if someone else is doing all of their worrying for them.

## Preparing Teens for Independence

As students watch the classroom clock's minute hand inch toward the final bell, many feel that they are caught in a time warp and that the school day will never ever end. At the same time, their parents watch the pages of the calendar fly by and realize that time is running out. Their fully developed daughter is big enough to wear her mother's clothes, and their son's height now approaches his father's. They pale to think that soon their overgrown kid will be moving out on her own. Concerns about middling grades, messy rooms, half-done chores, and other signs of immaturity create a sense of urgency as parents contemplate the implication for their child's future. How will the daughter who can't get herself up for school in the morning hold down a job? If she can't keep up with her room, how will she manage a household? If she only studies when someone is standing over her to crack the whip, how will she succeed in college? If she is moody, irritable, self-centered, and blames everyone else for everything that goes wrong, how will she get along in life?

Trying to motivate your teen by listing her personal failings won't help her become responsible. A better approach is to tackle the problems head-on one at a time. If she relies on you to drag her out of bed in the morning and repays you by treating you like the wicked witch, tell her you want to make things more pleasant for her in the morning and teach her to get herself out of bed. That way, she will be able to hold down a job and/or get herself to her college classes. Buy her a clock with an alarm loud enough to penetrate her dreams and agree to call her once (and only once) if she thinks a personal appearance from you would help. Discuss how she can get herself to school if she misses the bus or isn't ready to leave the house when you are. Instead of lecturing about the terrible fate that awaits students who chalk up too many unexcused absences, help her look on the bright side. Reassure her that she may be able to make up credits in summer school or simply graduate a semester late. Many teenagers become amazingly responsible once the possibility of upsetting their parents disappears and students realize that the only effect will be on their own future.

You crack the whip but your child's grades don't improve. You talk until you're blue in the face but the chores don't get done. Too much negativity alienates teens and causes them to feel defeated rather than motivating them. Zero in on a few issues and ignore the rest.

## Teaching Life Skills

Few teens learn household management skills in school. If your teen doesn't already know how to plan and shop for meals, do laundry, handle a family budget, place a telephone call to get information, and solve interpersonal problems, this is the time to teach him. If you don't know how to do some of these things, either, so much the better! Your ability to maintain a satisfying relationship with your adult child depends on your ability to relate more like equals. Learning together takes you out of the role of teacher and recasts you as a fellow student.

### Cooking

Stopping at McDonald's for a bag of food or popping something in the microwave is fine for an occasional meal, but adults need to know how to handle all aspects of meal preparation. Actively involve your teenager by having him choose a week's worth of recipes from a cookbook. Make grocery lists together and have your teen accompany you to the grocery store to shop. Read labels to look for foods with less fat and additives, and show him how to compare unit prices to decide which products to buy. Put your child in charge of the meal preparations. Let him tell you what to do next instead of serving as the master chef and relegating him to the role of busboy.

Knowing how to cook and clean isn't enough; to keep up with a house, teenagers must be able to cook and clean regularly. Assign some regular household chores. You'll both feel better about his future prospects when he can carry on even when he doesn't feel like it.

## Financial Management

If you're comfortable sharing information about your family's finances with your teenager, have him join you when you're paying bills and balancing the checkbook. He needs to see how these feats are accomplished. Have him put his algebra skills to good use by calculating how much it would cost to pay off the current credit card bill if you only made the minimum monthly payment. Include him in some of the decision-making about purchases so he can begin to learn the ins and outs of money management.

If you don't want your teen involved in your finances, an alternative is to provide hands-on practice by increasing his allowance so he can handle his personal expenses himself. Have him track and categorize his expenses for at least a month so you can calculate how much he needs. Have him create a budget by organizing his expenses into categories. Typical categories include school books and supplies, car expenses, clothing, entertainment, snacks, and miscellaneous. Open a checking account in your child's name and deposit enough money each month so he can pay for everything without having to come to you. Teach him how to write checks and balance a checkbook. If you end up providing a financial bail out because your teen overspent on clothes and couldn't afford some necessities for school, deduct the amount from his next month's allowance. Learning to make a budget and write checks is easy. Learning to live within a budget is much harder.

Do you need to make a restaurant or airline reservation? Is it time to comparison shop to see that you're getting the best insurance rates? Have your teen make the calls so he learns how to make appointments and conduct business on the phone.

### Home Office Management

Give your teenager a tour of the file cabinet so she can see how you file important family papers. Then provide her with some manilla folders and guidance so she can create a filing system of her own. That way, she learns a valuable skill and learns to organize her own important papers such as college materials (applications, catalogues, financial aid papers, and essays), "credentials" (letters of recommendation, transcripts, resume, awards, and certificates), receipts for big purchases (including warranty cards and records of serial numbers), income records (paycheck stubs and tax forms), and legal documents (birth certificate, car registration, extra automobile insurance cards, and social security card).

## Teaching Interpersonal Problem-Solving

Effective counselors are warm, nonjudgmental, and spend more time engaged in supportive hand-holding than dispensing advice. Reassuring your teenager that you love and appreciate her may be the salve she needs to rally and carry on without taking further action. Otherwise, knowing that you are on her side can provide her with the strength to confront and solve her difficulties without further help from you. Then, when she is upset later in life and you aren't on hand to kiss the emotional boo-boos, she will be able to replay your words of consolation and reassurance in her mind. Hopefully, she will be able to derive solace and the strength to confront her problems on her own.

FACT

Your teen may appear to ignore your words, but your tone will undoubtedly get through. Whether you comfort or condemn him when he has problems will largely determine whether he responds to future difficulties by comforting or condemning himself. Think before you speak!

If your sympathy and support aren't enough for your teenager to solve her problem of the moment, she may benefit from your services as a therapist. The first step is to help her sort out what she would like to see happen or how she would like to have the situation resolved. She probably already has a good grasp on who has wronged her and what everyone else needs to do. The next step is for her to understand her role in the difficulties and consider what she is willing to do to solve her problem. If she's open to hearing your opinions, share your views. Role-play conversations so she can practice trying to work things out.

## Teaching Conflict Resolution

Chances are that when your child was young, you shifted into high gear when you learned that something was amiss in her life. When she was upset about a problem, you leapt into action and talked to her teachers, friends, friends' parents, and anyone else who could shed light on the situation. If you thought she had been wronged by school personnel, other parents, or her peers, you raced to serve as her champion and advocate to defend her. If you thought she was the instigator or at fault, you issued apologies on her behalf and saw to it that she faced the music. Now your teen needs a different kind of help from you.

When teens are having problems at school or in the community, most are very adamant that they do not want their parents to try to fix things for them. This is as it should be. Soon your teenager will be on her own. You won't be there to solve her problems and mediate her conflicts with her professors and roommates, with her bosses and colleagues, much less with her husband and children. She must know how to solve interpersonal problems on her own. But what should you do when your teen lacks the courage to present her concerns and stand up for herself.

The best way to begin preparing your child for independence is by serving as her personal mediator when she has conflicts she can't solve on her own. That way, you can walk her and her antagonist through the steps of the problem-solving process so she can learn how to resolve disputes.

The main job of a mediator is to help disputants listen to one another. To do that, summarize each person's comments and ask them to do the same for one another. Diffuse tensions by restating any positive comments, such as compliments and apologies, and carefully note any areas of agreement. To help the parties move toward a mutually agreeable solution, discourage them from rehashing the past. Instead, encourage them to describe how they want things to be handled in the future. The following table gives some examples of how to use this technique.

**Parents as Mediators**

| Goal | Method | Example |
|---|---|---|
| Enhance communication | Summarize | "Mary says she doesn't like being teased." |
| Enhance communication | Ask parties to restate what they heard | "What did you hear Mary say?" |
| Diffuse tensions | Clarify areas of agreement | "You both want the conflict to stop."<br>"You want to be able to trust one another." |
| Diffuse tensions | Highlight positives | "Mary values your friendship."<br>"Mary is sorry she hurt your feelings." |
| Resolve issues | Emphasize the future | "What would you like to see happen?" "What would work for you?" |
| Resolve issues | Focus on solutions | "Mary would like you to return her phone calls."<br>"Mary wants you to keep her confidences." |

While mediating conflicts between your teen and others, be careful not to take sides. Insisting that, "My son is innocent and is being picked on" doesn't help anyone. Instead, support your teen by summarizing his explanations to be sure he is heard: "My son is saying that he believes he is innocent and feels he is being picked on." Summarize the responses if your teen is having difficulty hearing what his antagonist is saying to him.

Your job as mediator is to help the parties involved work through their differences and arrive at a solution that works for them. Your role is to help everyone speak and be heard without taking sides. Rather than solving your child's problems, your goal should be to facilitate the problem-solving process.

## Resolving Family Conflicts

The idea of the empty nest didn't make sense to William. His parents' nest would hardly be empty—they had many years to go before the last of their children would leave home. He believed that his mother doubted his ability to handle life on his own, which made William afraid even though he kept telling her he would be fine. William believed that his dad couldn't accept that his little boy had grown up enough to have opinions of his own, which hurt because William wanted his father's approval even if he didn't want to be a carbon copy of him. During an argument over William's failure to set the table properly, his mother suggested that everyone write down what they wanted to say in hopes of improving their communication. Beatrice wrote, "I'm having a hard time with the idea that you're growing up. I feel like there are a lot of things I didn't teach you. I guess I'm trying to make up for lost time." Bruce wrote, "I've gotten where I am today by doing things the way they're supposed to be done. Whether the fork goes on the left or right may seem silly to you, but getting the details right can take you a long way in life." William wrote, "When I'm on my own, I hope you'll think of me as the son who helped set the table, not as the kid who put the forks on the wrong side of the plates."

As Beatrice and Bruce contemplated what their son had written, they realized the wisdom of his words. Beatrice now understood why she had overreacted during their argument with William the previous day, but still felt embarrassed. "Maybe we should spend less time trying to teach William and more time trying to learn from him," Beatrice said. "I assume it's not too late for old dogs like us to learn some new tricks." Bruce smiled. "We managed to find our forks even though they were on the wrong side of our plates," he said. "I guess we can handle more than we thought."

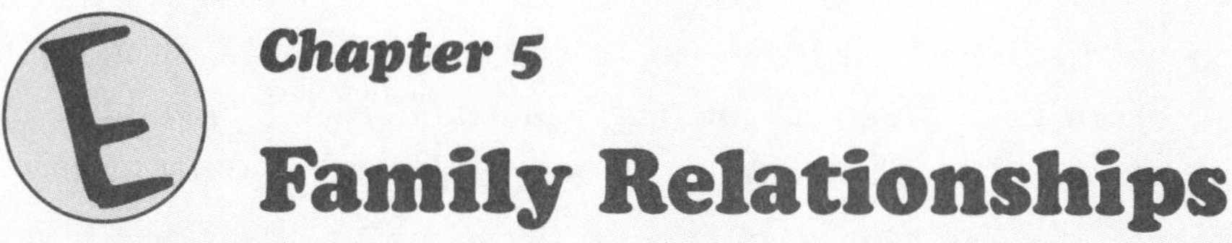

# Chapter 5
# Family Relationships

Consider the many benefits of sending your teen for an extended visit to a relative. Traveling alone will satisfy your child's quest for independence. He will learn about his roots, experience life in a different home, and forge a stronger relationship with an aunt, uncle, grandparent, or older sibling. He will have another caring adult to help guide him through adolescence if the trip goes well. If not—who knows? He just might miss you enough to be friendly when he returns.

## Sibling Relationships

George and Hannah had spent many years dreaming of the day when their kids would stop bickering long enough to decide they liked one another. Now that Sarita was approaching her eighteenth birthday, they supposed their wishes would never come true. Their three offspring continued to tease one another to the point of tears. They tattled on one another. They still argued about whose turn it was to sit in the front seat and who had received the bigger piece of pie. When cooped up together in the car on a family vacation, they drove one another and their parents to distraction.

Trying to be fair by creating the same rules for everyone can actually increase sibling rivalry. All children want to be treated as individuals, and this is particularly important to teens. To reduce competitiveness, make decisions according to each youngster's unique capabilities and needs.

Sarita's parents sometimes wondered if having three children so close together meant that Sarita had been forced to relinquish her baby days before she was ready. Despite Sarita's conflicts with her younger siblings, she got along famously with most everyone else. She was so popular at school that once she was nominated for homecoming queen and class president, victory was certain. She got along well with other adults and was liked by her teachers. She was even the favorite babysitter for a gaggle of neighborhood tweens and preschoolers, which proved she could get along with younger children—as long as they weren't related to her. George and Hannah feared that once Sarita moved out on her own, she would avoid holiday gatherings like the plague. They knew that some siblings were still arguing and trying to one-up each other as their parents lay on their deathbeds. George and Hannah hated to think their brood would never get along, but supposed they should accept that sad reality.

Comparing your children and settling their disputes increase sibling rivalry! While the top dog gloats, the loser will be itching for another round so he can beat his competitor. Affirm each child's strengths. Separate combatants so they can concoct a plan for settling their differences.

## Girls and Moms

If you think living under the roof with an adolescent daughter entitles you to a Presidential Medal of Honor, you're probably right. Amazing numbers of otherwise considerate, well-mannered, well-brought-up girls of good character decide their mothers are their arch enemies and turn on them like crazed warriors. The current norm for females is to spend all or part of their teenaged years being sullen, sarcastic, and condescending toward the person they once showered with wildflower bouquets and homemade Mother's Day cards. There will undoubtedly be some moments when your not-so-darling daughter waves the peace flag and opens both her heart and her bedroom door to you. During a brief, if unexpected, cessation of hostilities you might even score some real treasure: a hug, an affectionate tone of voice, some basic human consideration, or even a sincere apology for past war crimes. Nevertheless, sullen pouts and full-blown tantrums that would make a toddler proud are common.

Exercise daily, meditate regularly, cry on friends' shoulders, and do what you can to care for yourself through this difficult time. If you are one of the fortunate few with a daughter who treats you like a human being, support your long-suffering friends.

### Understanding Girls

No one really knows what drives teenaged girls' abominable behavior toward their mothers. Mothers spend inordinate amounts of time contemplating the "whys." Too often, they blame themselves. It can help to know that lots of experts are actively researching the problem. They may not have clear answers, but at least you can take comfort from knowing you're not alone.

One theory goes that girls have an especially hard time emotionally separating from their mothers because mother/daughter bonds tend to be particularly strong. This is true even if their relationship over the years has been riddled by conflict and ill will. When teen girls fight with their mother, they may be battling their own desire to remain within the safety of her protective shadow. From what girls share in therapy sessions, it is clear that those who are more insecure and fearful about growing up and becoming independent engage in the most heated battles with their mothers. Girls' repeated refrains, "I'm nothing like her" and "I can't stand her," seem to be an attempt to figure out who they are *not* as a first step toward figuring out who they are.

**QUESTION?**

**My daughter says I treat her like a child. What am I doing wrong?**
See if you can converse about the issues that undoubtedly concern her most: dating, drugs, alcohol, and sex. If you can avoid talking down to her, you may be able to restore some warmth to your relationship.

Another theory is that girls spend much of their childhoods dreaming of growing up to be Cinderella, Barbie, or Miss America. A real life mother reminds girls that they will grow up to be women, not goddesses. Noting and cataloguing a mother's warts and flaws may reflect girls' disappointment as they begin realizing what lies in store for them. As girls rage against and finally come to terms with their mother's imperfections, they come to terms with their own.

If this Cinderella theory is correct, having your daughter so preoccupied with your personal failings is healthy for her. Nevertheless, it is unacceptable for your daughter (or anyone else!) to insult, humiliate, and degrade you. Unfortunately, you may not be able to force respectful behavior. Retaliating in kind isn't likely to improve your relationship and may make it worse.

You can try sending your daughter to her room if she's having a tantrum, but if she won't go, you may have to barricade yourself in yours. Don't swear back at her or yell. A simple "I don't wish to hear any more of this—go to your room" should be enough to communicate your displeasure. You can (and probably should) let it be known that you expect an apology. Unfortunately, even if you get a genuine one, she may repeat the same obnoxious behavior an hour, day, week, or month later.

Unless you are made of stone, your daughter's sarcasm and haughty attitude can lead to haunting questions: "Am I raising a monster?" "Am I doing something terribly wrong?" "Do I deserve this kind of treatment?" Most certainly the answers will turn out to be, "No," "No," and "No."

Until your daughter matures, you may need to focus on protecting yourself. To that end, don't make yourself a target by asking for her opinion about your appearance, clothes, or behavior. Don't try to garner approval by using teen slang, adopting teen fashions, or trying to be the teen version of "cool." Trying to remake yourself in her image won't help her, you, or your relationship. She needs you to be a role model for her, not the other way around. Respect her need to be alone with her friends and don't say things to embarrass her, but when chauffeuring her about, don't hide out as if you were someone she has reason to be ashamed of. If she is embarrassed for her friends to see you, that is her problem, not yours. She needs to get over it. Eventually she will.

## Appreciating Mom

Mothers are understandably saddened when their once-adoring daughters withdraw during adolescence. Teen girls who distance themselves from their mothers may not think that they need guidance from a mature woman. Years later, many young women regret what they missed during adolescence and wonder why they felt compelled to hold their mothers at arms' length. "How could you stand me?" they ask. "I was so awful to you!" How long will you have to wait to hear those golden words? The typical pattern is for girls to become more appreciative of their mothers soon after moving out on their own. As daughters continue to mature, their respect and admiration for their mothers deepen.

## What Girls Think about Moms

**AGE 4:** My mommy knows everything!

**AGE 8:** My mom knows almost as much as my teacher!

**AGE 10:** My mom probably knows. I'll ask her.

**AGE 12:** My mother is wrong about a lot of things.

**AGE 14:** My old lady doesn't know much of anything.

**AGE 16:** That woman is clueless!

**AGE 18:** That old woman? What would she know?

**AGE 25:** Well, Mom might know. Maybe I'll ask her.

**AGE 35:** Before I decide, I'll ask Mother.

**AGE 45:** I wonder what Mother would say about this.

**AGE 65:** If only I could talk it over with Mother.

If your daughter doesn't fit the stereotype and she proudly claims you as a relative, either she is exceptionally easygoing or she trusts that you really are on her side in her struggle to become her own person. What can you do and say to convince your daughter you want what's best for her? Ask, and chances are she will say, "Just leave me alone!" Trust that she will be able to be close when she feels more secure in her own identity. In the meantime, if she won't discuss personal matters with you, see if you can find an older-but-wiser female confidante and guide for her.

## Family Triangles

When girls are so angry with their mother, are they trying to oust her so they can have their father all to themselves? Freud, the father of modern psychiatry, thought this might be the underlying issue, and lots of modern mothers are convinced that their daughters are competing with them for their husbands. In fact, picking arguments with mom and turning to dad for comfort is a common family dynamic, and many girls and fathers forge their relationship during long talks about how to get along with the witch who is ruining her daughter's life.

If girls are out to steal their father, they certainly aren't aware of this. The idea that anyone could find their father even slightly appealing strikes them as shocking; the idea that they might want him for themselves seems totally gross. More likely, girls tear their mother down because they fear they will never be as competent as she is and are trying to boost their own egos. Receiving dad's reassurance that they are worthy, capable, and lovable is what makes their relationship so important.

## Boys and Mothers

Sons tend to treat their mothers a bit better than daughters treat their mothers, but unfortunately that's not saying much. While girls rage to create more emotional distance, boys are more likely to withdraw. Creating more of a physical separation is easier for boys because parents typically allow sons more freedom to come and go. When tensions heat up at home, a boy can announce that he is going to stay at his girlfriend's and stamp out the door without provoking a major crisis. If a girl heads for her boyfriend's under similar circumstances, her parents are likely to try to stop her if they can and may call the police if they can't.

Boys distance themselves emotionally from their mothers by retreating into their shells. Boys may not hear her or even register the fact that she is standing right in front of them, trying to get their attention. A mother may feel that she is being purposely ignored, which can thoroughly frustrate her.

As a rule, boys are not as in touch with their feelings as girls, which can make them harder for mothers to deal with. Boys may not realize they are getting angry until they suddenly find themselves overwhelmed. They also have a harder time putting their feelings into words. When confronting your son, go easy. Push him too far, and he many punch a hole in a wall or break something in pure frustration. Don't be surprised if your son turns on his heels and heads toward his room or out the front door in the middle of an argument. When teens feel out of control and in danger of striking out physically, they need to learn to walk away until they regain control. Don't follow or try to stop him. It is better to heed your son's demands to be left alone than to carry on to the point that he loses control. Try another talk when he is calmer.

Adolescent boys' sexual impulses are very strong, and being close to any female can trigger sexual feelings. Boys are confused and extremely disturbed when they become aroused from mom's hug, kiss, or kindness. Respect your son's need for physical and emotional space.

An important developmental task for adolescent boys is to establish their identity as an adult male, and most boys are secretly obsessed with worries about their virility. Boys growing up with fathers who are physically or psychologically absent often lack male role models. Such boys may end up taking their cues about manliness from the characters they see on television programs and movies. Unfortunately, men are usually portrayed as violent rogues in dramas, as nincompoops in comedies, and as womanizers in both. Many adolescent boys behave like young macho men toward their moms in an effort to act like their heroes, while adopting a know-it-all attitude to convince her they aren't stupid.

Boys are under a lot of pressure to be virile, and most harbor secret worries about their masculinity and ability to assume the role of a full-fledged man. As a result, boys may try to act like he-men and are often fearful of their feminine side. To avoid appearing weak or effeminate, boys may hide their tender emotions from others and squelch them within themselves. That means they really need to avoid Mother, who knows they are weak and frightened and is uniquely able to evoke their tender emotions. Moreover, she undermines their manliness by expecting them to do chores boys consider to be "woman's work." Since their fragile male ego can't stand having a woman tell them what to do, they may not tolerate her assigning them any chores whatsoever. Try to assuage your son's anxieties by letting him know that his helpfulness around the house means that he will make a fine husband and father.

## Teens and Dads

With so much emphasis placed on the importance of good mothering over the last decades, fathers may feel that their contributions don't much matter. Nothing could be further from the truth! Experts now realize that dads are more powerful role models for their children than was previously thought. Girls' attitudes toward men and boys' attitudes toward women are largely formed by watching how their father treats their mother. A girl's expectations of how men ought to treat her are based on what she witnessed at home.

Dad's actions have a big impact on a girl's desire to be similar to or different from her mother. A girl is less likely to want to be like her mother if her father rejected her mother.

Like girls, boys take their cues from Father about how to relate to women. Boys tend to treat the central woman in their life the way their father treated their mother. Even if a boy grew up despising his father's physical or emotional abusiveness toward his mother, he is likely to repeat the pattern by mistreating his wife. In so doing, such a boy misses out on the joy of a satisfying love relationship. Worse, he may perpetuate the cycle of abuse by passing it on to his own sons.

Modern teens can seem overly materialistic, but contrary to what many people think, teens don't value dad according to the size of his paycheck. Research shows that teens' overall life satisfaction is more related to the quality of their relationship with their father than to their families' economic status. Teens who have a warm relationship with dear old dad tend to be more optimistic, self-confident, and able to influence what happens to them. Those who don't feel good about their relationship with their father are more pessimistic and don't feel so able to take charge of their lives, according to an article by Hasida Ben-Zur in the April 2003 *Journal of Youth and Adolescence*.

Telling your teen to respect your wife is important, but it is not enough. In this critical area, teens are more likely to do what their fathers do than what their fathers tell them to do. You must respect your wife with your words and deeds if you want your children to treat her respectfully.

Unfortunately, despite the fact that teens value their fathers, they are largely absent from children's lives. In *Father Hunger*, author Margo Maine indicates that only 20 percent of teens see their fathers at least once a week. By early adolescence, 50 percent of American children have no contact with their fathers whatsoever, and 30 percent have only sporadic contact. Over eleven million children are not in contact with their fathers on a daily basis.

## Girls and Dads

The challenge for adolescent females is to develop an appreciation for their minds and hearts as well as for their bodies. Fathers play a unique and important role in this process. Most men are initially shocked when they suddenly realize that their little girl has turned into a voluptuous young woman. It is important for them to appreciate that seeing her as attractive will help her see herself that way. Some men believe that to be aware of their daughter's sexuality is somehow abnormal or wrong. In fact, it is normal and right. When a father can simultaneously enjoy his daughter's personality and affirm her sexuality, he helps his daughter appreciate herself.

Some parents are concerned about their teenaged daughter's behavior toward their father, which at times may appear flirtatious, provocative, or even blatantly seductive. A closer look inevitably reveals that the daughters aren't doing anything differently than they've been doing all along; the difference is in the eyes of the beholders. When a gangly prepubescent child jumps on her father's lap and begins hugging and tickling him, everyone understands that she is being affectionately playful. When a young woman with breasts and hips does the same, she may appear to adults to be making sexual advances. She is not. In her mind, she is still daddy's little girl. To treat her as if she were doing something shameful or wrong will only confuse and upset her.

Pushing your daughter away when she sits on your lap may wound her deeply. Set limits by having her sit at your side while letting her know that you appreciate the beautiful young woman she has become.

Regardless of what clothes are in fashion with the younger crowd, having a half-naked teenaged girl bounding through the house or a bikini-clad daughter lounging about during a family vacation can be unsettling for one or both parents. Setting limits is important not only for their comfort but for helping your daughter realize that regardless of how she perceives herself, she is now a woman. Moreover, since other males will also see her as an adult, it is important for her to start becoming aware of the effect she has on adults. Unfortunately, setting limits is easier said than done. This is a potentially embarrassing subject for daughters and parents alike. Telling a daughter in a disgusted or angry tone that she needs to put on more clothes or change her behavior toward her father can make her feel that her sexuality is something shameful. Growing up shouldn't have to mean losing her father's hugs or affection. Be gentle.

Dads play an important role in helping adolescent daughters to separate from their mothers. Girls commonly turn to their fathers for support as mother/daughter conflicts intensify. By empathizing without taking sides, fathers help to diffuse tensions as the women struggle to create a new relationship as equals.

Disturbances in the father/daughter relationship are common among girls with eating disorders. The author of *Father Hunger: Fathers, Daughters and Food* notes that to become confident young women, "Girls need to be 'courted' by their fathers, in a non-seductive way." This helps girls to accept their changing bodies, which boosts their confidence with boys. In the absence of acceptance from the most important male in their lives, girls are at risk for self-doubt, self-deprecation, and even depression. Otherwise, they may retreat from social contacts, behave promiscuously, or develop an eating disorder.

How a father relates to his teenaged daughter can exert a profound influence on her future love relationships. Denying her sexuality is as destructive in its own way as being overly preoccupied with it. Your daughter needs you to accept her as a total person.

## Boys and Dads

It goes without saying that a boy needs both of his parents, not only to love him but also to accept him for who he is. True acceptance can be hard for a dad, especially if he began planning his son's future at birth. It is, in fact, common for fathers to dream of having a son to follow in their footsteps by attending the same college, joining the same fraternity, entering the same line of work, or taking over the family business. Many fathers sacrificed some of their cherished dreams on behalf of their family, laboring to ensure their son would one day travel the path they weren't personally able to pursue. Discovering that their son has a different plan for his future can be a blow. Many fathers take their son's wish to go in a different direction as a personal rejection. Unfortunately, the truth is usually a bit more brutal: Rather than rejecting their fathers' wishes, a son may never have given them much serious consideration in the first place. Boys tend to be quite independent. Only rarely will a flesh-and-blood child want to make the ultimate sacrifice of dedicating his life to pursuing his father's dreams.

In speaking of children, the poet Kahlil Gibran said, "You may give them your love but not your thoughts, for they have their own thoughts. You may house their bodies but not their souls. For their souls dwell in the house of tomorrow, which you cannot visit, not even in your dreams."

## Family Solutions

Sarita had passed her difficult stage and now got along well with her father and mother, but only as long as neither of her siblings was around. Enter a brother or sister, and Sarita turned back into a whining, tattling ten-year-old. In desperation, her parents vowed to stay out of all sibling disputes no matter who had started what and regardless of who had done what to whom. Instead, they sent all warring parties to their bedrooms until they could come up with a solution. Things came to a head when an evening dispute wasn't resolved, and all three children started in on one another at breakfast the next morning. "Family comes first," Hannah said. "No one leaves the house until this is worked out." Sarita was furious about being late to school. Hannah was worried about missing work and was dismayed when her son appeared delighted to stay home from school. But thirty minutes later he was bored and ready to work things out. The sacrifice was worth it, because after that, all three children made a real effort to get along when it appeared they might be sent to their bedrooms. Real friendship might still be a long way off, but George and Hannah thought it might yet be in their futures.

Chapter 6

# Communicating with Teens

If talking to your teen is like talking to a brick wall, you're not alone. Most young people close their bedroom doors to isolate themselves, secrete themselves behind walls of anger to hold family members at bay, and use slang and coded communications to prevent eavesdropping. If your attempts at lighthearted conversation draw grunts and frowns and your teen grows evasive when you broach a serious subject, don't try to tear through the shroud of silence. Instead, learn to listen without judging. That is the key to unlocking a teen's heart.

## Reading Between the Lines

Since Alex had turned thirteen, even simple conversations had a way of turning into arguments. One night Alex's mother reminded him that if he intended to go to an upcoming party as planned, he needed to do his chores as per their agreement. For some reason, that made Alex furious.

Alex made a sarcastic comment to the effect that his mother should mind her own business. A heated exchange followed. "Have it your way. I won't go to the party!" Alex said. His mother was mystified. "I want you to go to the party, Alex," she said. But Alex was adamant. "I knew you'd find a way to stop me!" he insisted. His mother said, "I think it would be fun for you." Alex rolled his eyes, crossed his arms, and said that dreaded word, "Whatever" before stamping off to his room.

FACT

Counselors have a saying that what people can't talk out, they act out. Your teen's behavior can give you clues as to her needs. If she seems content when she's grounded and becomes touchy and irritable when her privileges are restored, she probably needs more time at home.

The current dilemma for Alex's parents was whether or not to let him attend the upcoming party. Alex's father thought he should go. However, Alex's mother wasn't sure. Since Alex had insisted they would stop him from going to the party, she thought that might be a clue to say no. But who could be certain? They wished they could have a heart-to-heart with him. Without his input, they felt like they were stumbling through a darkened cave without a flashlight.

## Time to Talk

In busy households, finding time to talk can be a challenge. Most psychologists agree that families can't have quality time unless they have a sufficient quantity of time together.

## The Weekly "Date"

If your household is too chaotic for you and your teen to talk without a dozen interruptions, make a "date" and leave everyone else at home. Go out for donuts once a week or make it a habit to take a Sunday afternoon stroll. Your teen may be willing to accompany you on errands if you leave the other children at home. Keep the radio off. Having your teen accompany you on a business trip isn't something you could do often, but having an extended period of time together can sometimes get the conversational ball rolling well enough that afterwards, only small nudges are required to keep it going. Even a once-a-year day-long fishing trip may go a long way toward shoring up your relationship. Sometimes it doesn't matter what is said or how it's said. Quiet time together can provide a sense of closeness. A warm silence sometimes communicates more than a dozen conversations.

## Daily Talk Time

Note your teen's daily patterns to get a feel for when he is most receptive to chatting. In general, transition points are often the best time to have pleasant conversations, such as after homework is finished, right before bed, or first thing in the morning. After coming home from school, some teens are very touchy until they've had time to relax, unwind, and restore their sagging blood sugar via a snack. Others come home chattering away, and there is a small window of opportunity for a decent conversation before they settle into other projects. If you are at work during your teen's prime talking time, see if you can arrange to check in via the telephone. Shake yourself awake when your teen comes home from a date and see if he's up for chatting about his evening. If it's too late for him to call his friends to process what transpired, he might appreciate your company.

FACT

Most teens have radios or CD players in their bedrooms. Over a third also have VCRs, DVD players, and video games as well. Sixty-five percent have their own television and 21 percent have a computer. To free up time for family conversation, oust the electronics!

Make it a goal to spend fifteen minutes alone together each day. It's a sad statement on modern family life that in most households, that would be a tough goal to meet. Perhaps the only solution is to do a complete lifestyle overhaul. If so, declaring the television off-limits during the week may be just what the psychologist ordered to give the people who live under your roof a chance to function like a family. Calculate the number of months you can count on having your teen living under your roof, and you will see why it is important to make every day count.

## Conversation Starters

Parents often find themselves flailing about for an icebreaker so that they can connect with their teen. Even innocent comments and questions such as "Hi, how was your day" commonly draw angry, sarcastic, or other off-putting replies. Because teens are going through so many changes, their stress levels tend to be high, and most young people spend a lot of time on emotional overload. When teens are feeling overwhelmed, they typically become silent and uncommunicative. Like turtles, they pull into themselves, and they resent having people trying to get them to come out of their shells.

Be considerate of your teen's need to withdraw when he's feeling overwhelmed, but insist that he be considerate of you. If he bites your head off when you make an innocent comment, explain that the proper response is, "I don't feel like talking just now."

A teen's favorite topic of conversation is himself, but when your child is feeling touchy, almost any question you ask may be the wrong one. Ask how his chemistry exam went, and he may not want to admit that he thinks he failed. He may not want to say that he thought it was pretty easy, either, if when he said as much to his girlfriend, she called him a showoff or a nerd. The solution is to avoid asking questions! Modeling is the most potent form of teaching, so if you want your teen to talk about his day, demonstrate by talking about yours. Will your teen care how your day went? Perhaps not. But teens tend to be overly self-absorbed and benefit from reminders that other humans inhabit the planet, and that parents are actually members of the species. As long as you're not overwhelming your teen by sharing lots of heavy-duty personal problems, he may enjoy the experience. Being talked to like an adult is affirming; he gets a peek into the adult world he will soon join, and having an opportunity to give you some advice now and then will boost his self-confidence.

## Responding to Teen Dramas

Modern teens' special style of speech can make them sound as though their life is one crisis after another. This is particularly true for girls. By emphasizing every other word and ending every sentence with a verbal exclamation point, ordinary events come across like high-octane dramas.

Most parents can readily comprehend what is going on when a teen says, "I couldn't *believe* my *eyes*! I was just *standing* there when suddenly *there he was, THE hottest guy in school, right by my locker, looking at me*! I could have *died!*" Her facial expressions and gestures say more clearly than her words that she was delighted by the chance encounter.

FACT

Don't feel badly if your teen shares the details of his days with his friends instead of you. Do you really want to spend two hours rehashing his two-minute encounter with a cute girl? If so, don't yawn when he gives you the details. Otherwise, be glad for his friends!

Teens can be equally melodramatic when they are unhappy. Because their upsets may be frequent, triggered by minor events, and very short-lived, it is easy to become jaded. Do your best not to assume she is crying wolf. Instead, listen compassionately, then go on about your business. If you think your teen is making mountains out of molehills for attention, make sure you are responding when she is happy. Some teens can only get their parents' attention when they have a crisis brewing. Do not question that her feelings are real or suggest she is overreacting. Her problems are real to her. You can't have a good relationship with your child unless you fully accept that truth. If your teen can't trust you with small problems, she'll be less likely to share big ones.

When your teen says that everything is fine but she's clearly troubled, don't try to pry information out of her. Do reassure her that you are available to listen if she wants to talk. Let it be her decision.

It can be hard not to react when your teen finally brings up a subject that you have very strong feelings about and have been anxious to discuss. Be careful how you respond when you hear, "I'm so behind in English. It will take me *all night* to write the essay, and I'll *flunk* if I don't turn it in *tomorrow*." If you've been unhappy about your teen's study habits, you might be tempted to use this moment to interrogate her to find out why she's behind, lecture her about the importance of keeping up, chastise her for not devoting enough time to her studies, or tell her to stop complaining and get busy. Don't do it! Such negativity on your part will make her regret having mentioned her schoolwork to you. Instead, be glad she is concerned enough to consider it a problem. And tell her so! "I'm glad your grades matter to you and you're concerned about getting your work turned in on time."

If your teen cannot trust you to listen respectfully, she will find others to confide in. The people most likely to fill in the gap will be peers. While they may be supportive, older-and-wiser adults are in a better position to guide. Make a commitment to listen without criticizing and judging.

Your teen definitely needs an adult to talk to. If for whatever reason your child feels she cannot confide in you, you need to make sure she has someone. A teacher, coach, counselor, member of the clergy, or next-door neighbor can serve as a sounding board, and having someone to listen to her is even more important than having someone to talk to her. It is often hard for parents, however, when the child they love maintains a stony silence at home and pours out her heart to a stranger.

## Listening Skills

Most people have an extremely hard time listening to one another—so hard, that therapists spend untold hours and make their livings helping parents and children master this tricky business. The best tactic for getting teens to talk is simply to give them lots of time to respond. They aren't as adept as adults at mentally processing incoming messages, organizing their thoughts, and finding the words to express what they want to say. When they are emotional, their thinking typically slows to a snail's pace. It takes considerable time for them to unravel their emotions, find a pattern to their jumbled thoughts, and knit some words into a coherent response. After you ask a question or make a comment, pause for at least five seconds before saying anything else. That may sound easy, but it isn't! Time yourself, and you'll probably discover that the reason you have so many one-sided conversations is because you fill in all the pauses. Your teen literally cannot get a word in edgewise. If your teen doesn't respond in five seconds, ask if he heard you. Chances are good that his mind wandered off, either because he's learned from experience he doesn't have to participate or because his mind has carried him to a less stressful subject. Repeat your question and give him another five seconds.

FACT

Some popular teen expressions mean the exact opposite of what you might expect. For example, "That's bad!" means "That's good!" in some circles. Instead of barreling through conversations assuming you know what your teen is trying to tell you, make it a habit to summarize and ask if you understood correctly.

To be a good listener, let your teen know that you heard what he said and show that you are trying to understand him. To do that, you need to provide "listening" responses every time he pauses to come up for air. Those are responses that stick to what he said and do not go beyond it. They include simply restating what he said, summarizing the content of what he said, reflecting the feelings he expressed, and/or asking questions to clarify what he said without expanding on the meaning. Parents have such a hard time responding without inserting their own thoughts and ideas into the conversation, they often need a referee to hold them in check. If your conversations with your teen typically degenerate into shouting matches or silent seething, sign up for lessons. Every therapist in America dedicates most of the time in family counseling sessions to teaching them.

## Conversational Do's and Don'ts

Ask teens why they confide in their friends and not their parents, and almost everyone gives one of the following responses: "My friends listen." "My friends don't judge me." "My friends accept me for who I am." "My friends can relate to what I'm going through." "My friends don't have personal agendas." "My friends don't try to change me." Your teen may be wrong about her friends, but because she *thinks* they have those qualities, she trusts them. The question is how to convince her that you have them, too.

Few parent/teen interactions count as real conversations. Parents spend most of their time explaining, directing, instructing, and lecturing. Know-it-alls are hard to be around, which is why so many teens dislike their parents' company. Sometimes being right hurts more than it helps. Let your teen be the expert sometimes. Let him do some things his own way.

| DON'T . . . | DO . . . |
| --- | --- |
| "Multitask" your teen by trying to listen while simultaneously handling other chores. | Let the answering machine get the phone, put down the dust rag, tell your other children you are busy, and give your teen your undivided attention. |

| DON'T . . . | DO . . . |
|---|---|
| Tell your teen you understand what she is going through and expect to be believed. | Recount a time you confronted a similar dilemma or were in a situation that evoked similar feelings. |
| Insist that you can relate to your teen's problems if you cannot. | Tell your teen that you never had to go through anything like he's going through, and that you wish he didn't have to, either. |
| Try to nudge your teen in a particular direction. | Tell your teen that when people are upset, they fantasize about doing different things, but you trust her to make the decision that seems best for her and everyone concerned. |
| Tell your teen what to do. | Soften your suggestions by asking, "Have you considered . . . " "What would happen if you . . ." "What if . . ." |
| Betray her confidences if you can help it. | Let her know in advance if you must divulge something she told you. Give your reasons and affirm her right to feel angry and betrayed. |

## Responding to Teen Confessions

Alex's parents decided that if he asked for a ride to the party, they would drive him. He never said another word about it. He talked on the phone for a while and was in a fairly decent mood afterwards. Still, his mother couldn't decide whether to feel guilty or not. At bedtime she asked Alex how he felt about missing it. He said it worked out okay, because his friends understood he was grounded, and it turned out that they didn't need him there. "Didn't need you?" his mother asked. Alex then explained that two boys had gotten into an argument at school and agreed to settle their score at the party. "The guy is in a gang, and he was supposed to bring his homies. He didn't show, though. What a chicken." Alex's mother smiled. "Yeah. A chicken." As she turned out his light, she added, "Anytime something like that comes up again, you're automatically grounded. Do you understand? And if you're already out, you have an early curfew. Which means you are to come home *immediately*. If not sooner." Alex grunted. "I knew you'd be that way," he said. It was too dark to see if he looked as relieved as she felt.

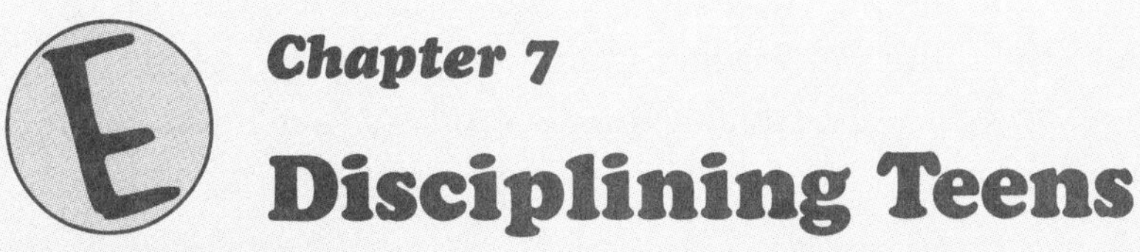

# Chapter 7
# Disciplining Teens

Many experts say that good parents must set limits and enforce consequences to keep their children on track. Most junior high school students benefit from some parental structure. However, by high school it's usually better for families to work together to decide what the rules and penalties should be. Actually, some parents have no other choice. If your teen ignores your rules and walks out the door when you ground him, it's time to face reality: You can no longer call all the shots.

## Controlling Your Teen

Kirsten thought she should be allowed to stay out on weekends until the town's teen curfew, but her parents thought that 1:00 A.M. was too late for a fifteen-year-old. School basketball games and movies ended long before then, and only the bars served customers after midnight. For a young woman to be out after 11:00 P.M. struck them as too dangerous. What was there to do in the wee hours of the morning except get into trouble? If Kirsten's friends were drinking, they feared she might join them. The thought of her in a car with a drunk teen driver terrified them.

Communicate your expectations clearly to your teenager so he knows what will please and disappoint you. If your teen defies your rules and seems not to care what you think, forget trying to be stricter. Concentrate on building a better relationship even if that means waiting to deal with some problem behaviors.

One Saturday night, Kirsten called home just before her curfew and asked if she could stay out later. Her parents were adamant that she return home. A few weeks later she came in an hour late with a flimsy excuse, so they grounded her. She accused them of treating her like a baby and not trusting her; her mother told Kirsten that by coming home late, she had proved herself untrustworthy. Kirsten's parents reassured themselves that their daughter might be furious with them, but at least she was safe. That comforting idea fell apart when they caught her sneaking out of her window at night a few weeks later. How to control a child who refuses to cooperate? How to protect her?

## Teens as Individuals

How nice it would be if there were rule books detailing what parents should and shouldn't allow teenagers of different ages to do! No such book exists because rules need to be based on what will help your particular child learn and grow. Of course your child must observe federal, state, and local laws like every other citizen; school rules like every other student; and household rules like other family members. But rules about curfew, driving, dating, studying, and so forth should be based on your teen's unique needs.

Teens are insistent about being treated as individuals, and rightly so. Does your teen actually need a curfew? If she is responsible, uses good judgment, and is careful about her safety, she may not need one. Let her decide when to come home.

No two teenagers are alike. When some sixteen-year-olds head out in the family car, they are more conscientious than adults who have driven for years without an accident or ticket. Such teens may not need any restrictions. Other teenaged drivers are so reckless that they are an accident waiting to happen. Handing them the keys to the family car is like handing a book of matches to a toddler and sending him out to play. Your teen's capabilities should determine your rules.

You do your teen a serious disservice by making decisions based on stereotypical ideas of what teenagers need. Some very pro-social teens protest by rebelling. It may seem to them that being a good kid and trying to do the right thing isn't worth the trouble.

Some teenagers only handle their homework and household chores responsibly when their parents outlaw television watching, long telephone conversations, and computer games on school nights. They must also be supervised to get their work done. Other children generally tend to their studies but sometimes need reminders to help them keep their priorities straight. Many students are conscientious about project deadlines, do all of their homework, and wouldn't dream of not preparing for a test. Asking the latter type of student a seemingly innocent question such as, "Don't you think you should get started on your homework?" understandably makes them furious. After all, how you would feel if a friend asked you, "Don't you think you should get started on the dishes now?" That sounds very condescending to an adult who feels capable of making decisions about when to wash dishes without outside help. If your teen handles her schoolwork like an adult, she deserves to be treated like one!

## The Punishment Problem

Psychologists have long warned that punishing children is not the most effective way to get them to behave. Heavy-handed methods may succeed at keeping some younger children in line but backfire as soon as they discover their parents can no longer control them. Nevertheless, many parents continue to yell, criticize, take away privileges, and ground teenagers to try to improve their behavior. Even if intimidation kept you in line, it is ineffective for most modern children.

Corporal punishment is an absolute no-no for adolescents. Being struck on the buttocks can trigger a sexual response despite the pain. The combined sensation can create serious problems in adult sexual functioning. Do not hit an adolescent!

To many parents, punishing misbehavior seems like a good way to ensure that justice is served. They believe that punishment helps youngsters to focus on what they have done wrong and learn the important truth that crime doesn't pay. That sounds logical, but children who get punished the most tend to have the worst behavior. Even if they behave while under their parents' watchful eye, as soon as they are on their own they do as they please. Elementary school students who constantly misbehave are regularly punished by their teachers, but their behavior usually gets worse as the years go by instead of improving. Lots of college students go wild when they are on their own.

Although threats and punishments keep some young children in line, most discover long before adolescence that they only get in trouble if they get caught. Some parents actually say, "If I catch you doing that again, you're going to get it." Teens who were punished a lot during childhood are often very deceitful. They have had lots of practice sneaking, lying, and covering their tracks to hide their misbehavior.

Many discipline problems are really moral problems in disguise. For instance, it is wrong for a student to express anger toward a teacher by disrupting class. A disliked teacher doesn't deserve maltreatment however unpleasant her personality, and disruptions are unfair to students who are trying to learn.

Punishing children for what they have done wrong doesn't teach them how to control themselves and behave correctly. Hence, punishments often fail because they don't address the real issues. For instance, lots of teens make poor grades because they don't know how to manage their time. They watch television, talk on the phone, and postpone studying until they are too tired to concentrate. They underestimate how long it will take them to read a chapter or do a report. They don't know how to break up large projects into small steps and do a little each day, so big projects overwhelm them. Punish your teenager for being lazy and not caring and you may both miss the point: He may need a tutor, study buddy, or a class in study skills.

You assume your teen won't clean his room because he doesn't want to be bothered. Surely a fifteen-year-old can handle the job! But a really messy room can be so overwhelming that teens may feel unsure about how and where to begin. Offering your teen help with getting started might be more effective than a punishment.

Perhaps the biggest problem with punishing children is that they often end up feeling angry with whoever punishes them. A week after you ground your teen, she might not remember what she did wrong, but she will probably remember how mistreated she felt when you wouldn't let her go to the movies with her friends. If you can't quite remember why she's grounded, there's a good chance you handed down a sentence in a moment of anger. That means you were probably more concerned about making her suffer than figuring out how to help her learn.

## The Blame Game

Many parents try to give teenagers constructive criticism, but some young people are too sensitive to benefit from it. All they learn is to blame their problems on everyone else. Instead of accepting responsibility for their actions, they blame their curfew violation on the car that broke down and their drug use on their parents' divorce ten years ago. Instead of playing the blame game when your child comes in past his curfew, have a straightforward discussion about the problems: Does your teen think his curfew is unfair? What time does he consider reasonable? If he were to be delayed, how could he handle the situation responsibly? What does he think the consequence should be for violating a curfew? If you let him stay out later, can you trust him not to drink or use drugs? Conclude such conversations by telling your teen you will rethink the problem and get back to him. Even if you do not extend his curfew, you have sent an important message: You respect his opinion and are trying to consider what is in his best interest. Tell him what he can do to earn your trust or merit whatever privilege he is seeking.

## Teen Bullying of Parents

Punishments may keep children in line as long as they feel too frightened to retaliate, but parents may have to be increasingly harsh to keep strong-willed youngsters in line. Teens in this situation experience their parents as cold and rejecting and try to avoid them as much as possible. In an effort to win the battle of wits and wills, frustrated parents ask, "What do I have to do to get you to listen to me?" "How can I get you to do what I say?"

Trying to control by intimidation and threats is called bullying, and children who feel bullied at home typically dedicate a lot of energy to trying to help themselves feel more powerful. They typically bully weaker classmates and younger siblings and may even try to bully their parents. When they are big enough, usually by middle or late adolescence, they may try to provoke a physical confrontation. They may be strong enough to win. It is common for bullying parents to abuse alcohol, to be perfectionists, or both. Either way, help is possible—and important. See your newspaper or yellow pages for contact information for Alcoholics Anonymous and other self-help and parenting groups. Your child needs a teacher, not a bully.

**How can I tell if I'm being too strict or too lenient?**
Pay attention to how your teen responds when you set limits and enforce rules. If her behavior improves, she probably benefited even though she complained. If her behavior doesn't change or worsens, you're either providing too little, too much, or the wrong kind of structure.

## Logical Consequences

Logical consequences is a parenting method designed to teach children self-discipline by helping them learn from their mistakes. The goal is for the consequence to fit the crime. For instance, if a teen steals money, a punishment might be having to listen to a lecture, being grounded, or losing a privilege. A consequence, on the other hand, might require him to apologize and repay the stolen money and a small fine. The repayment might be in the form of cash, deductions from the teen's allowance, or doing chores to work off the bill.

While your teenager might benefit from stricter limits, she might not be able to handle them. Some teens do better when their parents stop trying to set any kind of limits and focus on developing a positive relationship based on mutual respect.

In another example, punishing a teen for bad grades might consist of grounding him for a few weeks or declaring the telephone off limits on school nights. A consequence might be having a quiet hour each evening to ensure he has time to do his schoolwork. Often the difference is how the disciplinary measure is presented. Yelling, "That's it! You're grounded for two weeks, Buddy! No more going out for a whole semester!" is a punishment. Calmly stating, "Now that you're behind in school, you'll need more time to study so you can catch up. To help, I'll make sure you have an hour of quiet time each day. We'll keep the television and stereo off, leave the answering machine on, and I'll make sure no one interrupts you." Teens may feel punished either way, but the point is to teach them an important life lesson. Punishment teaches, "I'm mad so you're in trouble." Consequences teach, "You need to correct your errors and try to right any wrongs you've committed."

FACT

If you are angry about something your teenager has done, tell him in no uncertain terms. Wait until you've calmed down before deciding how to proceed so you can create consequences designed to help and teach. That way your child can't so easily discount your decisions by saying, "Mom's just angry."

Although logical consequences are very effective with younger children, parents need to modify the usual procedures for teenagers. They should be involved in the process of determining what went wrong, what will help them learn, and how they can avoid repeating the same mistake in the future. Ask your teen what he thinks the consequences should be for breaking a rule, failing to keep a commitment, behaving disrespectfully, or placing himself in a dangerous situation.

### BEHAVIOR: POOR GRADES

**REASON:** Didn't bring home books 'cause kids call him a nerd.

**POSSIBLE SOLUTIONS/CONSEQUENCES:** Study in library before or after school. Explain, "I'm trying for the nerd-of-the-year award." Buy an extra set of books with his own money to keep at home. Blame his parents for insisting that the books be brought home.

### BEHAVIOR: LATE TO SCHOOL

**REASON:** Wouldn't get out of bed when called in the morning.

**POSSIBLE SOLUTIONS/CONSEQUENCES:** Earlier "lights out" so he can relax even if he can't sleep. Set an alarm. Parent will not write letter asking tardiness to be excused. Parent notifies school's truant officer.

### BEHAVIOR: SWEARING AT PARENTS

**REASON:** Felt his parents were harassing him.

**POSSIBLE SOLUTIONS/CONSEQUENCES:** Apologize. Teen states when he feels harassed and asks to postpone the discussion until he is calmer. Difficult conversations are held via e-mail so he can think more clearly. Attend family counseling to learn to communicate.

### BEHAVIOR: WON'T HELP WITH CHORES WHEN ASKED

**REASON:** He is too busy.

**POSSIBLE SOLUTIONS/CONSEQUENCES:** He chooses the chores and negotiates a deadline for completing them each week. He cannot watch the television, talk on the phone, or use the computer until his chores are completed. He will give advance notice if he can't do his chores as promised and say how he will make it up to his parents.

## Respect!

Even though you raised your teenager to be considerate and respectful of you, you have probably been more tolerant than your own parents were about allowing their children to express their feelings and participate in decisions. Even if you haven't been tolerant at all, other parents in your child's generation have been. Your teen will probably feel entitled to express herself whether or not you want to hear what is on her mind at any given moment. Young people have been taught to just say no, and they're saying it every time their parents turn around! Worse, they don't even do it nicely. Consider this all-too-typical interchange:

**PARENT:** "I've got a really bad headache. I'm going to lie down for a few minutes."

**TEEN:** "You said you'd take me to get a haircut Saturday afternoon, remember? Well, it's Saturday afternoon!"

**PARENT:** "I'm sorry. I'm really feeling ill."

**TEEN:** "So what am I supposed to do?"

**PARENT:** "I guess I'll have to take you Monday. I really need to lie down."

**TEEN:** "Easy for you to say. You're not the one who needs a haircut!"

To give their teen a taste of their own medicine, some parents take the approach of, "If you can't do this for me, I'm not doing that for you." They hope their child will act less selfish and self-centered once they realize that respect and consideration work both ways. These parents may act surly and rude to their teen. They may respond with a tit for a tat, handling their child's refusal to help around the house by refusing to cook, do laundry, or provide transportation for her. There is something to be said for not allowing yourself to be treated like a doormat! On the other hand, by continuing to be considerate of your teen even when she cannot reciprocate, you can teach an important lesson about the value of selfless giving. She may not appreciate your actions now, but when she grows up and looks back at what transpired during these difficult years, she may similarly feel inclined to give to others without expectation of being paid back. Her respect for you may deepen.

QUESTION?

**What can I do about my daughter's sarcasm toward me?**
If a reprimand doesn't solve the problem, respond as you would to a toddler's tantrum: studiously ignore her. If she yells or exits the room muttering curses, so be it. Disrespectful behavior doesn't merit a response. Don't give her one.

## Protecting Your Teen

It is, of course, distressing to think your teen might do something illegal, endanger herself, jeopardize her future or her own moral standards, or betray values you hold sacred. In fact, it may be terrifying. Still, you must accept that you cannot make your teen's decisions for her; she must make them for herself. Your job is to alert her to dangers, teach her to protect herself, help her ponder the moral issues, and let her learn from her mistakes. As long as your child feels that you are on her side, you can at least hope to influence her. Whether or not you find the answers to your teen's problem of the moment, a serious discussion about whatever is troubling her is often all that is needed. Feeling emotionally supported by you can help your teen think more clearly so she can solve her problems herself.

## Creative Problem-Solving

Once Kirsten's parents accepted they could not control their daughter, they asked her what she thought a reasonable curfew would be. She said she thought 1:00 A.M. on weekends was fair. They asked if she could withstand pressure from her friends to do things she knew were wrong. Kirsten hesitated, so they told her that her curfew would be 11:30 P.M., but they wouldn't punish her for coming in late. That way, if she sensed trouble brewing, she could truthfully tell her friends she had to get home—that she was late and would be grounded forever, sent away to boarding school, or endure some other horrible fate. Each time Kirsten went out, her parents expressed confidence that she would make good decisions while tucking in a bit of advice on how to handle situations she might find difficult. "I know you are wise beyond your years and wouldn't get into a car with a driver who had been drinking like less mature kids," her mom said one evening. Kirsten looked proud, but nodded solemnly. "You know your father or I would gladly pick you up at any hour—no questions asked," her mother added. A month later, Kirsten did call for a ride. "And could you drive my friend home, too?" she asked. "He was actually going to ride home with John, even though John has been drinking. I told him that was totally immature." They weren't happy that a fifteen-year-old had attended a party where kids were drinking, but knew the biggest problem was solved. At last, they had found a way to reach her!

# Chapter 8
# Teen Dating

Beginning to date is simultaneously exciting and scary. Boys are often more interested in having sex and may see love as the route to scoring, while girls tend to seek love and may see sex as the route to achieving emotional closeness. Still, boys seek emotional intimacy and girls are physically attracted to them. Learning to manage sexual feelings and to relate to one another lovingly is a big challenge. It's hard for teenagers to escape some serious heartbreak along the way. Fortunately, broken hearts do mend.

## Dating Dilemmas

Kevin said that most students were in cliques because they were basically insecure and could only handle being around people who were pretty much like themselves. His mother knew that wasn't true, but was familiar with that attitude. Back when she was in high school, students had called the group she hung out with a clique, but they were really just a group of people who had grown close because they were on the cheerleading squad together. Be that as it may, Kevin was proud to be a "floater." His mother understood that to mean that at school Kevin mixed and mingled with students from many different social groups. Kevin's mother thought that sounded fine but began to worry when he started hanging out with some down and out kids who felt to her like trouble.

Most parental lectures about not giving in to peer pressure don't have much impact. Here's a new twist on an old saying to share with your teenager: "If all my friends were to jump off a bridge, I wouldn't jump with them. I'd be at the bottom to catch them."

Kevin admitted that the new kids he was spending time with used drugs. However, he assured his mother that he did not. She finally believed him when he said that "dopers" were too boring and he stopped spending time with them. Next he brought home some scary looking people who dressed in black leather and lots of metal studs and chains. She was relieved when Kevin lost interest in them, too. She admired his independence and ability to get along with lots of different people without compromising his values. But when he started dating a girl from a different ethnic and religious background, she felt that he had gone too far. She insisted he end the relationship immediately.

Kevin's mother tried to explain her objections to mixed marriages, but Kevin wouldn't listen. He accused his mother of being a bigot, said she couldn't tell him whom to date, and stamped out of the room. When he admitted that he was planning to take the girl to the prom, his mother grounded him. He said she was kidding herself if she thought she could break them up. She couldn't understand why he was being so rebellious. Worse, she didn't know how to stop him.

FACT

Would Romeo and Juliet have made it to the altar if their families hadn't interfered? Since most teen relationships fizzle in short order, probably not. Parents need to consider carefully before trying to separate an enamored couple. Interference is more likely to fan the flames of passion than squelch them.

## Flirting 101

Elementary school girls don't much care for boys, who are generally too rough and rowdy to hold much appeal. In junior high school, girls suddenly begin reconsidering the merits of the opposite sex. They smile their invitations at the boys or they send them via their girlfriends. Soon the boys circle about and begin flirting. That's when things quickly fall apart. When a young male attempts to win a girl's heart, he often acts as if he were on the football field playing a practice game with his buddies. He quickly discovers that girls who didn't like having their hair pulled at age eight don't enjoy being slammed into lockers at age thirteen. At age nine the girls didn't appreciate having their freckles or kinky hair made fun of; at fourteen they feel totally humiliated by jokes about their curves or lack thereof. As the insults fly back and forth, most everyone gets their feelings hurt.

Although boys sometimes bully a hapless girl and purposely try to make her miserable, in general they tease the girls they are attracted to. The same goes for girls. Unfortunately, it may be hard for your child to believe that what feels to her like mistreatment is actually a compliment. Inform your teen that young boys typically relate to one another by pushing, shoving, jostling, and name-calling, and it takes them a while to learn that women don't find such behavior endearing. If your teenager feels harassed, she may be able to command better treatment with a line like, "If you are trying to flirt with me, you need to find a better way." As always when setting limits verbally, body language must match with the words to be effective. Accordingly, students should turn on their heels and walk away from situations they dislike. Remind your child that just as no one has the right to abuse or humiliate her, she doesn't have the right to abuse or humiliate others. Physical violence and name-calling are more likely to provoke an enemy into retaliating than ending hostilities. Help your teen figure out what to say and how to say it when defending herself so that she can be firm without being cruel.

Boys lose confidence when girls accuse them of being "queer" or "dorky." Girls worry that something is wrong with them when boys tease and trip them. Explain to your teen that peoples' flirting skills are pretty clumsy at first. They can help one another improve their behavior by giving feedback.

## First Crushes

A first crush is often directed toward someone unattainable, hence, safe. Children can fantasize without the complication of having to relate to a real human being, which often reduces them to babbling and feeling idiotic. The object of a young teen's first affection may be a teacher, an adult neighbor, a cousin, a peer living a few cities or states away, or a member of the same sex. Some junior high school students have a steady boyfriend or girlfriend but most confine themselves to flirting, holding hands, and may exchange some kisses. Most young people don't begin going on real dates until high school if their parents set limits. Some teenagers aren't interested in dating until after high school.

Some homosexual play is common among young adolescents, especially boys. This doesn't mean that they are homosexual, but boys may not know this. Parents need to explain that there is a big difference between having a homosexual experience and being a homosexual. Sexual orientation does not become stable until early adulthood.

Many parents are disturbed by the boy-craziness of their daughter or the girl-craziness of their son. However, what appears to be strong, precocious sexual interest is more likely to be intense anxiety about sexuality and fearfulness about not being attractive to members of the opposite sex. Sexually abused children typically have very negative feelings about sexuality. Many try to work through past traumas by acting out sexually during junior high and high school; later in life they may develop problems with frigidity and impotence and seek help from a therapist. Getting help sooner rather than later can save a lot of heartache. Young people who haven't had a positive ongoing relationship with an adult member of the opposite sex often feel lost about how to relate to peers they feel attracted to. Having experienced true intimacy with an adult of the opposite sex helps them understand that male/female relationships can be truly intimate but not involve sex.

### Early Dating

Students who begin dating during junior high are at risk for precocious sexual activity, pregnancy, and sexually transmitted diseases. The vast majority of sexually active teens over age sixteen belatedly realize they were not emotionally ready for sex and regret their early involvements. Parents need to set limits to prevent young teenagers from becoming sexually active if they can. If they cannot, it is important to seek individual counseling for your teen and parent counseling for yourself to learn how to take a firm but loving stand. A male therapist is a good choice for boy-crazy girls as well as for girl-crazy boys. A warm relationship with an adult male affirms boys' masculinity and teaches that virility and having sex are very different. Meanwhile, a positive relationship with an adult male reassures girls about their acceptability to members of the opposite sex.

## Young "Studs" and "Sirens"

The first boys to enter puberty tend to be viewed as good catches by the girls, who may pursue them with a vengeance. Some boys are delighted to have so much female attention. Others dislike so much female attention and resent being viewed as sex objects. Although boys may enjoy the fact that being labeled a stud impresses their male friends, many boys don't become interested in girls for several years.

FACT

**The double standard is alive and well in adolescent crowds. Sexually experienced boys are admired, while experienced females are reviled. Reputations are hard to live down whether earned or completely undeserved.**

Sexual slurs and harassment in the school hallways, cafeteria, and locker room can cause serious depression and inflict psychological damage that lasts for decades. Many children suffer in silence, feeling too ashamed to let their parents know they are being victimized. Having one's sexual orientation attacked or one's reputation assailed by peers of the same sex can be even more devastating than when members of the opposite sex are involved. Most teenaged girls are more concerned about having girlfriends than boyfriends, and boys want to spend most of their time with other boys rather than with girls. If you learn that your child is the target of ongoing harassment or abuse, notify the school. Increased supervision during lunch, gym, and during other unstructured time may help. If school administrators cannot provide adequate protection—and often they cannot—move your child to a different school or homeschool him.

The first girls to enter puberty may or may not be interested in boys, but if they happen to be well endowed, they can easily become the focus of their peers' sexual anxieties. Peers may accuse such girls of being obsessed with sex and horrifically promiscuous and spread vicious rumors of outrageous sexual escapades that are impossible to combat. Once branded as promiscuous, the fact that a girl has no sexual experience whatsoever becomes irrelevant; the myth takes on a life of its own. Female classmates may beat her up as punishment for imagined attempts to steal their boyfriends while boys feel free to take sexual liberties with her. Such a girl often suffers such indignities as having her locker emblazoned with obscene signs and having her phone number posted on the bathroom walls and her picture put on the Internet. Whether or not they end up living up to the reputation they did nothing to deserve, they are nevertheless traumatized and may be haunted by the memories decades later.

## Dating Stages

By gradually moving through the stages of dating, teenagers have time to learn to relate to members of the opposite sex and to process and learn from their experiences, many of which may be very emotionally intense. During junior high, school dances and flirtations during lunch and recess provide opportunities for young people to mix and mingle with members of the opposite sex. The supervision can help ensure their physical safety, but the emotional toll is often high. Co-ed group outings to the mall, movies, or school events such as football games usually follow, along with supervised co-ed parties. During this stage, parents are still involved, if only as chauffeurs and funding sources.

QUESTION?

**My fourteen-year-old wants to date. Isn't that too young?**
Attending a school event with a co-ed group may be fine if parents are driving. Set age limits on the people your child can date. A difference of more than two years often ends up with the younger child getting hurt.

Double dating is the typical next stage of dating. The presence of another couple can help to dilute the intensity of the experience by giving participants other people to focus on and provides each child with an ally if something goes amiss. The next dating stage is going out alone as a couple. Teens may "hook up" for a trip to the movies to see whether they like one another. Compatible couples may start seeing one another with enough regularity to declare themselves boyfriend and girlfriend. Next comes making a commitment not to date other people, which past generations called "going steady." In junior high these committed relationships may only last a day or two. In high school they can last for months and may or may not lead to marriage.

## Teen Love Connections

Whether your teen has a secret crush on a teacher or is engaged to be married, the feelings of being in love are the same. The bliss of being in the loved one's presence, the agony of even short separations, and the longing for oneness are the same at age thirteen as at thirty. The heartbreak of breaking up is the same, too, even if the time factors differ dramatically for people of different ages. Losing a relationship that lasted a day can devastate a junior high school student, and the days required to recover can feel like a year. The end of a month-long relationship can plunge a sixteen-year-old into a state of grief and take a month to mourn, but that month can feel like a year. A six-month relationship can undo a young adult; the six months needed to recover can feel like a year.

Teaching your daughter to say "no" to her girlfriends is as important as teaching her to say "no" to her boyfriends. Many girls report feeling more pressured by their girlfriends to join the crowd by giving up their virginity.

It is often hard for teens who are in love to understand that expressing their love for one another by making love won't cement a relationship or even help hold it together. Still, it may be much more hurtful to have a consummated relationship end. Parents often try to deter teens from becoming involved sexually by talking to them about the importance of being emotionally ready to make love. The problem is that teens may feel ready because they are in love. A better question may be whether they are ready to cope with losing someone they have made love to. There is no guarantee that teens will be impressed by that line of reasoning, either, because when they are head-over-heels they are sure their love is too great to ever end. But teens need to at least be warned of that risk up front.

Although there is a difference between infatuation and true love, people cannot tell whether they are in lust or in love until the initial passion subsides enough for them to think clearly. It is easy for parents to write off their child's passion for a day-long affair of the heart as "puppy love," but there really is no such thing. Parents lose credibility when they try to pretend that their teenager's feelings are not real or are unimportant. Children used to fall in love and marry before age seventeen. Times have changed, but children have not. But because times have changed, there is little support for teenaged marriages. Even as the social stigma of being a teen mom or dad has virtually disappeared in many circles, the very real problems of becoming a parent before age twenty are as difficult as ever.

## Dating Readiness

There's really no way to assess a teenager's readiness to date. Some people aren't good at handling relationships long after their hair has turned gray and their face is covered with wrinkles. If your teen is pressing to be allowed to move on to the next stage of dating, try the following: Explain that dating makes people emotionally and physically vulnerable and tell your child she needs to demonstrate her ability to protect herself as well as her date, both physically and emotionally. Tying permission to date to responsible, considerate behavior in other areas may improve her behavior and can at least help your child focus on the interpersonal skills and personal attributes she needs to strive to develop. That doesn't mean she'll succeed during her teenaged years—or during her stay on the planet, for that matter. There are a number of issues to consider in determining whether a teen is ready to date:

- Does your child honor the trust you place in her by being where she says she will be, notifying you about changes in plans, and returning home at the appointed time? Or does she not honor the trust people who love her place in her?
- Does she honor her commitments and promises to her friends? Or does she forget her obligations and break promises when a more interesting opportunity presents itself?
- Is she loyal to her friends? Or does she betray them by talking about them behind their backs?
- Does she follow rules you feel strongly about, such as not hanging

out with boys in her bedroom? Can she assert herself with male friends by telling them that she isn't allowed in their bedroom when she visits? Or is she unable to abide by rules you consider important?

- Can your child refrain from drinking and using drugs? Can she call for help if she finds herself in a situation that could get her into trouble? Or does she do whatever is necessary to fit in with her peers?
- Can your child delay gratification even though she wants something very much? Or does she have a fit if she doesn't get what she wants when she wants it?
- Does your child remain respectful of other people's feelings even when she is angry with them? Or is she callous in her treatment of others when she feels hurt?
- Does she avoid dangerous situations? Or does she expose herself to risks and deny that there could be unpleasant consequences?
- Can she bounce back from emotional hurts? Or does being rejected undo her?
- Does she protect her body by making sure she eats well and gets enough sleep and exercise? Or does she use poor judgment when it comes to guarding her physical health?
- Does she choose positive friends who support her attempts to succeed at school and get along with her family? Or does she choose destructive people who undermine her attempts to achieve her goals?
- Can she separate from friends who turn out to be destructive for her? Or does she hang on to hurtful relationships?
- Is she able to fulfill other responsibilities when she's in love? Or does everything else fall by the wayside?

Lots of excellent books for teens are available that can teach them everything from dating etiquette to how to decide whether the current object of her affection might turn out to be Mr. Right. Even teens who don't like to read will probably manage to plow through them. Before you shop for birthday presents, see Resources for Teens at the end of the book.

## Foolish Kids, Wise Choices

Kevin's mother eventually realized that she had overreacted by worrying about her son marrying someone from a different religious and ethnic background when he just wanted to take a girl to a school dance. His mother let him go, and after the crisis had passed she stressed the importance of marrying within the faith. She felt reassured when Kevin said he wouldn't turn his back on his religion. His mother felt badly for rejecting a girl she didn't know because of her ethnic background. Realizing that the way to avoid stereotyping was to get to know her, Kevin's mother urged him to ask the girl over for dinner. Kevin said no, her new boyfriend might get jealous. "I liked her," Kevin said, "but I was so mad at you for trying to tell me I shouldn't, I imagined getting even by eloping with her." His mother paled at the thought.

You may be able to drive away dates you consider "losers," but the real solution is for your child to choose winners. Teens who feel like winners aren't likely to let losers drag them down even if they do get involved with them. Help your teen appreciate her strengths and work to overcome or accept her limitations.

For the first time, Kevin's mother understood why teen rebellion was so dangerous. She decided to make an effort to get to know her son's friends, get along with them, and appreciate whatever good qualities Kevin saw in them. That way, when she expressed concerns about them, Kevin might see her as an ally instead of a threat. When Kevin had friends over, she suggested he ask them to stay to dinner. Beneath the purple hair and sparkly makeup, most of the kids were pretty nice. When she heard one of Kevin's friends say, "Your mom is pretty cool," she decided having them get to know her was even better than getting to know them. Maybe their attitude would rub off on Kevin.

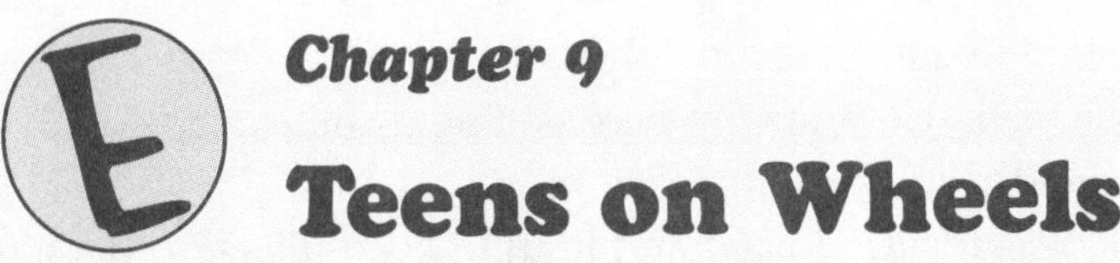

# Chapter 9
# Teens on Wheels

For adding gray hairs to your head, there's nothing like having the child who once toddled at your knees take the steering wheel and head into traffic. Check the accident statistics and you might go completely gray. You simply must not let your teenager drive if he drinks, uses drugs, doesn't buckle his seat belt, or is a reckless risk-taker. Access to a car is a great bargaining chip for commanding responsible behavior both at school and home. Don't hesitate to use it!

## A Parent's Nightmare

The day Blain's practice permit arrived, he couldn't wait to go out for a spin. His dad had confidence in his son's ability to handle himself behind the wheel. However, when Blain climbed into the driver's seat, his father did a double-take. Blain looked so very young and vulnerable. He seemed overly eager, too, as if the car were a great new adventure. His father decided he must convince his son that a car was transportation, not entertainment. He knew he was stalling as he explained the importance of properly adjusting the seat, mirrors, and seat belt. Blain could tell his dad was totally freaked and tried to keep his cool. But after driving a block listening to a dozen warnings and instructions, Blain felt frustrated. "I know what I'm doing, Dad," he said. He increased his speed to twenty-five miles per hour despite his father's warning not to go so fast. An argument ensued, and Blain got so distracted he nearly had an accident. His dad took the wheel and ended the "lesson."

Assailing teen drivers with too many warnings can turn overconfident kids into rebels and scare uncertain ones so they can't think clearly enough to drive safely. If you can't keep your cool during behind-the-wheel practice, enroll your teen in driver's education or find someone else to coach him.

It seemed to Blain that his dad was trying to find an excuse to keep his little boy from growing up. He felt insulted, but knew a lot was at stake so he carefully obeyed his father during practice sessions. When Blain got his license and permission to run an errand by himself, he inched out of the driveway and down the street in case his dad was watching. As soon as Blain turned the corner, he whooped with joy and put the petal to the metal. Finally, he was free!

## Rights of Passage

In most cultures, solemn initiation ceremonies followed by grand celebrations mark the exact moment at which children are officially declared adults. In Western societies, the transition takes place in a series of small steps that span many years. Depending on their family's religious affiliation, children are declared spiritual adults during confirmation and bar mitzvahs. The onset of menstruation marks girls' physical coming-of-age. Other special transitions include starting high school, starting to date, turning sweet sixteen, having a coming-out party, getting a job, graduating from high school, registering to vote, being old enough to join the military, and reaching the legal drinking age. While all of these transition points are highly significant to teenagers, the big moment for most is when they get a driver's license and access to a car.

**FACT**

Many parents aren't eager to have their teenager start to drive because of safety concerns. For teens, driving is about cutting apron strings, autonomy, independence, and freedom. Parent/teen conflicts over cars bog down because they have such different agendas. Let your child know you respect his desire to grow up. Help him do it safely.

Like tentative toddlers afraid of falling, some beginning drivers are fearful about maneuvering an expensive, powerful machine through traffic. However, some teens, especially boys, often feel an exhilarating surge akin to what toddlers feel on taking their first steps. The difference is that toddlers discover the joy of independent travel while crossing the living room unassisted, while teens eagerly anticipate their freedom for months or even years in advance. Add to that a long-term love affair with machines, wheels, and speed, and having to wait for the magical moment of being legally able to drive becomes almost unbearable. Once it has finally arrived, teenagers can become as frustrated as toddlers by parental restrictions, warnings, and prohibitions. Many parents are aware that the danger is real but are caught up in a struggle with themselves about not feeling ready for their child to come of age. They don't want their child to drive but know they are overreacting. They withhold permission to drive one minute and toss him the car keys the next.

Not being allowed to get a driver's license or being denied access to a car can create the same kind of helpless frustration and righteous indignation toddlers feel when their parents won't let them run around freely in the grocery store. It's not surprising that some teenagers feel justified in taking the car keys and heading out without permission. Some go so far as to steal an automobile and take it for a joy ride. What can seem like a conscienceless crime to an adult may seem like justice to a teen. Spell out exactly what your child needs to do in order to earn driving privileges so he has a sense of personal control. Investigate the cost of insuring your teen sooner rather than later and let him know if you expect him to help with the cost. Reassure him that if he is mature enough to handle a car responsibly and you can afford the insurance, you will let him drive. Describe what "mature enough" means to you and be very specific and concrete.

If you've often threatened consequences but failed to follow through, your teen may not regard the limits you set regarding the car as serious. Practice holding firm about other issues well in advance so when you describe the consequences of using the car irresponsibly, she will know you are serious.

## Putting Your Teen in the Driver's Seat

Long before your teen begins driver's education or applies for a practice permit, make a list of the characteristics and personal qualities of a safe driver. Mark the ones your teen currently lacks and describe what he could do to demonstrate that he has developed them. For instance, to drive safely requires good temper control. An impulsive teen who hurls insults and breaks things when angry is likely to lash out when another driver gets in his way or does something irritating. On the other hand, a teen who argues or stamps out of the room when he is angry is successfully handling a situation without losing control. Let your teen know the kind of behavior you need to see in order to be sure that he is capable of owning a vehicle or using the family car.

**How can I convince my son to drive carefully?**
Write your own rules of the road and consequences for breaking them. "Make the honor roll = Use of the car for school activities, errands, and dates." "Drink = No driving for two months."

## Experience as Teacher

Like toddlers, new teen drivers often use poor judgment because they lack the experience required to anticipate danger and recognize the importance of not getting distracted. It's fine for kids to learn many things by experience, but discovering what happens when they become distracted, speed, and tailgate aren't on the list. How do you teach a teen who won't listen to what you say and seems to need to learn by experience? Fortunately, there is a way.

Teen drivers need to minimize distractions by keeping the radio and cell phone off and not trying to eat while they drive. Until hitting the brake becomes automatic, they may freeze or press the accelerator by mistake. They need to practice, practice, practice!

Insurance companies have put decades and millions of dollars into determining which drivers are at the greatest risk for having auto accidents. The bad news is that teenaged boys are at the top of the list, with teenaged girls close on their heels. The good news is that a number of factors are known to decrease the risk. You can use the insurance industry's vast experience to protect your teen. If your child meets the following criteria, his chances of being in an accident lessen:

- **Completing driver's education.** Even chronic underachievers don't want to fail this class, so your teen should be highly motivated to learn the rules of the road, which are all about safety. You might also notify your child that you will contact the driver's education instructor for an opinion about whether your teen's classroom behavior was serious and responsible. Explain that if you learn that he was more focused on his peers than on learning, you will assume he needs an additional six months to mature before it is safe for him to drive.

- **Completing a defensive driving course.** Though the classes are so boring that most students doze off, having grisly descriptions of accidents and lists of death-and-injury statistics infiltrate one's dreams is still a sobering experience. Require your teen to take and pass a defensive driving course before allowing him to take the wheel without you by his side.

- **Completing a drug and alcohol driving awareness course.** Even though many students swagger into the classroom, the "Don't Drink and Drive" messages still have a way of sinking in. Inform your teen that if he rides in a car with a driver who has been drinking, you will assume he doesn't understand the risks and will not allow him to drive until he takes the class.

- **Driving a vehicle equipped with airbags.** They can't prevent accidents, but they reduce the devastation of a crash. It's worthwhile to invest in a car equipped with them if you can afford it.

- **Driving a vehicle equipped with automatic seat belts.** Since teens feel invincible, seat belts can seem to them like just an irritating nuisance. The automatic kind help ensure they buckle up anyway. Tell your teen that if you discover he is riding or driving without being properly buckled up, he will not be allowed to drive for a month.

- **Driving a vehicle equipped with anti-lock brakes.** Novice drivers and daredevils alike are prone to hit the brake so late and hard as to send the car into a skid that can cause them to lose control of the car. Depending on your child's perspective, anti-lock brakes lessen the danger or the fun.

- **Driving a vehicle equipped with daytime running lights.** Lights that stay on whenever the motor is running enhance the visibility of your teen's car. Of course, having lights on during the day isn't as effective as painting the car with signs that say "Teenaged Driver," but anything you can do to make other drivers more aware that your baby is on the road can only help!

- **Annual mileage driven.** Spending more time on the road increases the risk of accidents. But don't forget that your teen needs lots of practice. A safe way to get it is while chauffeuring you around town!

- **Good grades in school.** Academic success has more to do with behavior than ability. Good students pay attention to the task before them, avoid distractions, follow directions, delay gratification, work methodically, and are conscientious—all of which are needed to drive safely. It's not surprising that insurance companies give good students big discounts. In fact, a 3.5 grade point average can earn a 10 percent insurance discount with some companies. Let your child know that you will consider him responsible enough to drive when he can be responsible in his classroom behavior.

- **Membership in approved youth groups.** Birds of a feather flock together, so it's not surprising that belonging to a gang won't entitle your child to an automobile insurance discount. Being on the student council or involved in a church youth group might. Does your freshman want to drive when he turns sixteen? Have him contact your insurance agent to inquire about these discounts so he can consider whether it might be worth his while to join.

- **How the car is used.** Business/pleasure/work or school. Using the vehicle for occasional outings rather than relying on it for transportation to work or school typically reduces the miles driven each week. That lowers the risk of an accident, which can translate into lower insurance premiums.

- **Living at home or being a student away at school.** Teens who are completely on their own are at risk for getting into all sorts of trouble, including car accidents. Inform your child that if he drops out of high school or doesn't continue his education after graduating, the insurance companies will consider him a big risk and so will you. Unless you are sure your child is exceptionally responsible, make sure the car is only available as transportation to work.

- **The type and age of the car.** The type of car your child drives is also a risk factor. If you allow your child to buy one with a huge engine and monster-sized mag wheels, you must expect him to test its capabilities.

Both committing a moving violation in the car (regardless of the reason) and being in an accident (no matter who caused it) increase your child's future risk of being in a collision. If either stemmed from inexperience, provide more supervised practice. If it stemmed from becoming distracted or behaving recklessly, don't let your teen take the wheel unless an adult is present to supervise for a time. Either way, hold your child responsible for paying for any tickets he receives while driving and any charges stemming from accidents, including insurance price increases.

Forty percent of all teen motor vehicle fatalities occur between 9 P.M. and 6 A.M., usually on Friday, Saturday, or Sunday. Having teenaged passengers aboard increases the possibility of an accident. They distract the driver and are notorious for urging their chauffeur to speed. Most teen passenger deaths occur when another teen is at the wheel.

## Dollars and Cents

At a time when insuring a sixteen-year-old can cost $1,200 per year, most people are looking for ways to cut costs. Fortunately, there are a number of ways to save money. The first place to check rates is with your current insurance carrier, since discounts are mandatory for having two or more qualifying cars on the same policy. However, you should then call other companies to comparison shop since rates vary dramatically. Independent agents may represent several companies, while some company representatives and agents may represent only a single company or company group. To check as many companies' rates as possible, ask to see the rates for all the companies the agent represents.

Ask about special discounts for teenagers. For instance, State Farm Insurance offers a 15 percent discount to students who successfully complete their "Steer Clear" program. It involves keeping a log for thirty days and taking a test.

The most expensive insurance category is "nonstandard" for high-risk drivers. The next rating is "standard," which is for moderate-risk drivers. "Preferred" rates are lowest. Ask the insurance agent what you can do to get a better rating, but be aware that if you and your teen are on a joint policy and either of you were in an accident, were ticketed for a moving violation, or submitted an auto insurance claim within the past three years, you may not qualify for a preferred rate. If you have a clean driving record, avoid companies that cater to high-risk drivers, since the rates are higher. You can lower your rate by paying a higher deductible, but if you do have an accident you have to pay more money out of pocket. Another way to save is by paying your insurance policy quarterly or twice a year instead of monthly.

## Accidents Happen

While it's true that accidents happen, they are expensive in dollars and suffering. Motor vehicle accidents are the leading cause of death among fifteen to twenty-year-olds, according to the Insurance Information Institute (*www.iii.org*). Thirty-six percent of teen deaths involve a car accident. Sixteen- and seventeen-year-olds are three times more likely to crash than eighteen- and nineteen-year-olds. The main reasons are immaturity and lack of driving experience. Sixteen-year-old boys have a well-deserved reputation as being hellions behind the wheel, but sixteen-year-old girls are now closing the statistics gap.

To try to combat the tremendous teen accident problem, three-dozen states now have Graduated Drivers Licensing programs (GDLs). In a typical scenario, teenagers are given a learner's permit, which entitles them to drive with a supervising adult in the car. After the passage of time and a test, they graduate to an intermediate license, which places restrictions on the number of passengers allowed in the vehicle and may exclude nighttime driving. Only after holding the intermediate license for a specified period can teens qualify for an unrestricted license. Most states with GDLs also have a zero-tolerance for alcohol policy for teens. You certainly should have one in your home even if your state does not! You may not be able to revoke your teenager's driver's license, but you can certainly revoke access to the car.

FACT

Fifty percent of motorcycle accidents involve liquor. Most occur during short trips, for example, to school or the grocery store. The usual cause is that a driver of a car didn't see the motorcyclist, but motorcycle driver error is often a factor. Taking a course in motorcycle safety can substantially reduce the risk of an accident. For more information, visit *www.motorcycle-accidents.com*.

Being behind the wheel with just one or two alcoholic drinks in your teen's system greatly increases the risk of having an accident. According to First Eagle insurance services (*www.firsteagle.com*), teenage boys with a blood alcohol level of .05–.10, which is below the legal limit for adults, are eighteen times more likely to be in a single vehicle crash than their sober counterparts while teenage girls are fifty-four times more likely to have an accident! According to *www.factsontap.org*, 25 percent of fatal accidents involved a teen driver with a blood alcohol level of .08 or higher. Most states now have special zero-tolerance laws to control drinking among teenaged drivers. A teenager with a blood alcohol level of .02 percent will fail a breathalyzer test. That means that a 160-pound boy who slowly consumes a single drink over the course of an hour before driving would be categorized as drunk. Have a disposable breathalyzer test on hand and conduct random tests to motivate your teen to stay sober. You can avoid all of the "I think you were/no I was not" arguments for less than three dollars per test. (Type "disposable breathalyzer" into your favorite Internet search engine to find a company that carries them.)

## Car Troubles

When young children encounter a problem, they quickly settle on the first solution that comes to mind. They may lack the skills to consider whether their solution is even valid, much less the best. As a result, they make lots of bad decisions. If an immature teen decides he wants a car, he may go for what seems to be the obvious solution: He gets a job and races to a dealership, paycheck in hand. But unless the job pays exceptionally well, or unless he works many, many hours each week, he soon finds that he can't keep up with the payments. Warn your teen that if he gets behind on payments he could ruin his credit, and lose both the car and the money he put into it–and he'll probably conclude you are just trying to throw a wet blanket on his wonderful plan. And since doing your teen's thinking for him does keep him from growing up, there is some truth to this claim!

Instead of allowing your teen to devote his energy to arguing about a car being affordable, help him calculate how many hours he would have to work each week in order to pay the bills for one. Have him do the footwork to locate the figures. He can check at dealerships to find out the monthly payments of cars he is interested in and the estimated miles per gallon each one gets to determine how much it will cost to drive one mile. Have him contact your insurance agent to check on insurance costs and use his computer skills to request some additional quotes online. Help him find the number for the Department of Public Safety so he can determine the cost of license plates and state taxes.

| | Can Your Teen Afford a Car? |
|---|---|
| Car payment | $200 (Monthly payment) |
| Insurance premium | $150 (Yearly premium divided by twelve) |
| Taxes and tags | $10 (Yearly cost divided by twelve) |
| Oil changes | $10 (Quarterly cost divided by three) |
| Gas | $20 (Cost of one gallon of gas divided by the miles per gallon the car gets = cost to drive one mile. Multiply that cost by the number of miles your teen expects to drive each month.) |
| **Total** | **$390** (Total monthly cost, excluding repairs) |

Next, help your teenager calculate how many hours he would have to work each month to pay for his car. To guesstimate his salary and take-home pay, he can answer some newspaper employment ads or ask friends who work:

**HOURLY SALARY BEFORE TAXES:** $7.00
**HOURLY TAKE-HOME PAY:** $6.50

Divide the monthly car cost by the hourly take-home pay to calculate the number of hours your teen would have to work to pay for his car. In the example above, a teen would have to work sixty hours per month or fifteen hours a week. If the car needed any sort of repair (which he can expect when buying such an inexpensive car) or he were to use more than 1½ tanks of gas a month, he would have to work more hours to keep the wheels turning.

Once your teen has done the math, he may decide on a less expensive car or decide not to get a car at all. If he were to work and invest his paychecks in himself by attending post-secondary education, he could earn better wages and afford a better car after he graduated and got a job. Even if he barrels ahead, overextends himself while trying to keep up with car payments, loses the car, and ruins his credit, learning to do all the calculations won't have been wasted. He'll know how to test out the soundness of his financial decisions in advance so he can make better purchasing decisions throughout his life.

## Hard Lessons the Easy Way

The first time Blain raced into the driveway, screeched to a halt, and got out without having to unbuckle his seat belt because he had failed to buckle it in the first place, his father canceled his car insurance. "We'll try again in six months," he told his son. Blain was irate. He yelled that this was another example of how his father ruined his life by overreacting. "It wasn't like I was drinking and driving or speeding or doing anything wrong," Blain said. "Yes, you did. You weren't wearing your seat belt." Blain swore he would never speak to his father again. But Blain's attitude had already softened when some of his friends were in a car accident a month later. One ended up with a spinal cord injury. Blain thought he had learned the seat belt lesson the hard way, but it turned out to be the easy way. (E)

# Chapter 10
# School Daze

Some teenagers very much enjoy academics and find learning inherently rewarding. But most students need to know how they can use what they learn in the real world. Otherwise, they lose interest and motivation. You may need to set limits to get an underachiever to study and to help an overachiever adopt a more relaxed approach to school. Your other educational duties include supporting your child's teachers and mediating conflicts without undermining the educational process.

## When Teens Won't Study

Jenna's mother and father couldn't understand why their daughter had slacked off on her studies. She had always enjoyed learning and looked forward to school, but now she was often tardy, sometimes cut classes, was disrespectful toward her teachers, and didn't do much homework. Nothing her parents did or said made a difference. On a typical evening they would ask if she had homework and send her to her room to study if she said yes. When they checked on her later, she was often lying on her bed staring at the ceiling with the phone to her ear. Then she stopped bringing home her books, saying she had forgotten them or claiming to have finished her homework in class.

**Try to talk to your teenager about school and you may get nonanswers ("It's okay.") or face a wall of anger ("Leave me alone!"). Though you might be tempted to back off, you need to find out what the problem is and try to help solve it.**

Jenna's parents confiscated the telephone, limited the amount of time she could spend online, and outlawed television-watching on school nights. Nothing helped. She spent the extra time writing in her journal, painting her fingernails, or moping around the house. Her teachers called and wrote notes warning that Jenna was in danger of failing three classes. Parental involvement was supposed to be so important, but what were her parents supposed to do? If they had a magic wand, they would certainly wave it.

## Diagnosing School Problems

When teenagers won't study, many frustrated parents begin doling out punishments. That won't light a fire under your child unless he is anxious for your approval and is capable of doing the work. Sometimes another problem interferes with students' ability to concentrate and triggers misbehavior at school. If your child's peers think academic achievement is "uncool" and he is more concerned about pleasing them than you, if he has simply lost interest in academics, or if he is distracted by another problem, punishments may only make a bad situation worse.

When confronted about school grades or behavior, many teenagers become defensive. They deny there is a problem, blame their difficulties on someone else, or try to justify their behavior. In the process they may end up believing their own claims that "I'm doing fine," "I can handle my problems myself," "The teacher picks on me," or "The homework isn't graded anyway." There isn't much point in discussing an issue when your child is defensive, so tell him that the two of you can try talking again when he is calmer. If the second conversation isn't any better, state that you will contact his teachers so they can reassure you that your concerns are overblown. If they do know of a problem, you can solicit their suggestions for solving it. Let your child know you will expect him to attend school conferences so he can hear what is said.

By high school, most students can reach out to teachers and administrators for help with school-related problems. However, some teenagers are still too immature. They can't overcome their shyness or don't know what to say. Schedule a conference and have your child attend so you can walk him through the process.

Announcing that you will contact your teen's teachers to find out how he is doing and to solicit recommendations may well be the bomb that crashes through your teen's defenses and opens the way to a more forthright conversation. Most students feel that they should be able to manage school without their parents having to intervene. Faced with the embarrassing prospect of a school visit, many young people become motivated to be more responsible about their studies. They may summon the courage to contact their teachers or administrators for assistance with academic and social problems.

**QUESTION?**

**My child won't do homework. Period. What can I do?**
Mentors often motivate students when other approaches fail. Contact the principal or your school district's central administration offices to inquire about programs for at-risk youth. Alternatively, contact Big Brothers or Big Sisters at *www.bbbsa.org*.

Most teachers are willing to help students who have fallen behind if they seem serious about doing better. Even if your teen has alienated his teachers by disrupting the classroom, an apology and a promise of better behavior can move them to provide extra help, accept late papers, or offer extra credit so he can catch up or salvage his grade. However, sometimes students need more assistance than a regular classroom teacher can provide. Resource help through the special education department may be an option, but in some schools the stigma is intense and students refuse to attend. A professional or peer tutor may be a solution. Contact your child's school guidance counselor, the district's educational diagnostician, or special education coordinators for referrals. Making the financial sacrifice to pay for professional tutoring is worth it when your child's high school career is at stake.

## School Conferences

If your child is clearly floundering and can't solve his academic problems himself, call the principal. You may need to go to the school to confer with teachers about ways to help your teenager no matter how loudly he protests. Set up a time to meet with teachers in advance rather than dropping by. Prepare for each conference by talking to your teen about the issues that need to be addressed. Bring specific questions and ideas about how to improve his school experience.

Arrive with a positive attitude, and try to shore up your teen's attitude by reminding him that chalkboard heroes aren't in the classroom for the money or prestige. They deserve respect if for no other reason than that they are human beings. During the meeting, be respectful and solution-focused. Blaming or arguing with the teacher undermines her authority.

Serving as a good role model is critical. By watching you, your child will learn how to approach authority figures with a problem. He will need this skill for interacting with other teachers and with bosses throughout his life.

Even if you are convinced that a teacher has wronged your child, do not attack the teacher. Help your child figure out how to cope with a bad situation or strive to make it better. He may end up feeling mistreated by an employer down the road. He needs to learn how to resolve conflicts when you're not there to run interference for him.

In the past, a few students suffered because they ended up in a classroom headed by an incompetent teacher. Now most students suffer because parents have systematically undermined classroom discipline and eroded educational standards. They have done this by traipsing to the school and demanding that teachers be held accountable for expecting too much academically or behaviorally. "How dare you give my child a C on this paper! He worked hard on it! You're ruining his self-esteem," parents say. They charge emotional abuse because a teacher spoke sharply to a misbehaving student. Even as parents demand that teachers be held accountable, they deter educators from holding their children accountable. Even as parents find themselves unable to discipline their children, they deter teachers from disciplining them. You really do need to support your child's teachers if you can and help to mediate disputes without taking sides if you cannot.

## Instituting a Home Study Hall

You cannot force your child to study, but you can lead him to the educational waters to increase the likelihood that he will drink. If your child isn't bringing home his books and studying, institute a supervised study hall at home every school night. Turn the television and music off. Turn the answering machine on. Institute a quiet hour for the entire family.

Have your child study at the kitchen table so you can supervise while doing dishes, preparing lunches, or tending to other chores. Or sit with him and read, pay bills, or open the laptop so you can tend to other business.

Bright students can do well in elementary school without putting forth much effort, but to succeed in junior high and high school, doing well on exams isn't enough. To get good grades, they must turn in homework assignments and reports. That is as it should be. Knowledge doesn't drive success; it's what people do with what they know that counts.

Tell your child that education is a great benefit of living in America, and you intend to make certain he gets it—that you won't let anyone or anything cheat him out of it. Set a timer and tell him he needs to study for an hour. Stop the clock whenever any sort of interruption impinges on his study time: going to the bathroom or conversing with someone (even if you or a sibling started the conversation). If your teen has no homework, he can review the day's lessons or work ahead. If he has no books, suggest he spend the time *thinking* about what he learned that day.

If your teen isn't keeping up with his schoolwork, set up a quiet hour so he has time to study. Families must pull together to support a teen who is having academic troubles. Express appreciation to your teen's siblings for observing quiet time. They may benefit from a supervised study hall, too.

Students may complain loudly the first day or two of an enforced study hall at home. If the parent has to keep stopping the clock and extending the time, an hour-long study hall can end up lasting all evening. Teens may then test limits by not bringing home their books and insisting it is ridiculous to go through the motions of a study hall. If a slow reader has nothing to do, letting him have a book or magazine can strengthen his reading skills, which is critical for school success. Otherwise, let your child sit out the time with nothing to do. Disallow naps, however. Extend the study hall to make up time spent sleeping and establish an earlier bedtime. Studiously avoid conversation and don't get "hooked" by comments designed to provoke an argument. After six or seven days of parental consistency, virtually every teenager realizes that they can't wiggle out of the study hall. At that point, they begin bringing schoolwork home and studying a bit. Boredom, it turns out, is the best motivator of all.

## A Real Motivational Boost

Many students won't study because they are rebelling. Others are too caught up in having fun to dedicate themselves to something as boring as schoolwork. Either way, they may disregard parental warnings about the disasters that will befall them if they don't settle down and shape up. Sometimes the best solution is to place the responsibility squarely in your child's lap and let the chips fall where they may.

Community colleges across the country have opened their doors to high school students. Many offer remedial classes in math, reading, and writing that can be taken for high school credit. Attending college often provides a motivational boost as well as an educational one by eliminating high school students' fear of entering an alien environment.

If you get an indication that your child isn't doing well because he simply can't be bothered with paying attention in class and doing his schoolwork, reverse psychology may be just what the therapist ordered. Reassure your teenager that failing a couple of classes isn't the end of the world. Tell him that summer school is an option if he wants to graduate with his class. If graduating on schedule isn't a priority, let him know that you think it would be great if he would stick around for an extra semester or year of high school. Help him consider the advantages: Extra time in high school making up a few failed courses may mean he'll have room in his schedule to take some fun classes or a study hall so he can finish his homework at school. He can continue to live at home and won't have to worry about the expense of an apartment or college tuition for a while longer. Lots of students suddenly undergo a dramatic attitude readjustment when faced with the prospect of attending summer school or delaying graduation. They suddenly become very intent on passing.

Girls' traditional downhill academic slide has been the source of much concern among parents and educators alike. Teachers have tried to make classrooms more girl-friendly and are providing extra doses of encouragement and support. The results have been impressive–so much so that girls are now leaving boys behind in the academic dust. Some preliminary research suggests that both sexes do better in segregated classrooms. Boys are bolder about asking questions and participating when they aren't worried about how the girls might react. Girls are less likely to hold themselves back for fear of outshining the boys. Those who remember the separate but oh-so-unequal problems when segregation was routine are appalled at the thought of going back to the past. Still, it is worth rethinking the advantages of an all-boy private school for a lad who is lagging academically.

## Overachievers

It's hard for parents of underachievers to believe that parents of overachieving teenagers have anything to worry about. Teachers may also be skeptical when parents express concern about students who try to do too much too perfectly. But those who push themselves too hard are at risk for burning out. Some become ill. Perfectionists can become sufficiently desperate when they realize they can't do everything well that they become depressed or even suicidal. First-born children are at greatest risk, but it is possible for anyone to forget they are fallible and have limitations.

Some parents place undue pressure on their children. They are satisfied with nothing less than A's and expect their youngsters to excel at everything they do. They may convince their seventh grader that to get into college requires academic excellence and participation in lots of extracurricular activities. Some children pressure themselves in hopes of winning approval from an aloof, unaffectionate parent. Some overachievers are intent on not upsetting parents who seem vulnerable and easily overwhelmed.

Some intellectual types love learning. They are never happier than when reading technical books, spouting facts, and discussing esoteric subjects. Overachievers dedicate similar time to academics but their attitude is very different. They are more preoccupied with grades. Their approach to their studies is grim, rather than enthusiastic.

Overachievers may have developed their obsessive approach to academics in response to external pressures. By high school the problem usually resides within the students themselves. Parental efforts to get them to relax and lighten up don't help. Reassurance that it is okay to make a B—or even a C or a D—may fail to have an impact. This is because many overachievers have come to assess their worth as human beings in terms of their good grades. Doing poorly triggers feelings of personal worthlessness. To help your overachiever, focus less on what she does and more on how she feels:

- **Ask,** "Did you have fun at school?" **not** "How did you do on the test?"
- **Ask,** "Did you learn anything interesting while studying?" **not** "Are you ready for the test?"
- **Ask,** "Don't you think you deserve a break?" **not** "Don't you think you'd better get busy?"
- **Say**, "I love your sweet smile and good heart," **not** "I'm proud of you for being such a good student."
- **Say,** "I'd rather you took a lighter load and enjoyed yourself," **not** "Will that course help you get into college?"
- **Say,** "Have a good time!" **not** "Do your best!"

Set limits to ensure your teenager gets enough sleep at night by establishing ironclad rules about bedtime. Insist that she join you at the dinner table rather than skipping meals so she can continue studying. Get her out of the house if necessary to separate her from her schoolwork and competitive activities. If all else fails, watch for signs of depression (see Chapter 18) and seek counseling.

## Selecting Classes

Part of the excitement of starting junior high and high school is the prospect of getting to choose what courses to take. The reality is often a big disappointment. Junior high school students may not get any electives if they are on an academic track headed toward college. High school is a little better, but not much. Between the many courses required for graduation and those that are virtual necessities to get into college, students have little room in their schedules for electives. Students who do not aspire to attend college have a bit more leeway.

To help your child develop a high school course schedule, the first step is to learn what is required for graduation. Some requirements are established by the state Department of Education. For instance, California requires thirteen courses, including three in English, two in science, two in mathematics, three in social studies, two in physical education, and one in visual or performing arts or foreign language. Students also have to pass a test of basic skills. Fulfilling state requirements isn't enough, however, since individual high schools add requirements of their own. For instance, most California high schools require twenty to twenty-four courses. Many schools around the country include a course in computer literacy among their requirements.

## Solving Social Problems

After the security of elementary school, being shuffled into different classrooms and having to adapt to many different teachers and classmates requires a big adjustment. Not being well liked can be so devastating as to interfere with your teenager's ability to concentrate on academics. Even popular students struggle with social pressures that distract them from their schoolwork, discourage academic achievement, and deliver repeated blows to their self-esteem. If your child appears unhappy and bares his fangs when you rattle his cage to find out what's wrong, don't be put off. He may really need your support, advice, and help.

Peer pressure causes large percentages of previously self-confident seventh and eighth grade girls to become blind to their talents and relinquish their academic goals. Their new preoccupation is with trying to fit in. In many schools, friends are the only protection against being isolated, bullied, and harassed, so young teens are strongly motivated to sacrifice their values and beliefs to affiliate with a group. Joining a clique or gang ensures they won't have to endure the ultimate humiliation: eating lunch alone in front of a gawking cafeteria crowd who might duly note their isolation, spread word of their worthlessness, and target them for special tortures.

Be sure your teen knows to contact a principal or counselor if he feels threatened by a classmate, is being harassed, or feels isolated and alone. Even when faced with an extremely serious interpersonal problem, some students are reluctant to reach out. In a national survey, only 17 percent of students said they would alert an adult if they thought another student had taken a gun to school.

Boys are not exempt from being harassed and scapegoated, and many suffer mightily. They may be made to feel that their intelligence and academic abilities are more socially handicapping than helpful. Maltreatment is most often driven by envy. Students who don't see much of a future for themselves may strive to destroy those who appear destined to go far. Today's high school nerd is likely to be tomorrow's computer genius, accountant, artist, or entrepreneur. Boys and girls alike should be encouraged to join extracurricular activities where they will be likely to find people who appreciate their talents and are less preoccupied with whether they are wearing the "right" clothes and carrying the "right" sort of book bag.

## Social Survival

The key to social survival in junior high and high school is having at least one like-minded friend and a few other peers that your teen can enjoy enough to hang out with. A companion can stave off loneliness during unstructured times, such as at lunch, on the school bus, and before and after school. Let your teenager know that so much emphasis on popularity and the tendency to disrespect students who are in any way different reflect the tremendous personal insecurity of this age. Those who pick on other students are the most personally insecure of all. They try to feel better about themselves by putting others down.

Reassure your child that social success in high school has little to do with popularity as an adult, a loving spouse, or anything else that your child needs to feel happy. Lots of Hollywood giants were made to feel like misfits during adolescence. Sissy Spacek couldn't even snag a part in her high school play.

The key is for students to strike up conversations with peers, reach out to those who share similar interests, and work on turning them into friends. Even in schools where 70 percent of the students drop out, a serious student can find some people with similar academic aspirations. Good friends support one another to achieve their individual goals. They do not drag them down. The challenge is to find them in the first place, and not to abandon them if a peer with a better position in the high school social hierarchy comes along.

## Support from Home

After Jenna's parents set up a study hall at home, she began doing her homework but she continued to cut classes. When they announced that they had scheduled a school conference, she confessed that other students were taunting her because of her obesity. She was so miserable that she was having suicidal thoughts. Her parents called the guidance counselor, and he invited Jenna to attend a supervised teen discussion group. The group became her haven. She volunteered to serve as an office aide, and finally had a niche. At that point her attitude and attendance improved, and she devoted more energy to schoolwork. Her parents still felt badly about having assumed Jenna's academic problems were due to laziness. They became more insistent that she share what was really happening in her life. (E)

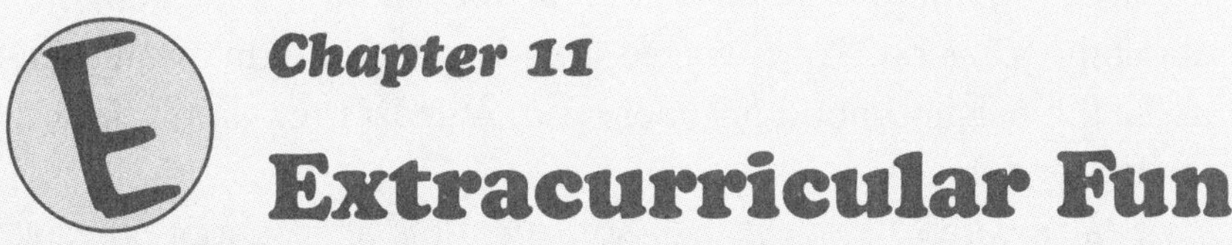

# Chapter 11
# Extracurricular Fun

Enjoyable extracurricular outlets are important for everyone and essential for those who dislike academics. Without some structured activities that get their juices flowing, young people are likely to do whatever necessary to create some excitement. Often they direct their energy to stirring up trouble. Finding healthy outlets your teen enjoys can be challenging—you may have to sell your teen on the idea, provide transportation, and foot the bills. Although teenagers simply must have a pastime they feel passionate about, don't overschedule your child. That isn't healthy, either.

## Teen Boredom

When fourteen-year-old Sean wasn't planted in front of the television watching cartoons, he was in front of the set playing video games. When he wasn't doing either, he was in the den playing computer games. His parents were concerned that Sean was so isolated, got so little exercise, and frittered away so much time. Still, they were not altogether unhappy about the situation. They worked long hours and didn't want him roaming about the neighborhood unsupervised. At least they didn't have to worry about him when he was at home.

Sean's parents *thought* their son spent his after-school hours at home, but they later discovered they were mistaken. His usual pattern was to stop at home after school and forward the phones to his cell phone so he could answer if his parents called to check on him. Then he headed down the street to be with some friends he knew his parents would not approve of. The boys hung out at the home of a child whose parents were at work, so the group had the house to themselves. They mostly played on the computer or drove to the mall in town. Sean was careful to arrive home before his parents, and his activities only came to light after he and his friends were picked up by the police. They had shot out some windows of a nearby home with a BB gun. Sean of course insisted that he hadn't fired the gun. When his parents asked him why his friends had done such a thing, he said, "I don't know. I guess just for fun. They were bored."

## The Benefits of Extracurricular Involvements

The benefits of extracurricular activities are almost too numerous to mention. At the very least, enjoyable pastimes help teenagers relax by taking their minds off of school and family problems and break the monotony of everyday life. Besides reducing stress, the social benefits can be invaluable. The chance to interact with peers in a semistructured situation helps teens develop better social skills. Feeling connected to a group can provide an important sense of belonging for young people who don't feel accepted by other students at school. Having a niche can do more to strengthen teens to withstand peer pressure than dozens of parental lectures. Community involvement creates a sense of connection to the world outside of school. Colleges usually give points to potential students for being active in their school and community. Be sure your teen saves his awards, plaques, and certificates of recognition. In addition, he should ask sponsors and coaches for letters of recommendation to save for his files.

Adult sponsors, teachers, and coaches often become significant sources of moral support and serve as important teen role models. They can form a bridge to the older generation that opens the way for alienated teens to form better relationships with their parents and teachers.

The feeling of accomplishment that comes from exercising nonacademic talents can provide a much-needed ego boost if your student struggles with schoolwork and has a hard time keeping up. Extracurricular activities can also provide a positive focus, direction, and sense of purpose. Participating helps many teens define career interests, and sometimes an activity becomes a steppingstone to a job or lifelong career. Activities that are simply fun enhance the quality of your teen's life by adding to its joy. Don't minimize the value of fun!

## High School Sports

Since funding cuts have eliminated extra school bus runs in many districts, participation in clubs and activities that meet before and after school has decreased. At the same time, the pool of available sponsors and chaperones has dried up because so many parents work. As a result, fewer choices for extracurricular school activities are available for today's youth than past generations enjoyed.

Despite cutbacks in extracurricular activities, most public schools maintain active athletics programs. They offer students a variety of ways to participate. If not actually playing on a team, students may be chosen for the cheerleading squad or join the drill team. Coaches are important as authority figures and often serve as mentors and guides for their charges. Besides the health benefits of rigorous physical workouts for team members, participants learn to consider the needs of the group. They are helped to understand the importance of contributing by supporting one another instead of trying to make an individual splash. Teenagers tend to be very self-centered, so learning to cooperate for the greater good is a valuable lesson.

From playing on a team to selling hot dogs in the stands, sporting events offer opportunities for healthy social involvements that help young people feel connected to their school. Identifying with their institution creates an increased commitment to its goals. That lessens students' motivation to join gangs and drop out.

Sports aren't only for the athletically inclined. Student volunteers take tickets, work in the concession stands, deliver water to the players, twirl batons, serve as mascots, or play in the band. Such activities build self-esteem by giving young people positive outlets for their energies and providing recognition for their efforts as volunteers.

## Other School Activities

While athletics programs are the most visible extracurricular activity, most high schools also have a debate team and a group that produces the yearbook. Depending on the social climate at your child's school, members of both may be teased for being involved, but they are tomorrow's lawyers and writers. Schools have student councils and prom committees, homecoming floats that need to be built, and peers in need of tutoring. There is something for most everyone willing to donate time.

Some regular credit courses involve out-of-class time that enables students to interact around a worthy cause. The orchestra and choir prepare for and give concerts. Drama classes rehearse and put on plays. Art classes design murals and decorate bulletin boards. English students enter contests and publish literary magazines. If your teen claims there are no extracurricular opportunities, talk to the guidance counselor to find out what's available. Some students don't realize the many opportunities that exist on campus.

Other volunteer opportunities at school expand students' social horizons while teaching them valuable vocational skills. Office aides, hall monitors, and nurse's assistants learn about office procedures. They acquire responsibility and discipline and chances to exercise some authority. Volunteers establish relationships with one another and get to know staff members as people. Many students especially enjoy the status of being able to roam the halls, deliver messages, and escort visitors and other students to and from classrooms. En route, their opportunities to meet peers one-on-one open the way to friendships.

A dedicated French teacher may sponsor a French or foreign language club, a math teacher a math club, a science teacher a rocket-building club. If your child sees a need for a club relating to a school subject, she should approach a teacher or discuss the matter with the principal. If you've got the time, volunteer!

## Community Clubs and Organizations

When searching for extracurricular involvements, parents and teens need to expand their thinking beyond high school activities and consider the many community clubs, special interest groups, and civic organizations in the larger community. Although there are fewer high school clubs than in the past, opportunities for teenagers to participate in activities outside of school are virtually unlimited.

### Parks and Recreation Departments

Many parks and recreations departments operate youth centers and offer classes in everything from line dancing to puppeteering. Personnel are usually grateful to have teenagers help out with classes designed for younger children. Staff members appreciate teens' help chaperoning special events, such as nature hikes and outings to museums. City sports programs for soccer, softball, and swimming abound, and students who can't make the team at school can play. Open gymnasiums give teenagers a place to meet, mingle, and shoot hoops while staff provide a bit of supervision.

If your teenager is hesitant about going alone to a recreation center, see if he can find a companion for the first visit. Alternatively, assign him the chore of taking a younger sibling. After the first trip, your teenager may feel comfortable enough to go alone.

## Church Youth Groups

You don't have to be a member of a church or synagogue to have your child attend an affiliated youth group. Most religious organizations are happy to have young people attend just for fun. Choirs need singers. Sunday schools need teachers. Nurseries need sitters. Softball teams need players. Youth groups usually welcome new members heartily. Other than an opening and closing prayer and the fact that proceeds from car washes may benefit missionaries, most groups are about socializing, not religion. Your teen doesn't have to worry that someone will "try to shove religion down my throat," as young people typically anticipate. If you're not a member of a church or synagogue, call around to find what they have in the way of a youth program.

## Youth Clubs

After your teen has dropped out of boy scouting and campfire girls (both of which have excellent teen programs), youth groups like Future Farmers of America and 4-H clubs continue to draw large crowds. Many areas have a YMCA or YWCA, Boys and Girls Club of America, and Salvation Army. Many adult clubs are appropriate for teens, too.

## Adult Activities for Teens

Lots of community clubs and organizations will readily accept teenagers as members. However, calling in advance to ask if it would be possible for your teenager to attend is usually a bad idea. Asking permission for your teenager to attend suggests that she might pose problems or require special consideration, supervision, and treatment. Accordingly, whoever you contact will probably consult with the organizers or the entire membership before deciding. Often a crisis ensues as groups debate the consequences of having a bunch of misbehaving fourteen-year-olds in their midst. Adult members assume they would have to clean up their language and avoid controversial topics so as not to upset the teenagers' parents. Many adults don't realize that teenagers' language and the topics they discuss are far more extreme than in most adult organizations. The typical answer is "no teenagers allowed."

**There are decided advantages to being the only teenager in a group of adults. Being younger than everyone else does draw some extra attention, but young people are generally treated as equals. Most rise to the occasion and behave like adults.**

Consider placing a call to a community organization to learn the schedule and to find out when potential members can visit to see about joining. Instead of asking permission for your teen to attend, simply drop him at the door and retrieve him afterwards. A bicycle club won't mind having a teen pedal with them, a running club will welcome a teen runner; however, a hiking club might want a permission slip signed by a parent for a youth under age eighteen.

Alternatively, accompany a shy teen to the first meeting as if both of you were considering joining. Who knows? You may end up doing just that. By taking your teen to a meeting without creating a stir about his age in advance, the group will welcome him like any other guest, relate to him like any other potential member, and consider him for membership on his own merits. That is much better than having them base their decision about whether to let him attend according to their stereotypes of teenagers—which are often decidedly negative.

Take your teen who likes to sing to the auditions or organizational meeting for your local community chorus. Chauffeur a teen musician to the community orchestra, band, wind ensemble, or meeting of the local guitar society. Writers' groups abound for aspiring poets and authors. Community theaters need volunteers to help with advertising and props as well as actors. Art clubs are available for painters, book clubs for readers, sailing clubs for sailors, and hot air balloon clubs for balloonists. It doesn't matter that your child doesn't sail and has only seen a hot air balloon at the state fair. Participants in these sports are desperate for crew. Take your politically minded teen to a local meeting of Democrats, Republicans, Greens, or the League of Women Voters. Check the entertainment section of the local paper for announcements and contact the Chamber of Commerce for lists of other area clubs and organizations.

## Private Lessons

Karate lessons. Guitar lessons. Singing lessons. Ceramics classes. Clogging. Gymnastics. Yoga. Modeling. There's lots of fun stuff out there, and adolescents spend so much time in classrooms, they usually feel comfortable in learning environments. If your teen doesn't go for the usual ballet and piano lessons, use your imagination. If a single flying lesson seems expensive, consider that for the price of two video games he'll have an experience he'll never forget if he lives to be 100. He may save up for a second lesson. Once your teen finds something that lights his fire, he may feel inspired to do well in school so he can work in the field some day.

## Something for Everyone

Might your teen enjoy flying remote-control airplanes? Learning to play the keyboard? Raising cocker spaniels? Trying his hand at sculpture? Learning carpentry? Going hunting? Fixing up an old car? Building a boat in a bottle? If you can't find a specific subject that captures your teen's interest, try to come up with something new for him to investigate each week if possible. Otherwise, set a goal of having an activity planned for him at least once a month. Visit a dog show. Sign him up for a private keyboarding lesson. Have him spend a day hanging out with a friend who is into sculpture or pottery. See if he can accompany a carpenter friend to work. Ask if your neighbor will let him hang around and help out while he works on his car. Ask a colleague at work to consider taking him along when he and his male friends go fishing. See if your vet will let your teen shadow him at work for a day. That will give your teen something to look forward to or dread—either way the anticipation will help to relieve his boredom.

Community college courses are open to high school students. With your permission, your child can take a course that meets evenings or weekends in jewelry making, small engine repair, computers, or Spanish. He might even earn some college credit!

Sampling a range of activities, hobbies, events, clubs, jobs, and organizations will help your child define his vocational interests if he doesn't have a specific goal. Discovering what he does *not* like or enjoy will help him narrow the range of career possibilities. Eliminating careers can be a first important step for helping people to decide what they might like to do with their lives.

## Conquering the Summertime Blues

Boredom is a particular problem for teenagers during the summer. They need to have an unending supply of friends and lots of fun things to do for entertainment. Unless they are involved in some structured activities, attend summer school, have a job, or volunteer on a regular basis, the surge of excitement they feel when summer vacation begins soon wears off. Irritability or depression is likely to set in as adolescents are forced to confront their most dangerous foe: boredom. For ideas for summertime jobs, see Chapter 13.

### Summer School

Summer is a great time to take a course for fun or to get a difficult high school class out of the way. Either way, summer study can free up time during the regular school year so students have room in their schedules for an elective or study hall. It might seem that taking an academic course in summer school would be overly challenging—how to learn calculus in eight weeks when most students require a full academic year? In actuality, summer school usually turns out to be less difficult than students anticipate. Being able to concentrate exclusively on one subject can make things considerably easier. In addition, it is common for teachers to scale back their usual requirements during summer courses. Teachers may decide at the outset not to cover some of the chapters in the text. Many simply run out of time before getting through all of them. Teachers may also tend to assign fewer homework problems, shorten the required length for the term paper, or find other ways to reduce the pressure. In general, summer school students and teachers alike seem more cheerful, the rules more relaxed, and there are fewer discipline problems than during the regular school year. This may be due to the short school day, the better weather, the smaller classes, or the fact that only the more motivated students attend in the first place. This is true in high school as well as college summer classes. Attending a single course for four hours a day can sound miserable when students are used to sitting for an hour at most, but teachers provide lots of breaks.

Summer school has some additional benefits for younger students. Those who would be stuck at home all day because they aren't yet driving can more easily arrange to get together with classmates before and after school. Signing up with a friend can be a good way to have a study buddy as well as some good companionship. Attending a college summer class can be a great introduction to college. Students don't feel so lost when the crowds have departed for the summer. It gives them a chance to meet some people and get to know the campus.

## Summer Learning Camps

Whether your teen wants to attend summer camp or work at one, find one in The American Camping Association's searchable database. You or your teen can go to *www.acacamps.org* and search over 2,000 summer camps by location or area of interest. Specialty camps cater to at-risk youth, talented and gifted, and teens needing help with such problems as grief or weight loss. From the same Web address your teen can find a summer job as a camp counselor. The site even has advice on everything from interviewing to counseling children at camp.

You can send your computer star to computer camp, your hockey wiz to hockey camp, your science fan to NASA to study space technology or to the sea to study oceanography. Simply type "summer camp" and "oceanography" into an Internet search engine such as *www.google.com*, and voila! A list.

Lots of teenagers love to travel, and an exotic trip to study in a foreign land may be just the social and academic cure your child needs. Typical programs designed to cater to American high school students place teens with local families that have been carefully screened. Students study foreign language and culture for a period ranging from a few weeks to all summer. Simply go to your favorite search engine and type in "summer study," "high school," and the name of the language your child would like to study or the country he wants to visit. Be sure to ask for references and talk to some families about their child's experiences. If you want more careful supervision, contact the American Institute for Foreign Study at *www.aifs.org* or call 800-727-AIFS. Students are housed in foreign dorms at colleges and universities. There's truly no better way to learn a foreign language than to take classes while living in the country!

## Signs of Burnout

And yes, some teenagers do too much, too intensely. The "hurried child syndrome" first coined by psychologist David Elkind in his book, *The Hurried Child: Growing Up Too Fast Too Soon,* describes the problem of parents who push too hard and overschedule their children. Kibbutzing from the sidelines is in bad taste. Let the coach or teacher handle that job. When you're at your child's game or recital, stick to applauding successes and consoling her over mistakes and mishaps. If you are pushing too hard, you may note the following signs of passive resistance in her:

- Forgets about meetings, practices, or events
- Loses required materials, such as uniforms, equipment, and permission slips
- Won't help line up transportation

- Loses schedules and directions to meets
- Drags her feet when it's time to leave the house
- Complains of headaches or stomach aches on the days of scheduled activities

Of course, some overly enthusiastic teens push themselves too hard. Be alert to signs of burnout and safeguard your child's health, but don't discourage a child who is reaching for the stars. Few junior Olympic athletes and concert pianists get pushed to the top by their parents. Au contraire. Most drag their reluctant parents to the car and insist on being driven to the next lesson.

## Teen Hobbies

Sean's only genuine interest was watching cartoons. His parents were able to capitalize on that unlikely hobby by signing him up for a cartooning correspondence course. Suddenly Sean was off and running. He spent three months drawing cartoons by hand, then began creating digital ones on the computer. He entered a contest through a local artist's organization and won an honorable mention. During his senior year he picked up a freelance assignment illustrating an article for a local magazine. Suddenly he knew what he wanted to be when he grew up: He would illustrate children's books. His parents were still nudging him toward college but decided if he postponed it a while it wouldn't be the end of the world. Sean had joined the National Society of Children's Book Writers and Illustrators and was sending his portfolio out to New York publishers. His parents were delighted that he had found his niche.

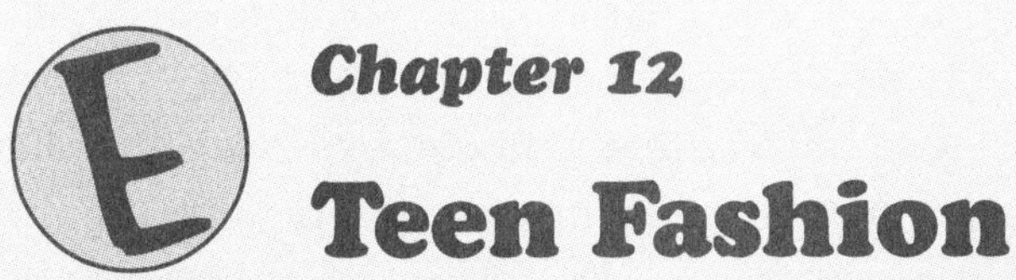

# Chapter 12
# Teen Fashion

Fashion is a major source of friction in many families. Yet the pattern has been for today's teen fashion revolution to ripple across the generations and become tomorrow's fashion statement for people of all ages. Battles over mini-skirts and dreadlocks typically stem from parental difficulties with accepting their teens' emerging independence, autonomy, individuality, and sexuality. Instead of arguing about eyebrow rings and purple hair, see if you can identify and come to terms with the real issues.

## Fashion Offenses

Kevin was the youngest of three boys, so his parents were seasoned pros when it came to dealing with teenagers. The main thing they had learned was not to sweat the small stuff. Accordingly, when Kevin shaved off his lovely brown hair and ended up with a blue crew cut a month later, his parents did their best to grin and bear it. Kevin was a good kid, a decent student, and they understood that trying on new identities for size was part of being a teenager. They felt a bit embarrassed by Kevin's appearance when he went through what he called his "grunge" period and worried about what their friends might think. Nevertheless, they kept their concerns to themselves. They didn't want to set a bad example by caving into pressure from their own peers. Kevin's parents were glad when he traded in his "grunge" look for a clean-cut "preppy" look a few months later. Just when they thought his fashion experiments were over, he announced plans to get both arms tattooed up to his elbows and have a nipple pierced. He had an answer for all of their arguments but agreed to wait a month to see if he changed his mind before doing something so painful and permanent. That crisis seemed like nothing compared to what happened next. As the family was getting into the car to go to Thanksgiving dinner at grandmother's, Kevin's father did a double-take and his mother gasped. "What in the world—?" his dad thundered. "You're wearing makeup?" They stared in amazement at Kevin's eyes, which were ringed with eyeliner and topped with eye shadow. Kevin insisted it was no big deal, but having a son wear makeup was a very big deal to his parents. They were horrified.

### The Fashion Wars

Perhaps parents require more time to adjust to new fashions than teens because older people are generally more resistant to change. For whatever reason, adults tend to prefer styles that were popular during their own teenaged years. Many look askance at modern clothing, criticizing it for being too tight, too baggy, too black, too gaudy, or too revealing. The same goes for fashions in music, and many adults declare teenaged tunes unacceptable. Yet it is virtually impossible for even the most determined parent to win the fashion wars. Teenagers may defer to their parents' wishes in order to eliminate conflict at home. Then students borrow outfits from friends or buy them on the sly, tuck the outlawed clothing or makeup into a backpack, and do a quick makeover in the school restroom. When parents forbid body art, some teenagers have holes bored in areas they can readily conceal, such as a nipple or navel. They get tattoos on their lower back or upper arm, evading discovery by carefully tucking in their shirts and rolling down their sleeves while at home.

**How do I get my teenager to dress respectably?**
Styles that the older generation considers attractive may look hopelessly old-fashioned to your child. Wars over clothes can alienate your teen and are very hard to win. Usually there are other, more pressing issues to tackle. Choose your battles carefully.

## The Call to Battle

If a parent and teenager are having conflicts over major issues, such as grades, curfews, dating, or drugs, it is usually unwise to add to the turmoil by simultaneously trying to enforce a dress code. In the grand scheme of things, it rarely matters that your teenager prefers black or green lipstick to pink and red. It does matter that he is eating properly, getting enough sleep, and handling his school and home responsibilities.

FACT

Controversy continues over whether or not music can warp young minds. The lyrics of some popular teenaged songs are extremely sexual and violent. It is known that watching violent television shows and movies increases aggressiveness. Whether listening to music has a similar effect is unknown. Some experts think that it may provide a safe outlet for impulses that would be dangerous if acted out.

Some parents say that there may be merit to making a big to-do over minor issues such as clothes, hair, makeup, and music. They point out that since teenagers feel compelled to rebel, parents may be able to channel the rebellion into a relatively harmless area by holding firm about fashion and music. Certainly it's better for your teen to defy you by slipping on a forbidden T-shirt behind your back than by violating his curfew. It's better for him to defy your rules about haircuts than about cutting classes. But if you're already struggling over curfews and cut classes, it's probably unwise to also argue about clothing.

### Winning the War

Intergenerational fashion wars are very common, but they are not universal. Some teenagers' fashion tastes are more like their parents' than their peers'. These teenagers may seek their parents' opinions of what to buy and wear and care more about what they think than their friends. Usually this is because the teenagers spend most of their time with their families or are immersed in an activity that usurps the majority of their time and energy. Homeschooled students with limited peer contact may emulate their parents. The same goes for aspiring concert violinists, champion figure skaters, Olympic hopefuls, teenaged stars, and other super-achievers, who model themselves after the adults in their lives. Their lives are very different from the average teenager, who spends less than 5 percent of the time with his parents, according to Taffel, the author of *The Second Family*. After spending all day at school, most of the evening in their bedrooms studying and talking on the phone, and all night sleeping, little time remains for communing with dear old mom and dad! If you are concerned about your child's clothes and the values that they seem to express, the first step is to rethink your own values and how you express them. Make spending time with your child a priority. For your child to choose to spend time with you, work to improve your relationship by honing your communication skills (Chapter 6), your methods of disciplining (Chapter 7), and engaging in some joint extracurricular fun (Chapter 11).

## Family Issues

As teenagers don extreme styles and parents strive to get them to tone down their appearance, teen identity issues often collide with parent/child separation issues. Parents often believe the underlying problem stems from values clashes. Sometimes this is the case, but more often separation and identity issues cause simple differences of opinion over clothes, hair, makeup, music, and body art to escalate into major confrontations.

## Separation Issues

Some professionals are now questioning the longstanding assumption that it is necessary for teenagers to separate emotionally from their parents. It has long been believed that an emotional separation is required before a healthy parent/adult child relationship can develop, so some rebellion and defiance were viewed as positive. However, experts have come to realize that many teenagers never rebel, rarely if ever defy their parents' rules, enjoy spending time with them, and make a fairly effortless transition to relating to their parents more like equals. These happy situations seem to develop when parents are able to treat their teenagers like young adults. Many teenagers struggle with their parents to gain more emotional distance and force their parents to see them as people in their own right. Too often, teenagers feel that they are being treated as mere reflections of the people that gave them life. Often, the teenagers are right.

**My child ignores my opinions. How can I get her to listen to me?** The first step is to accept that her opinions are as valid as yours. Only then will she have confidence that you are objective enough to be able to guide her.

Until a parent is clear in her own mind about the difference between herself and her teenager, she may automatically project her thoughts and feelings onto her child. Thus, a mother who stopped wearing makeup and combing her hair during a bout of depression is terribly worried because her daughter stopped wearing makeup and looks like she isn't combing her hair. Although her daughter insists that she is going for the natural look, the mother doesn't feel reassured. She sees her daughter as a miniature version of herself and can't accept that the two of them are very different. Similarly, the father who wore psychedelic clothes back when he took hallucinogenic drugs accuses his child of looking like a druggie because of his extreme outfits instead of accepting that the style is popular among kids who never touch drugs. If only promiscuous girls wore plunging necklines and stiletto heels back when you were in high school, don't assume that your daughter is advertising her sexual availability because she likes see-through tops and fishnet stockings. It's a new generation. To assume your teenager is just like you almost always breeds resentment and escalates conflicts. If your teenager keeps insisting, "I am not you," you may need to work on coming to terms with that reality.

FACT

In some tribal societies the women go about naked from the waist up, the men wear loincloths, and no one thinks anything about it. Similarly, American teenagers who grew up with MTV and R-rated movies may not consider very revealing fashions to be provocative. However, members of the older generation may feel offended or titillated by them.

If you are concerned that your child's appearance signals problems with depression, drugs, promiscuity, gangs, or another problem, you need to address your concerns directly. Talk with her often to find out what is on her mind and in her heart, as well as on her daily agenda. Express your worries, doubts, and uncertainties directly, and feel free to ask questions: "When I was your age, only promiscuous girls wore blouses with plunging necklines and went braless. How do boys your age react to tops like the one you're wearing?" Even if she doesn't provide a reassuring answer, hopefully your questions will induce her to consider how others might react to her appearance.

## Identity Issues

Clothes may not make the man or the woman, but appearance can accurately reflect what is happening inside of him or her. How people dress says a lot about how they feel on a given day, what kind of person they perceive themselves to be, what social group they belong to, and so forth. Clothing reflects people's mood and important aspects of their personal identity. However, try to draw conclusions about what is happening inside someone else based on her appearance, and you will probably be wrong as often as you are right. Does your teenager's unkempt appearance reflect low self-esteem as you fear? Or does she prefer to put her energy into other activities? Perhaps she is a major clothes hound, and her disheveled look is actually a cutting-edge fashion statement that will soon be sweeping the country. Looks really can be deceiving.

Trying to sort out what is going on inside your teenager by scrutinizing his attire isn't likely to get you very far. If he says that he shaved his head because he thinks it's cool, you need to accept his explanation. If you fear he has joined the Nazis, ask him to share his thoughts about race instead of focusing on his baldness.

Clothing is an intensely personal matter. What your teen chooses to wear expresses her identity. If she is still experimenting with different identities and trying to decide who she is, her taste in clothes as well as makeup, hair, and music are likely to change. While your only concern may be that your teen's outfit is too sloppy or revealing, your child is likely to take criticism as a personal rejection. From your teenager's point of view, clothing conflicts are likely to be about independence ("Mom and Dad are treating me like a baby"), autonomy ("They're trying to control my entire life"), and personal acceptance ("My parents don't love me, just an image of me. All they care about is how I look").

As the pressure mounts to make major life decisions, it is normal for teens to try on several different identities for size. That can translate into major changes in style of dress. Add that to all of the many other dramatic physical and emotional changes your child is going through, and your teenager may feel like a stranger. Asking him to wear styles that seem more familiar to you may not seem like much. In fact, it is asking a lot. It is also an attempt to sidestep the important challenge of this phase of parenthood: releasing your grip on the baby you adored, on the child you nurtured, and getting to know and appreciate the adult your teenager is becoming.

If you forbid your teen to wear gang clothes or "colors," remember that clothes are not the issue. She can still put on the forbidden articles of clothing when you're not around, leading you to believe a serious problem is solved when it is not. Before taking action, discuss the matter with a school counselor.

## Peer Pressure

Most parents are convinced that the teenaged obsession with wearing just the right clothes, hairstyle, and makeup is driven by peer pressure, and the idea that their youngster is so influenced by friends worries them deeply. Will today's mindless conformity to the dictates of fashion become tomorrow's willingness to follow the crowd into serious trouble? Accordingly, parents struggle to convince their teens not to choose styles just because they have the in-crowd's seal of approval.

Don't be surprised if your teen cares more about her friends' opinions than yours. She is less secure about where she stands with her friends than with you. Further, to develop emotionally and become her own person, she may need to turn her focus away from what you think and feel for a time.

It is true that most younger teens are extremely sensitive to friends' reactions and work hard to live up to their peers' exacting standards regarding looks, manner of speech, preferences in music and movies, and most everything else. Still, it is a mistake to conclude that your teenager's taste in clothes is driven by peer pressure. Your teen developed his ideas about what is totally gorgeous and what is horribly gross from television shows, movies, rock videos, and magazines. Teenagers don't see a particular outfit, tattoo, or hairstyle and think, "I think that's ugly, but I want it because the peers I need to impress would love it." Just like adults, teenagers are attracted to styles that they personally find pleasing. Only then do they contemplate how the people they would like to impress might react. The desire to please peers is real enough, but it is secondary.

## Problematic Attire

Some schools have tried to solve the teenaged fashion problem by mandating that students wear uniforms. Insisting that everyone conform to a dress code can eliminate lots of conflict at home, and many teachers and principals report fewer behavior problems and improved school spirit. Uniforms don't do much to lessen the peer pressure, however. Instead of deriding one another for wearing the wrong shirt, students criticize one another for wearing a shirt that is too loose or tight, too wrinkled or ironed, hanging out instead of tucked in.

If after chastising your teenager for conforming to peer pressure, you pressure her to conform to your taste in clothes, she may rightly view you as a hypocrite. It doesn't make sense to lecture your child about the evils of conformity while insisting she conform to styles that you and your friends like.

Even when school uniforms eliminate parental objections to the clothing their child wears to school, fashion can be a problem at home and in the community. If your daughter wants to wear clothes that seem designed to invite more sexual attention than she could safely manage, talk to her about your concerns. If you insist that she change outfits without further explanation, she may think you're just trying to control her. She needs to understand that if others react to her clothing as you do, they may think she is signaling her sexual availability. At the same time, it is important to remember that some styles that raise eyebrows among members of your generation may seem tame to her peers.

Like adults, teenagers choose clothes that they like and that they think friends will appreciate. If you believe in strict rules about clothing, only buy clothes you can both agree on. Let your son pick the outfits but retain veto power. Affirm your child's right to choose—but within limits.

## The Person Inside

Before proceeding to Thanksgiving dinner, Kevin's parents insisted that he wash off his eye makeup. Kevin exploded. He said if his parents didn't want to be seen with him, he would stay home. "That's not what we want, Kevin," his dad insisted. But Kevin said they didn't want *him*, just somebody to show off to their relatives. He said that he would find a picture of himself and they could take that to show off to the relatives and he would stay at home.

Suddenly Kevin's ten-year-old brother piped up, "Mom and Dad don't want Grandma to know that you're gay." Kevin's parents were too shocked to speak.

"I'm questioning, that's all," Kevin said quickly. "It's not like I've done anything." Then he crossed his arms over his chest. "You said you loved me no matter what!"

His parents exchanged glances. Was this just an adolescent phase like all the rest? They guessed they would find out in time. "Well, one thing is certain, Kevin," his father said. "Wearing makeup doesn't have anything to do with being gay. If you were a champion skater, I wouldn't expect you to wear kneepads and a helmet to your grandmother's house for Thanksgiving dinner. I'd appreciate it if you would wash your face." Kevin paused to consider, then walked back inside to clean up. When he was gone, Kevin's mother said she guessed these kinds of challenges were meant to help them grow as people. Kevin's father replied, "Maybe so. I don't know about you, but personally, I'm a bit tired of growing."

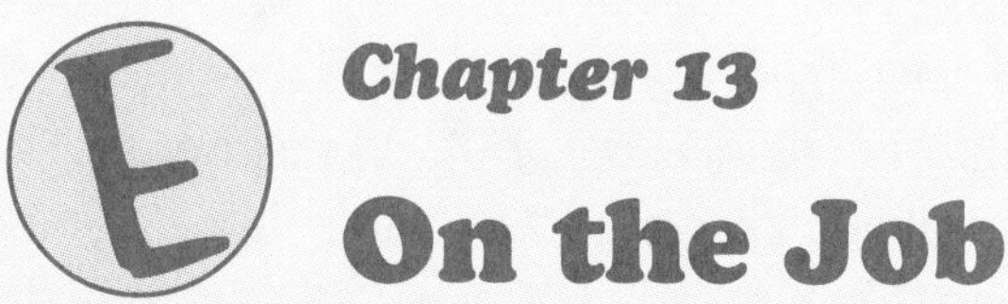

# Chapter 13
# On the Job

Most teenagers are eager for a regular paycheck, but finding and keeping a job can be difficult. Teen unemployment statistics are abysmal, and the available jobs often entail unpleasant work and low pay. Worse, negative employer attitudes toward teenagers often mean that they aren't helped to succeed when they are hired. You may need to teach job skills, help your teen find work, and be supportive if he ends up getting laid off or fired.

## Balancing Work and School

Meagan had never liked school, her grades weren't wonderful, and she refused to consider college after high school graduation. Her academic difficulties had taken a toll on her self-esteem, and her parents were pleased when she got her first job. It was just at a fast-food restaurant, but they hoped a successful work experience would help Meagan feel better about herself by providing a sense of accomplishment. It might open her eyes to the importance of education and inspire her to attend some sort of vocational training program after high school. In the meantime, her parents believed a job would provide some much-needed structure on evenings and weekends. She would spend less time hanging out with her friends, some of whom were getting into trouble. Meagan's parents congratulated her heartily.

Excellent students may be able to work twenty hours a week if they don't have any extracurricular involvements. Marginal students can work that much if they are in a work/study program. Otherwise, working more than ten hours a week tends to have a negative effect on students' grades.

After Meagan's first exhausting week at work, she adjusted and began to enjoy her job. Most of her co-workers were teens, and although the kids worked hard, they also found time to socialize. The downside was that on top of her twenty hours of work each week, Meagan was frequently called in to take extra shifts. Her hours on school nights were supposed to be from 5:00–9:00 P.M., but after the restaurant closed, the employees had to stay on to clean up. Meagan rarely got home before 11:00 P.M.—often as late as 11:30 or midnight. She assured her parents her schoolwork wasn't being affected, but her report card told a different story. She insisted she would be fired if she said she had to leave at 10:00 or refused to go into work when her supervisor needed her. Her parents didn't want to insist that she quit a job that she obviously enjoyed and that gave her such an ego boost. On the other hand, if she didn't graduate from high school, her future employment options would be dim. Their problem was solved when Meagan came home sobbing. "The boss was always on everybody's case, except for his one favorite, who can do no wrong," she said. "He was picking on Jill. I asked him if he got off on making girls cry. He fired me on the spot."

"That's no way to talk to a boss!" Meagan's mother said. Meagan shot back an obscenity and disappeared into her room. Her parents weren't pleased about what had happened but figured it was for the best. She would have more time for her studies. However, Meagan didn't use the extra time to study. She didn't even look worried when her parents warned her about failing. She had completely lost interest in school.

## Teen Employment

When it comes to the benefits of working, a paycheck is usually the first thing teenagers consider, but there are others that are equally important. Working gives teenagers an opportunity to contribute to society. If schoolwork seems divorced from the real world, having a job puts them in the mainstream of life. It gives teens a sense of being grown up and of doing something useful even as it helps them grow up and teaches them life skills.

From doing household chores to babysitting, lots of enterprising young teenagers find ways to do some work and get paid for it. Still, the vast majority have their first "real job" when they can legally hold a job at age sixteen. Some students begin applying the day after their sixteenth birthday. Many make a brief stab at working the following summer, while others show a notable lack of enthusiasm. Parents may end up charging their nineteen-year-old rent and threatening to evict their child for nonpayment to inspire him or her to look for a job. There are no set patterns. Teen enthusiasm varies dramatically, as do the issues they face on the job.

Some of the job settings generally regarded as least desirable may actually offer the best opportunities. The turnover in fast-food restaurants, convenience stores, and department stores is so high that responsible employees with any staying power often find themselves on the fast track to advancement. Depending on the job setting, they may be promoted to assistant manager, then to department or shift manager in a matter of months. Large companies often have training programs or provide educational assistance to help faithful employees climb the corporate ladder. Many young people see their minimum wage job quickly convert into a career.

FACT

Most of the jobs available to teenagers are in the service industry—primarily at fast-food restaurants and clerking in stores. The low pay and unrewarding work inspire many young people to continue their education. Meanwhile, teens who show some initiative can often earn hefty raises and move into management positions in short order.

## Job Problems!

"Help wanted" signs dot the landscape on city streets, yet many teenagers have great difficulty finding any job, much less a good one. When employers need to hire someone for a higher paying job, they favor young adults in their early to mid-twenties even if they don't have any more education than younger applicants. In fact, teenagers may be turned down and then hired for the same job a few years later even though they have no more education and the only difference is their age.

### Discrimination

Teenagers can be as productive, efficient, and responsible as older entry-level employees. When workers were in short supply during both World Wars, employers had a strong incentive to hire teenaged help. Young people managed jobs that today would be reserved for older, far more educated people. Teenaged workers currently do well in skilled jobs in Germany, where employers nurture young workers and put effort into helping them succeed. Meanwhile, negative stereotypes about teenagers in the United States, combined with the high unemployment rate, stack the deck against them. Employers often require workers to have some post-secondary education even though schooling doesn't teach the skills they need for a particular job. Young people are routinely blamed and fired for problems they did not cause, that were unavoidable, or that would have been overlooked if an older worker were involved, according to a January 1988 interim report on the school-to-work transition. In a double-whammy, parents are also likely to blame their teenager when work problems develop or their child is fired.

FACT

Experts predict that 60 percent of the jobs in 2030 don't even exist today; vast percentages of today's jobs will disappear. Workers can expect to have to retrain and change careers as well as jobs. Flexibility and a positive attitude toward education will be more beneficial in the long run than a specific set of job skills.

## Inexperienced Employees

Some employers understand the special needs and problems of teenaged workers. Compassionate bosses go out of their way to accommodate their young charges and try to provide positive learning experiences. Happy employees, most employers know, are more productive and more likely to stay. Given the cost of interviewing, hiring, and setting up new workers on the payroll and the man-hours required to train them, companies have a financial interest in going the extra mile to retain the people they hire. Trading a current employee for the next willing pair of hands that appears at the door is a very expensive way to do business.

Nevertheless, teenaged employees require some special nurturing by employers. Young people lack experience and basic job skills. Many are immature, and that can translate into being somewhat irresponsible about details like arriving to work on time and staying on task. They may dress inappropriately or commit other workplace faux pas. If bosses broach problems tactfully, teens typically respond very positively. But because of the negative attitudes toward young people, employers often react to their mistakes by treating them like unruly children. Since the pool of available workers is so large, many bosses decide that devoting themselves to training young employees isn't worth the trouble and forego it altogether. Instead, they allow newly hired teenaged workers to sink or swim and fire them the first time a problem arises. This policy is most unfortunate for working teens.

### Demanding Employers

It is unfortunately very common for bosses to make demands on teenaged employees that are clearly unreasonable. They promise a certain number of hours and don't deliver, change work schedules without informing workers, expect them to handle extra shifts on short notice, and demand overtime. Many supervisors are inflexible about letting students leave early enough so they can get to bed at a reasonable hour on school nights. They refuse requests for schedule changes despite adequate advanced notice—or worse, they agree to honor scheduling requests, forget, and fire the youth for getting upset or failing to appear.

Teens who feel used and abused at work may sound like they're blaming their boss, but in reality could be secretly holding themselves responsible for not being able to cope. Whether they are fired or quit, losing a job can create the kind of despair and self-doubt that turns into serious trouble.

## The First "Real" Job

Getting their first "real" job means a lot to young people. It is especially significant for a marginal student who has spent years dreaming of being in an environment where he can finally succeed. Many disaffected students really do not want to be in school and eagerly anticipate working. They only continue in high school because they understand that a diploma is a virtual requirement for any kind of halfway decent job. Until then, they are happy to get their feet wet by taking whatever job they can find.

Having a negative job experience during high school can readily convince students who have long teetered on the academic edge that the world of work is as unrewarding as school. They assume that they simply aren't cut out to work and that, like school, the workplace will be another exercise in failure and defeat. A study reported in the January 1998 issue of *Industrial and Labor Relations Review* indicated that if a teenager loses a job to a more skilled worker, the teen is more likely to give up on school, drop out, and end up unemployed. It is critical that high school students with poor academic records have positive work experiences.

High school work/study programs can help buffer teens from negative work experiences. They learn basic skills, get help finding a job, and teachers provide encouragement and support. If a conflict arises at work, the teacher may be able to help.

To help protect your teen, tell her that many supervisors are impatient with teenaged employees. Explain that while you expect your child to do her best, she shouldn't take it personally if things don't work out. If you are very anxious for your child to get a job, you may be reluctant to convey some of the hard realities about teen employment for fear of discouraging her from getting out and pounding the pavement.

If your child is fired, don't treat him like a failure even if you think your child lost the job due to irresponsibility and improper conduct, which are typical signs of immaturity that criticism doesn't usually improve. Let him know that first jobs are opportunities to learn. Reassure him that as he matures, his attitude and behavior on the job are likely to become more serious. As he continues to develop as a person, he will have better skills for dealing with conflict and solving problems. Then cross your fingers and hope it is true!

## Parents as Job Consultants

School should still remain a priority for teenagers. By devoting too much time and energy to a job, even superachievers can spread themselves too thin. Working more than twenty hours per week usually causes academic problems. However, ten hours may be too much for a teen carrying an exceptionally heavy academic load, who has many extracurricular involvements, or who is barely keeping up in school. You may need to set limits to help your teenager make school a priority.

The best way to ensure your teenager has a good work experience is to use your contacts to help your child find a job. The best jobs usually come from people with whom a teenager or his parents have a personal connection. Friends, relatives, and colleagues are more likely to take your child under their wing and go the extra mile to try to train her and help her succeed.

## Motivating Your Teen to Work

Telling your child about the hard realities of most jobs open to teens may not sound like a way to motivate him to check out the want ads, but you really should do just that! The reason some teens won't try to get a job is because they lack confidence about their ability to handle a job. If they don't do well in school, they may be especially afraid of proving themselves incapable in yet another major area of life. Discussing the unpleasant realities of most entry-level, unskilled jobs can prove more comforting than daunting. Reassure your child that if he gets a job and it doesn't work out, that doesn't mean he has failed. Point out that even a very negative job experience isn't the end of the world and can in fact help him learn the process of filling out applications, undergoing employment interviews, and gaining work experience, while earning some money. If he can leave a bad job on good terms, he can use the employer as a reference. That helps open the way to better jobs in the future.

Negative job experiences can motivate good students to continue their education, especially if their parents choose the right moment to make a case for post-secondary training. Point out that entry-level jobs for unskilled workers tend to be extremely taxing and that better trained workers typically get not only bigger paychecks but also better treatment.

Pushing a teenager to get a job can feel like pushing a reluctant mule up a mountain. You can drive your child to businesses with "help wanted" signs in the window and drop him at the door so he can get an application, but that doesn't mean he will fill it out and return it. You can line up a job for him yourself and lecture about being respectful toward bosses and conscientious about his work until you're blue in the face. Still, you can't prevent him from cussing out his supervisor and taking breaks when he's supposed to be working. If your child is not ready, try to accept it. Nagging won't help him mature.

What you can do is offer your teenager ways to make money at home and give him lots of positive strokes by pointing out whatever he does right. You can pay him big bucks for small jobs and it won't cost much if you simultaneously have him assume some of his personal expenses. This is a great way to teach money management, too.

FACT

Teenagers spent $141 billion in 2002. According to the June 2003 issue of *Update* magazine, they averaged ninety-four dollars per week spending money. To motivate your teenager to work, try having him foot the bills for his car, computer, and Cokes. With a paycheck, he may be able to have the lifestyle to which he would like to become accustomed.

When teens are reluctant to work, it is often because they feel shy about approaching employers to ask for a job. It is easy for adults to forget that job hunting can be very intimidating to inexperienced teenagers. Take the pressure off your child by dropping him at the door of an office or business where he does *not* want to work so he can experience the process of inquiring about job opportunities and retrieve an employment application. Freed from the pressure to land a job, teens can concentrate on learning how to job hunt. The next step is to help your child fill out the application. Again, be patient and supportive. Questions that seem obvious to you may not seem at all clear to your child. Next, role-play an employment interview:

- "Why do you want to work here?"
- "What qualifies you for this job?"
- "What personal assets and challenges would you bring to the job?"
- "Do you have any related experience?"
- "Do you have reliable transportation?"

Some of these are tough questions for anyone, and they are especially hard for teens who simply want a paycheck, don't know what assets and challenges are relevant, and have no experience. You may need to apply some creativity to helping your teen figure out what to say.

If your teen agrees to get a job but won't take any steps in that direction, he may lack confidence. Many teens don't know how to begin job hunting or how to handle a particular aspect of employment. Describe the process in detail and see if you can elicit and answer some of your child's "But what if . . .?" questions.

If your child won't follow your great advice about how to get and keep a job, most high schools offer vocational classes that demystify the world of work, provide career awareness, and teach students how to find and keep a job. Classmates serve as a built-in support system. High school work/study and internship programs provide gentle introductions to the world of work. Community colleges offer career exploration classes and teach students to write resumes, handle job interviews, and communicate with colleagues and employers. Local Labor Department offices (a.k.a., the unemployment office) also offer seminars and workshops that teach how to fill out applications, write resumes, and conduct job searches. Opportunities abound. Help your teen hook up with them.

## The Best Summer Jobs

Lots of teenagers get their first "real" job during the summer. Those who are especially resourceful or just plain lucky manage to land good ones. If you don't know someone who can give your child a decent job, there is another strategy that can work. Instead of suggesting that your teenager head for the nearest fast-food restaurant to pick up an application, help him consider what kind of work he might enjoy doing. Has he ever thought about becoming a real estate agent? A veterinarian or a dog groomer? Would he like to be a nurse or doctor? Would he like to travel and see the world? Has he thought of working in insurance? Every realty office needs someone to cover the phones while the receptionist goes on vacation. So do animal clinics. And doctor's offices. And travel agencies. And insurance offices.

If your teen thinks anything with an engine and wheels is the best thing since pizza, have him check jobs at tire stores, oil and lube shops, independent dealerships, and auto parts stores. If he can communicate his enthusiasm, he'll be more likely to get a job he likes—and keep it.

Your teenager may not know how to approach a potential employer for a job in a professional setting, so you might consider placing a call on her behalf to get the ball rolling: "Hello, my daughter is considering a career in insurance. She's very motivated, but she's only sixteen. Might your company have any sort of summer employment opportunities that would give her some exposure to the business? Perhaps answering phones or working in the mail room?"

Construction jobs are plentiful in the summer. If your teenager doesn't like the idea of sizzling under the sun while mixing concrete and swinging a hammer, help him consider the better-than-average muscles he'll have by summer's end and the better-than-average paychecks he'll earn along the way.

If the idea of calling on behalf of your child seems a bit strange, consider that networking is the best way for people of all ages to get jobs. Making a preliminary inquiry is really a way to network. However, if you get a positive response, don't pass the phone to your child. Get the contact information so your teenager can call on her own. Otherwise, it might seem as though a pushy mom is trying to force her child to get a job. That won't play well in the minds of most employers.

Working during the summer can be great fun for teenagers who land a job that falls into the definitely delightful category:

- Jobs at summer camps (where the counselors seem to have more fun than the campers)
- Jobs at amusement parks (where the workers seem to have more fun than the paying customers)
- Jobs at national parks (where the rafting guides, trail guides, and even the cafeteria help are as intent on their own fun as on caring for the visitors)
- Jobs at the local country club (where golf caddies work on their swing and life guards work on their tans)
- Jobs at movie theaters (where the teens take tickets and sell popcorn when they're not watching movies and munching from buttery tubs)

Many independent teenagers prefer to work for themselves, and summertime can be a great time for a young entrepreneur to start a business. Some teenagers go beyond the usual babysitting businesses and lawn mowing services. They paint houses, pet-sit while people are on vacation, help care for the elderly, wash cars, and sell products on eBay.

## Job Resources for Teens

When Meagan came home and announced she had decided to drop out of high school, her parents were distraught. Fortunately, they contacted the head of the vocational/technical department at their daughter's high school and asked if he would meet with them to see about a work/study program. As the school year was ending, it was too late for her to change her schedule, but he informed her of some great opportunities. In six to twelve weeks during the summer she could get her license to be a nursing assistant. She could participate in an internship program through the city. The school counselor could give her some vocational tests to help her start the process of identifying a career. In the fall she could work and go to school. Meagan agreed to remain enrolled. Finally, it sounded as though school had something to offer that she might want: help to formulate some goals and a start toward fulfilling them.

Volunteers at hospitals, libraries, and nonprofit organizations learn job skills, gain solid work experience, and are often hired for paying jobs. If your teen needs more structure and a positive outlet for his energies, help him find a situation where his contributions will be truly appreciated. Enter your zip code on the *www.volunteermatch.org* Web site. It lists 21,000 volunteer opportunities in Phoenix alone.

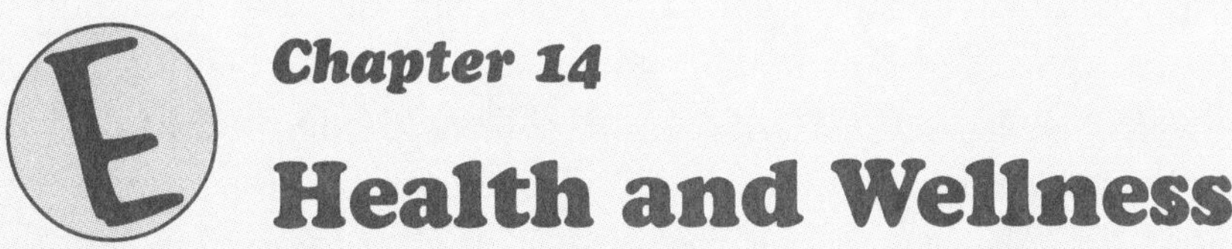

# Chapter 14
# Health and Wellness

Most teenagers know salad is healthier than pizza and milk is better for them than soda. They understand they are supposed to get enough sleep and exercise daily, and can recite the dangers of drugs, alcohol, and unprotected sex. Knowing what they should do doesn't mean they will do it, however. If you're wondering why, just look in the mirror. Few people are as responsible about their health as they should be. Fortunately, your teen has an advantage over you. He has you to help make sure that he takes care of himself.

## Teen Weight Watchers

Shawana didn't smile when the doctor said she shouldn't think of the fifteen pounds she had gained as fat but as curves. She didn't feel better knowing that her weight gain was normal for girls after puberty. Learning about how pictures of models in magazines are airbrushed and digitally altered to make them look slender didn't comfort her, either. Since her Barbie doll days, Shawana had been forming an image about what pretty girls looked like. All she had to do was look in the mirror to see that she didn't come close. Her parents' reassurance that she was in fact very lovely didn't reassure her, either. She couldn't stand herself, and didn't really believe anyone else could find her attractive.

Given the prevalence of eating disorders and substance abuse, competitive teens involved in activities that emphasize physique should be monitored. Anorexia is a problem for many ballerinas, gymnasts, and track team members. Likewise, football players may be tempted to use drugs or supplements to increase body mass.

Shawana embarked upon a self-improvement campaign and went on a diet. She lost five pounds in three weeks, and was elated when her parents and some friends complimented her on her appearance. Losing the next five pounds was harder, so she skipped breakfast and limited herself to an apple at lunch and small salad for dinner. Still, the scale didn't budge for days. It took her a month to lose another five pounds. Her mother blamed Shawana's irritability on her severe diet and fussed at Shawana to eat more. They clashed until a friend taught Shawana how to make herself throw up after meals. It sounded disgusting but was actually a relief. She could please her mother while continuing to shed pounds. Two months later, her mother saw Shawana when she was changing her clothes and gasped in horror on seeing her daughter's shrunken body. Shawana couldn't comprehend her mother's upset. She still felt fat.

## Teen Diets

Girls can expect to add seven inches to their height during their growth spurt, which usually takes place between ages eleven and thirteen. They approach their final adult height at age sixteen. Boys' growth spurt comes later, between ages thirteen and fifteen, and they basically finish growing by age eighteen, though they may add a few centimeters until age twenty-one. During the growth spurt, girls typically gain thirteen to eighteen pounds per year and boys gain fifteen to twenty pounds. Many young people are upset about their weight even before puberty begins—as many as one-third of girls are actively dieting in third grade. Twenty percent of children are obese, and the hormonal changes that come with puberty cause all girls to develop a layer of fat. Even if they were quite thin to begin with, they may be distressed about gaining weight in the current climate of super-thin models. Many adolescent boys worry about their weight, too. In a survey reported in the April 2003 issue of the *Journal of Youth and Adolescence*, about 20 percent reported wanting to lose and a third reported wanting to gain weight.

QUESTION?

**My son wants to gain weight. What should he do?**
Most boys simply eat more, but exercise is the route to getting the muscles boys dream of having. Working out regularly with weights is a good way to build upper body mass.

Contrary to what most boys think, eating isn't the solution for gaining weight. What most boys actually want is muscle mass. Exercise builds muscle mass, not diet. As for losing weight, dieting is notoriously ineffective. As soon as people cut their calories, the body thinks a famine is afoot. After the first few pounds are shed, metabolism slows to try to prevent starvation. Fewer calories are burned, so it becomes increasingly hard to lose weight as time goes by. After people stop dieting and resume normal eating habits, the weight quickly returns because the metabolism was reset for the lower intake of calories. The human palate is genetically primed to steer people toward sweet and fatty foods. The next time a diet begins, the body quickly goes into conservation mode to try to hold onto the fat. With each subsequent attempt to diet, losing weight becomes a bit harder.

The only effective way to control weight via food is to adopt healthy eating habits and stick with them for a lifetime. Avoid fast foods, which are notoriously high in fat. Only about 30 percent of calories consumed each day should come from fat. Teach your teen to read food labels.

A major culprit in obesity is prepackaged foods. They aren't very filling because so much bulk is removed during processing, so people can easily consume a large bag of chips or a dozen cookies in a single sitting. Because the fiber is broken down or removed, all of the food gets absorbed into the system. Even orange juice is inferior to Mother Nature's original, the orange. Thirsty teens can easily down several glasses and still feel hungry. Were they to eat one or two oranges and have a glass of water instead, they would feel full. That's why fresh fruits and vegetables and whole grains are great for dieters—not to mention everyone else.

A healthy diet should be combined with exercise. Besides the many cardiovascular health benefits, exercise increases the metabolism so food is burned more efficiently. The average teen averages two hours a day watching television. Cutting back to ninety minutes and spending the extra half hour exercising would yield some real health and fitness benefits. Consider inviting your teen to accompany you for a brisk after-dinner walk.

## Eating Disorders

The typical cause of teen obesity is too much junk food and too little exercise. As masses of teenagers struggle with their weight, eating disorders have reached epidemic proportions. Instead of consuming calories to fulfill their need for physical sustenance, compulsive eaters use food for comfort, relaxation, and solace. The health repercussions can be devastating. So many young people have high cholesterol that physicians anticipate seeing lots of heart disease in the not-so-distant future.

Meanwhile, the desire to be thin like the models and movie stars causes many to go on dangerously restrictive diets. Some literally starve themselves in an effort to achieve the look they consider required for beauty. Not eating can give girls who feel helpless in other areas of their lives a sense of being in control. Extreme weight loss deprives girls of their curves and even their periods, putting young women with conflicts about femininity at risk for developing anorexia, which literally means self-starvation. Anorexia is extremely dangerous. Many girls (and increasing numbers of boys) vomit and use laxatives to control food absorption. The physical toll is tremendous. Their hair thins, the enamel on their teeth dissolves, and their electrolytes are depleted. Untreated, anorexia is often fatal. Another serious eating disorder that can have serious health consequences, bulimia, involves alternately binge eating and purging. Get your child to a doctor immediately if you suspect an eating problem.

You cannot control what your teenager eats—and you shouldn't try. You can, however, control what you buy and serve. You owe it to your family (and yourself!) to make sure that all of the items stored in the cupboards and placed on the table are healthy choices.

While anorexics regard themselves as fat even when they are severely emaciated, teenagers suffering from bulimia binge on food and then try to compensate by purging. Bulimics are also at risk for a variety of health problems. Parents can't fend off the pressures to be thin spread by the popular media and reinforced by peers. They can't control what their teenager eats or how much exercise he gets. Still, there are a number of things you can do to lessen the likelihood that your child will develop a weight problem or an eating disorder. Number one on the list is to avoid making comments to the effect that your teen could stand to lose or gain a few pounds. It's hard enough for children when peers make disparaging comments, but when parents say hurtful things, teens' worries can turn into obsessions. Instead, take action. Stop buying sodas, chips, cookies, and assorted junk food. Simply explain that you are concerned about everyone's health and make some simple changes that are good for everyone.

- Switch from whole to 2 percent or skim milk.
- Switch from white to whole grain bread, from instant to whole grain rice.
- Broil meat instead of frying it.
- Season vegetables with herbs instead of creamed sauces.
- Instead of offering food to console your child, provide kind words.
- Eliminate trips to fast-food restaurants and cook at home instead.
- Ditch the sweets and keep sliced veggies in the fridge for snacks.

Unless the fare served in the school cafeteria is far more healthful than is typical, stop supplying lunch money. Have your teen carry lunch from home. Keep your concerns about your own weight to yourself. You may not think your teen looks to you as a role model, but your values and attitudes do sink in.

### Dietary Supplements

Teens are at risk for nutritional deficiencies if they have an eating disorder, chronic medical conditions, follow a vegan diet, or abuse alcohol and drugs. Athletes will, of course, need substantially more fuel to keep them in peak performance.

## Vitamins and Minerals

The best way to ensure that your child gets sufficient vitamins and minerals is through a well-balanced diet. Nevertheless, teens may benefit from a calcium supplement to support healthy bone development, especially during their growth spurt. Insufficient iron is a widespread problem, which causes anemia. About 6 percent of adolescents are anemic, which can stunt their growth and leave them feeling tired and lethargic. Menstruating girls lose iron through blood loss. Because adolescent boys are building muscle mass, they need a lot of iron, too. Consult your teen's doctor to see whether calcium and/or iron supplements are in order.

Many young athletes use dietary supplements to try to increase stamina and build muscle mass. If your teenager wants to take Andro-stenedione, widely available in health food stores, know that it has been banned by the International Olympic Committee, the National Football League, and the National Collegiate Athletic Association. Athletes are also at risk for insufficient chromium, and may want to take it to reduce fat and increase muscle mass. Some studies indicate that dosages of 200–400 micrograms of chromium daily may enhance lean muscle mass and decrease body fat, though not all studies support these findings. Taking a chromium supplement is currently regarded as safe.

Lots of athletes are consuming pricey supplements. The effects of long-term use are being tested but remain unknown. While you're waiting for the results, consider the merits of food. Supplement your child's diet with extra servings of meat, vegetables, low-fat milk, whole grains, fruit, and water.

Creatine, which is found in meats and fish, is sold as a dietary supplement. Despite some encouraging studies that suggest it is useful for increasing energy during intense exercise, long-term effects have not been established. Glutamine, an amino acid, has been found to prevent the loss of muscle mass from strenuous workouts. It is produced by the body naturally, and it appears to be benign when taken as recommended. HMB (beta hydroxy-beta-methylbutyrate) decreases body fat and increases lean muscle mass. It may decrease muscle breakdown stemming from intense exercise. Although creatine has been widely tested on animals, the actual mechanism of how it is metabolized and the long-term effects are unknown.

## Teens and Sleep

Teens' schedules are out of sync with other humans because their internal clocks run on a 24.6-hour day. Most complain of not feeling sleepy at bedtime. Left to their own devices, they would stay up a bit later each night and sleep a little later each morning until they were up all night and sleeping all day. Nevertheless, school starts early in the morning, whether or not they feel ready to rise. Even if your teen can't sleep, he should spend enough hours in bed so he can get enough rest.

QUESTION?

**How much sleep do teenagers need?**
The recommended amount of sleep for teens is 9.2 hours per night—far more than most of them get. Large percentages are chronically sleep-deprived but are unaware of the toll this takes on them.

When researchers have studied sleep-deprived teens, they score lower on tests of cognitive performance, effort, and concentration than those who get proper rest. They have more problems with crankiness and irritability. However, sleep-deprived teens rate their performance as high as their rested counterparts. They are completely unaware that the lack of sufficient sleep has affected them! Reduced sleep has been linked to poorer grades, higher drug use, more frequent driving errors, and more troubled moods according to Lynne Lamberg's research, reported in the January 2002 issue of *Odyssey*.

## Sleep Cures

You can't expect your teenager to be sleepy at bedtime and certainly can't make him go to sleep. But if he won't retire at a decent hour, remove distractions from his room, such as the television, telephone, stereo, and computer. To cure insomnia, the first step is to avoid stimulants after dinner, including chocolate and caffeinated beverages. Lots of sodas contain caffeine, so read labels carefully. The better beverage to promote relaxation is chamomile tea. A bedtime snack that combines a complex carbohydrate and protein can help. The combination induces sleepiness and a feeling of well-being. Next, a warm bath can help him unwind. While lying in bed, teens who are auditory learners can listen to music in order to block out distracting thoughts. Imagining sheep jumping over a fence and counting each one may work better for a visual teen. Reading a textbook in bed puts many teens to sleep faster than any sleeping pill could hope to do.

### Controlling Bedtimes

When you tell your daughter it's bedtime, does she say she needs to stay up to finish her homework? Going along with that plan may solve the immediate problem but doesn't help her learn to prioritize her activities and manage her life. Instead of preaching to her about her poor time-management skills, remain upbeat as you set limits: "If you can't finish up by bedtime, maybe your teacher will accept a late paper or let you do something for extra credit to make up the work. Now it's time for bed."

If your teen simply has too much going on and there aren't enough hours in a day, she obviously can't set limits when choosing activities and making commitments. If she needs to drop an honors class or withdraw from cheerleading, so be it. Her health is more important. Often the mere suggestion that you will ensure she is protected if she can't safeguard her own health is enough.

## Sexual Health

Talking about sex with children is hard for many parents, and most teens feel uncomfortable when their parents broach the subject. Common teen ploys to end conversations include pretending to already know it all, adopting a condescending attitude, and picking a fight. Although most students received some basic sex education in middle school and regularly talk about sex with peers, many young people are very ignorant about sexual matters. Forge ahead even if your teen acts as though you couldn't possibly have anything useful to teach. It is critical that your child be given accurate information about sexual health and hygiene.

### Medical Exams

Boys should have a medical examination if they notice a discharge from the penis or any type of skin changes in the genital area, including itching, bumps, blisters, sores, or a rash. Girls should have a pelvic exam if they have any type of menstrual problems or pain. They should see a doctor if they have itching, bumps, blisters, sores, or a rash around the genital area, a vaginal discharge, or burning urination. (An occasional small vaginal discharge that is white in color is normal.) Otherwise, girls don't need to have a pelvic exam until they become sexually active or turn eighteen, whichever comes first.

## The Myth of Safe Sex

Warnings about "unprotected sex" are highly misleading because they imply that "protected sex" is safe. Condoms may be better than nothing, but they aren't much better. Depending on the disease, the chances of contracting a sexually transmitted disease (STD) from an infected partner while using a condom run from 30 to 50 percent, according to articles in the February and August 1987 issues of the *Journal of the American Medical Association*. In actuality, the concept of "safe sex" conveyed by the makers and sellers of condoms is a scandalous myth. While combining a spermacide with a condom can substantially reduce the chances of pregnancy, spermacides don't provide protection against STDs. The only real protection is abstinence.

Although almost everyone is aware of AIDS, many teens don't know that there are many other STDs. Even if they do know that AIDS is just the tip of the STD problem, teens may have the mistaken notion that oral sex is safe. This belief is particularly prevalent among younger teenagers, and many middle school students have contracted oral herpes, pharyngeal gonorrhea, and HIV by taking semen into the mouth even if they don't swallow it.

## Self-Exams for Cancer

Females are at risk for breast cancer and should start checking themselves for lumps or changes after they begin menstruating. While standing in front of a mirror, they should examine their breasts first with their arms down, then with their hands up behind the head, and finally with their hands on their hips and the shoulders and elbows forward. They should look for bumps, dimples, rough skin, sores, swelling, or changes in shape from the previous month. Next, they should raise the right arm above the head and feel the right breast with the fingertips of the left hand, making small circles as they search for a small, hard lump or an area that feels thick. They need to be sure to check the area under the breast, and between the breast and armpit. Because breasts change throughout the month, girls should do the exams at the same point in their menstrual cycle. Finally, they should squeeze each nipple to look for discharge.

Of approximately fifteen million new cases of sexually transmitted diseases (STDs) reported each year, about four million are teenagers. Many young people mistakenly believe that birth control or douching will protect them. The failure rate of condoms is 50 percent for some infections.

Males should check themselves for lumps once a month beginning in adolescence to look for signs of testicular cancer, which is readily treated if caught early. A self-exam is easiest to do after a warm shower when the testes are hanging lower. Using the fingertips and thumb, your son should spend about a minute gently feeling around each testicle. Explain that it is easy to mistake the spongy tissue located on top of each testicle for lumps, but this tissue is normal. If your son discovers anything unusual, schedule a doctor's appointment. Boys should bathe regularly and carefully dry the pubic area to prevent infection. For further information, contact the Cancer Information Center at ✆800-422-6237 or see *www.cancer.gov*.

## Teen Hygiene

Thoroughly drying the pubic area after washing prevents fungal growth. Teenagers should wipe from front to back when they go to the bathroom to keep waste away from the urethra, which can cause a urinary infection. Douching is not recommended for girls; washing away the good bacteria increases the possibility of infection. Additionally, during menstruation tampons and sanitary pads should be changed every few hours.

Periodontal disease from improper oral hygiene is the leading cause of tooth decay and loss. Your teenager needs to brush at least twice and floss daily. Wisdom teeth grow in after age seventeen. Without enough room they become impacted, which can cause infection. Regular dental check-ups are important!

The increased production of sweat and oil during puberty necessitates daily showers to control odor and keep hair clean. Pimples and acne are the bane of a teen's existence, and although they are caused by hormonal changes, the best treatment is to wash affected areas twice a day with warm water and a mild soap made especially for acne. Washing should be done with gentle circular motions since scrubbing can cause the skin to become irritated. After cleansing, the American Academy of Dermatology (AAD) recommends that teens apply an over-the-counter lotion containing benzoyl peroxide.

Scoliosis, a curvature of the spine that ranges from minor to severe, is often first detected during early adolescence. The rate in the general population is only 2 percent but the risk is 20 percent if it runs in the family. Symptoms are uneven shoulders, prominent shoulder blade or blades, uneven waist, elevated hips, and leaning to one side.

To control bacterial growth, teens should avoid touching their face with their fingers without first washing, especially before applying makeup. Noncomedogenic or nonacnegenic brands of makeup are best. Teenagers should avoid pressing their faces against objects that collect sebum and skin residue, such as the telephone receiver, headbands, and tight caps. Oil collects under hair, so it should be kept off of the face. Glasses and sunglasses need to be cleaned frequently to keep oil from clogging the pores around the eyes and nose. Wash pillowcases, sheets, and blankets often to rid them of dirt, dead skin, and oil that collect on them at night. Teens with acne on other parts of the body should wear loose clothes so the skin can breathe. Popping pimples can cause skin to become red, inflamed, and infected to the point of leaving scars. Also, popping pimples can push infected material further into the skin, leading to more swelling and redness. Drinking lots of water helps flush out the system, removing impurities.

## Immunizations for Adolescents

If your teen isn't up to date on his vaccinations, now is the time to play catch up, according to the Center for Disease Control's recommendations for 2003. Check to be sure your child ages thirteen to eighteen has had all of the following immunizations:

- Hepatitis B (HepB Series)
- Tetanus/Diptheria (Td)
- Measle, Mumps, Rubella (MMR #2)
- Varicella
- Pneumococcal (PPV)
- Hepatitis A (HepA Series)

In addition, a yearly influenza vaccination is recommended for youth with certain risk factors, such as asthma, cardiac disease, and sickle cell disease. See *www.cdc.gov* for further information about immunizations for teenagers.

## Immune System Safeguards

Given the stresses inherent in this life stage, it is important for teenagers to keep their immune systems healthy. Despite the plethora of supplements that claim to do just that, the best protection is daily self-care. When teenagers are under- or overexercised, get too little sleep, have poor diets, or go through emotionally stressful periods, the immune system is less able to ward off illnesses. Rubbing elbows with so many people in crowded school hallways increases exposure to assorted cold and flu viruses. Help your child understand that all the pills, powders, and potions in the world cannot compensate for an unhealthy lifestyle. The time to begin developing the good habits that will last a lifetime is now.

The first symptoms of mono are flu-like, followed by a raging fever and extremely sore throat. Get your teen to the doctor, move the television into his bedroom, and stock up on books. He's likely to be bedridden for weeks.

An especially serious virus that is most likely to infect people between ages ten and twenty-five is mononucleosis. Because it is spread through saliva, mononucleosis has been nicknamed the "kissing disease." The usual route of contagion is from sharing eating utensils or drinking through someone else's straw. This illness affects blood cells and saliva glands.

## Happier Is Healthier

Shawana's weight dropped so low she had to enter a treatment center for teenagers with eating disorders. There she was shocked to learn that as American culture reached around the globe via movies, television programs, and music, eating disorders followed. Seeing the devastating price the other patients had paid for judging themselves based on their looks had a big impact on Shawana. She decided it was time to consider the truth of the old saying that, "Beauty is only skin deep." She understood the proper goal was to focus on her health and let her looks take care of themselves. It was a struggle, but she knew that was the route to real happiness.

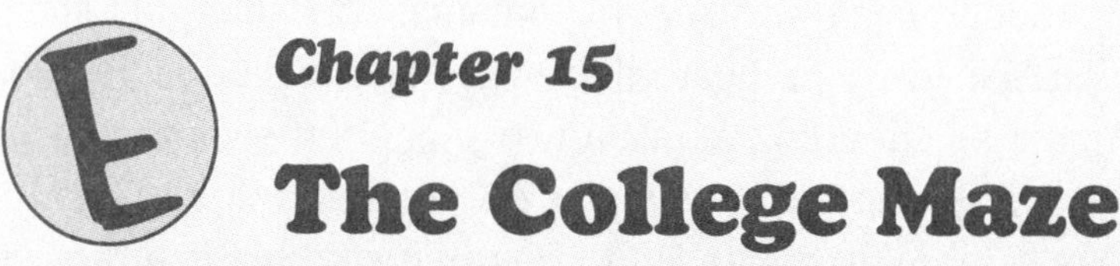

# Chapter 15
# The College Maze

Going to college will give your teen a lifelong economic boost even if she doesn't finish a degree. Employers prefer to hire and promote college-educated workers and pay them better wages. Taking college entrance exams, applying, lining up housing, and arranging for financial aid can be intimidating. Be sure your teen does the bulk of the work, while you provide guidance, support, and the information she needs to fill out the forms. Doing the research, compiling information, following directions, and meeting deadlines are basic college survival skills. Applying to college is a good preparation for what lies ahead.

## College-Bound High School Students

Robert wanted to attend college, but since his parents hadn't even finished high school, he had no idea how to get started. He had heard it cost a fortune and that scholarships and loans were available, but other than keeping his grades up he didn't know how to go about finding them. He tried to talk to his school guidance counselor, but she just said, "Take the SATs." Later he heard there were tests called ACTs, too. Then he found out he should have taken two years of the same foreign language instead of studying Spanish for one year and then switching to French. As determined as he felt to be the first in his family to get a college diploma, and as much as he wanted to become a doctor, the prospect of figuring out how to get into school felt daunting. Just filling out the forms to take the SAT was overwhelming. He was supposed to put down which college he planned to attend so his scores could be sent there. What should he put down when he didn't even know?

## Early Planning

Advanced planning for college is good, but some parents push their children too much and too soon. Forcing your teenager to take college preparatory classes in high school regardless of his interests is unwise. Insisting she make top grades even though this precipitates anxiety and keeps her feeling stressed is a mistake. Large numbers of disaffected high school students rebel and drop out. Others are so miserable that although they graduate, they vow never to enter another educational institution. Parents need to balance their wishes with their child's wants and needs.

If a high school student makes average (or even poor) grades and hasn't had some courses the college she wants to attend requires, all is not lost. She can make up missed courses and prove her academic ability by taking some courses at a community college.

Even without parents actively applying pressure, most teenagers feel under the gun to make college and career decisions. Their worries about making concrete plans escalate as high school progresses. This is unfortunate. Adolescence is a time to develop a personal identity and start defining interests and goals, not to set them into stone. Few fifteen-year-olds know what they might like to do at age thirty-five—or even at age eighteen, for that matter. Even students who think they know where they are headed often change their minds. Most college students change majors at least once. Encourage your child to take her time.

## College Preparatory Classes

In an ideal world, eighth graders would know what college they will attend and what their major will be. That way, they would know which high school courses to take so they could meet the specific admission requirements and take the high school courses recommended for their college major. If your teenager does want to attend a specific college, she should check the school's online catalogue or contact the college by letter and request one so she can check its admission requirements. The reality is that few eighth graders have any idea what college they might want to go to or what they might major in. Even if they think they know, their interests and goals are likely to change dramatically before high school graduation. By looking at catalogues from an assortment of colleges, young teens can start thinking about college and exploring the wealth of fascinating subjects they might like to study.

Two-year community colleges (called "junior colleges" in days gone by) usually take anyone who applies—including students without high school diplomas! They offer a wide range of remedial, vocational, and freshman/sophomore level courses. Anyone who wants to go to college can go!

When it is time to apply to college, high school juniors and seniors can make sure they meet the college's admission requirements by checking the catalogue. They need not be discouraged if they are lacking a particular course. Students who didn't take a course or who failed it can usually make it up at a community college. In this day of expanded educational options and opportunities, any student who wishes to go to college can attend regardless of his high school record. Nevertheless, when deciding what to take in high school to prepare for college, your child should know that most four-year colleges and universities expect incoming freshmen to have at least earned credits in basic academic courses:

- Four years of English, including English composition
- Algebra, geometry, trigonometry
- Biology and chemistry
- U.S. history and government
- Two years of the same foreign language

High school students can increase their chances of getting into a college with an exceptionally good reputation by exceeding the basic requirements, and should take mostly solid academic courses. Hence, a course in an academic subject such as psychology or economics is usually more advantageous than a vocational course, such as wood shop or interior decorating. Vocational classes focus on teaching practical skills and prepare students for jobs or to enter technical training, not college. However, some vocational classes that relate to a student's proposed college major can be acceptable. For instance, a college admissions committee might think that a high school course in interior design is an asset for a student planning to major in textiles. A course in wood shop might be appropriate for a student planning to major in construction management, and future physical education majors might take some extra P.E. courses. Aspiring fine arts majors really should take some high school music, art, dance, or drama courses unless they're enrolled in lots of private classes outside of school.

## Honors Classes

Most high schools offer honors classes so that outstanding students can get the best possible preparation for college. Although the pace in these classes is faster, more motivated students often prefer them. Because the course work emphasizes critical thinking and analysis with less time devoted to acquiring information and memorizing facts, some students actually find honors classes easier. They may find them more to their liking since there tend to be fewer discipline problems in honors classes, which primarily attract highly motivated students. More class time can be spent on teaching and learning with fewer disruptions by unruly students. It is easier for highly intellectual students to make like-minded friends.

Students sometimes avoid honors classes for fear they will hurt their grade point average (GPA) by getting lower grades than they could make in less demanding courses. There is no reason for them to do this. Colleges understand that high school honors classes are harder so they may consider a B in honors English to be the equivalent of an A- or A in regular English. Check with your school's guidance counselor for specifics as to how grades in honors courses are calculated into the high school GPA, and be sure to ask how participation in honors classes is noted on high school transcripts that are sent out to colleges.

QUESTION?

**Can my college-bound son take lots of vocational courses?**
More competitive colleges want students to have solid academic backgrounds, but a burned-out student may decide not to go to college at all. Electives your child considers fun are important, too.

If your child is academically inclined and highly motivated to achieve, he may enjoy more demanding classroom environments. Even if his past grades and achievement test scores aren't high enough for his high school to recommend him automatically for honors classes, he can probably still take them if he wishes. Placing high school students into classes according to their academic ability, or "tracking," as it was once called, has largely ended. Research shows that poor performers benefit from being in classes with more able students. If you ask the high school administration to let your child into one or more honors classes, most districts will comply.

Late bloomers may do well in honors classes even though their academic records and achievement test scores aren't wonderful. Discuss the matter with your child first. Genius really is, as the saying goes, 10 percent inspiration and 90 percent perspiration.

If your child enjoys sweating over schoolwork, she might thrive in honors classes. The risk for borderline students is that they may have to struggle so much that they become discouraged or burn out. If the school doesn't recommend that your child take honors classes, don't push unless your teen really wants to try. Just like for younger students, the most important educational goal is for teenagers to love learning. A happy high school experience helps to motivate students to continue their education. Respect your child's opinion about what courses she wants to take.

QUESTION?

**Is it true that students can earn college credit while in high school?**
Approximately 60 percent of the nation's 22,000 high schools offer advanced placement (AP) courses. They allow high school students, usually seniors, to earn college credit before high school graduation. In some school districts, it is possible for students to take actual college classes while they are still in high school through AP classes. Sometimes a university professor goes to the high school to teach it; sometimes the students are bussed to a nearby college so they can take the class. Some AP classes that meet in high schools are taught by regular high school teachers.

## College Credit for High School Students

Students who take honors classes should consider taking the College Level Educational Placement (CLEP) tests. The same goes for students who excel in a particular subject even if they haven't taken honors classes. For instance, tests are offered in such subjects as English composition, so a student who took regular English but who is an exceptional writer might do well. Tests are also offered for foreign languages, economics, biology, chemistry, algebra, trigonometry, accounting, management—and more. Students can request that the results of their tests be sent to colleges they are thinking of attending and have them evaluated. If a college deems the test scores high enough, it will award college credit if the student enrolls at the school. Some students earn so many credits this way, they are a long way toward earning a college degree before they arrive on campus!

Credit for AP classes may be automatically granted by a sponsoring college. Otherwise, students must take and pass an end-of-semester exam offered through the College Board Advanced Placement Program (CEEB Advanced Placement Program). The final decision is up to the individual college. Different colleges have different cut-off scores for awarding credit.

## College Entrance Tests

Some high schools are harder than others, so besides evaluating students' high school transcripts to see what courses they took and what grades they made, most four-year colleges require students to submit standardized test results. Accordingly, students must take either the Scholastic Achievement Test (SAT) or the ACT (which originally stood for Academic College Testing but has since been shortened to "ACT"). Most high schools are designated testing sites, and the school counselors have application forms and information. Alternatively, students can go to *www.act.org* to find out everything they need to know about the ACT and to *www.collegeboard.com* to find out about the SAT—as well as about the Practice Scholastic Achievement Test (PSAT). The PSAT gives students an opportunity to experience the testing situation, which can lessen their anxiety during the SAT. PSAT scores don't count, but students may be offered scholarships if they make good scores. They can use their test results to target their studies as they prepare for the SAT. Test schedules and locations and practice tests are on the previously mentioned Web sites. Students can even apply to take the tests online. SATs and ACTs may only be administered at a location near you once or twice a year and students must apply well in advance to be able to take the tests. Track the dates carefully! Most students take the tests during their junior year.

It's a good idea for students to study for their college entrance exams, but lots of intensive preparation beginning a few weeks beforehand will probably do more to increase your child's anxiety than his score. Studying should take place over an extended period of time to be effective. Consider buying a study guide during your child's sophomore year so he can pace himself as he goes through the material. Some exam preparation classes are excellent, some are poor, but most are very expensive. Crash courses usually yield poor results. Ask the sponsoring company for data to find out about their track record.

To get into a really good college, great grades and test scores are not enough! Your child should keep a list of clubs and organizations he has participated in and special awards he has received. He should collect letters of recommendation from teachers and sponsors. Admission essays should be carefully written and proofed.

Many students retake the college boards during their senior year hoping to make better scores. When taking the ACT a second time, 55 percent improved their composite test score, 22 percent had no change, and 23 percent lost points. If your child had a problem during the test, he should certainly consider retaking it. He can ask to have the best ACT score sent to the colleges he is applying to.

## Affording College

Community colleges pride themselves on making education available to people of all ages and from all walks of life. With convenient locations that make it possible for most students to live at home and with tuition partially subsidized by the government, these institutions of higher learning are usually the easiest on the family pocketbook. Many courses are offered on nights and weekends so that students can earn money by working while they attend school. Some students who go away to college return home during the summer and attend summer school at a community college. By taking a couple of courses each summer, your student may be able to graduate early and save a semester's worth of tuition and living expenses. However, most community colleges only offer freshman- and sophomore-level courses, so your child will have to do some advanced planning. In order for a junior to find the right community college courses, he might have to postpone taking some lower-level courses at his regular school.

There are many ways for students to get financial assistance with college. The major categories are scholarships, grants, student loans, and work/study programs. Most of the hassle of applying for financial aid has been eliminated since the information is available at two central online locations. The government Web site at *www.fafsa.ed.gov* makes applying for any kind of federal financial help a breeze. Students enter their information, and after processing they receive information about eligibility for government aid from the schools in which they have expressed an interest. At *www.fastweb.com*, the computer matches your teenager's information and generates a list of scholarships, grants, loans, work/study programs, and other sources of economic assistance for which he might qualify. Tens of thousands of individuals, organizations, companies, and colleges offer scholarships. Some grantors will consider anyone who applies; most have very specific requirements. Scholarships are available to help deserving Catholics, budding pianists, and Asian studies majors, just to name a few. To get an accurate reading of what scholarships your child might qualify for, he must answer lots of personal questions. That can get a bit tedious, but urge your teenager to provide *all* of the requested information no matter how irrelevant it might seem. There could be a scholarship for red-headed banjo players, and if he meets those qualifications and applies, he might win it!

When figuring the cost of a particular college, consider how many advanced credits it is offering your child. A college that grants a semester's worth of credit for work done in high school can save half a year of tuition fees and living expenses!

State colleges and universities typically charge a bit more for tuition than community colleges. The bigger problem for many families is the high cost of supporting a child living on her own. Some state schools have branch campuses around the state, which makes it possible for students to live at home while they finish their degree. Otherwise, dormitories are usually cheaper than fraternities, sororities, and apartments. Although not all state schools have dorms, many that do require freshmen to live in them.

The cost of private colleges varies dramatically. The tuition is prohibitive for many students, but if your child is offered some good scholarships, either for merit or because of your difficult financial situation, a private school could actually turn out to be less expensive.

## Choosing a College

Besides the price, there are several other factors to consider in choosing a college. Size is one relevant factor. Some students feel more comfortable at small schools where the classes are smaller and there are opportunities to get to know the faculty. Smaller colleges can't offer the same range of courses as big universities, but some have outstanding reputations for excellence in certain departments. They may specialize in training teachers or have good contacts to help a student majoring in drama get a good job after graduation. Some colleges offer special internships so that chemical engineering students can work at a company while earning college credit and step right into an excellent job when their degree is complete. Other students prefer big schools because the selection of courses, majors, and extracurricular activities is so great. While the population is more diverse at a big school, enabling students to meet a range of people, it is also easier for them to find people who share their interests.

Some schools are very competitive academically, with campus atmospheres that are highly intellectual. Other colleges have reputations as party schools at which the environment is more social. Like at elementary and high school, the kind of education students get out of college depends on what they put into it. While less demanding colleges may be more tolerant of mediocre students, a serious student can still get an excellent education.

If your child knows what she wants to major in, she should check for schools noted for academic excellence in her area of interest. Some teenagers feel certain that they will want to go to graduate school, so selecting a school with a good track record of getting students admitted is important. This is especially true for students who hope to do graduate work in a particularly competitive field, such as medicine or psychology.

The SAT Web site, ✐ *www.collegeboard.com,* has a college finder that uses your child's information to create a list of colleges that are likely to be of interest. The computer ranks the schools so that it is easy to comparison shop. Links to the college Web sites are provided, so more detailed information is a mouse click away.

When college brochures begin arriving, encourage your child to look at all of them, including those she wouldn't want to attend. They can begin to familiarize her with the kinds of opportunities colleges offer. Once she has narrowed her choices down to several schools, the next step is to go for a visit. Contact the college to see what arrangements can be made for guided tours and talks with recruiters and campus personnel.

## Opportunity Unlimited

Robert felt embarrassed about not knowing what to do to get into college because his parents couldn't help him. He felt better when he looked at the information on the Web sites for the SAT, ACT, and for financial aid. Apparently lots of students had the same kinds of questions he did, because he easily found answers to all of his questions. In fact, there were answers to questions he hadn't even thought to ask. He decided to apply to two small private colleges, two big private colleges, two big out-of-state public universities, the big state public university where most of his friends would be going, one small private college close to home, and one branch campus of the state university. His friends thought he was crazy, but he wanted to keep his options open. Applying to so many schools cost a fortune and created a mountain of paper work. He wanted to go to an expensive private school in another state, but everything depended on the cost. He would have to see which one offered the best financial aid opportunities. If insufficient money came through, he might live at home and attend the branch campus. That didn't sound half-bad, because it turned out that the school had an arrangement with some universities in other states, so in two years he could transfer and attend a pricey school for the same cost. The branch campus also had opportunities for students to spend their junior year studying abroad, and he was thinking he might prefer to spend money on that than on housing for the first two years. The opportunities were unlimited, and instead of feeling daunted, he was excited.

Robert now felt a bit sorry for his friends. When he asked them why they were choosing a particular college, most shrugged and said, “My dad said it was good,” or “My brother went there.” He felt lucky that his parents had given him lots of encouragement and support but little concrete help. By doing his own research he had unearthed a ton of great opportunities and had a much clearer idea about his goals. He knew where he wanted to go and why, and he had backup plans that he was comfortable with. He no longer felt queasy when he thought about the future. Instead, he was confident that he was on the right track.

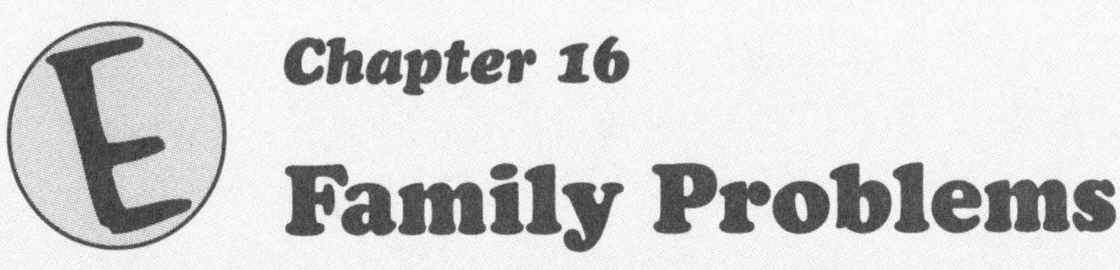

# Chapter 16
# Family Problems

Now that your teen is so wrapped up in her own life, the family may seem to rank last on her list of priorities. As long as everything at home is pretty much business as usual, you may be right. But at this sensitive stage, teens react strongly to family problems. Parental separation or divorce, bankruptcy, unemployment, remarriage, or a move that involves a change of schools can create a major setback. Coming of age in a single-parent home poses special challenges.

## Family Disruptions

David wasn't surprised when his parents announced that they were getting a divorce, and he actually felt a bit relieved. It had been hard listening to them argue all the time, as they had been doing for the last six months. He figured things would probably be better once they were apart. After all, when his dad went out of town on business the arguing stopped, the tension dissolved, and everything at home was fine. When David's father called home from his trips, he sounded fine, too. His parents explained they were divorcing one another, not David and his sister.

When their family is in crisis, teenagers' behavior usually deteriorates. Professionals know that young people often drink and use drugs to cope with family stress. Teens commonly act out to distract the family from other problems in an attempt to help them unite. Accordingly, probation officers typically require the families of delinquent teens to attend counseling.

Having his parents get divorced turned out to be harder than David could have imagined. His mom had filed, but she was all torn up about it. Listening to her cry and carry on tore David up, too. He tried to keep his little sister out of his mom's hair as much as possible and did what he could to help out around the house. His mom seemed like she might just lose it, and what would happen to them then? Money was terribly tight now that his dad had rented an apartment. When David asked if he could still go to college, they said they wouldn't be able to afford to send him.

Consider staying together for the sake of the children if one of those children is a teenager. Divorce is hard on everyone whenever it happens, but teens have an especially difficult time coping. Once they have finished high school, their lives aren't so severely impacted.

David was crushed about not being able to go away to college, but knew he couldn't leave his mother even if the financial problems were somehow solved. His mother could barely take care of herself, much less his sister. Just when he thought things couldn't get worse, his mom said they might have to sell the house. The thought of having to change high schools made David's head hurt. In fact, he was getting so many headaches that his grades were suffering. It felt like his whole world had fallen apart in three months.

## Parental Arguments

Every teenager reacts differently to family conflict, but in general this age group is more vulnerable to stress and has more adjustment difficulties than older and younger children. Hence, they are more disturbed by parental arguments. At a time when 50 percent of marriages end in divorce, most teens are acutely aware that arguments could lead to a family breakup. The possibility of losing the security of their family is especially difficult at a time of life when young people are already feeling very insecure.

Some teenagers feel the tension even if they aren't privy to their parents' arguments. They feel better if they can hear what is going on. Other children can't stand to hear their parents' heated discussions. If you must argue, ask your teen if she would rather have you do it in private so that she doesn't have to listen.

When parents are at war with one another, many teens find they can tip the balance of power by siding with one parent against the other. Being in such a powerful position may feel good in the short run, but eventually the guilt for having betrayed one or both parents can become overwhelming. If your teen's readiness to complain about the other parent leads you to believe that your child is your trusted ally, be prepared for a big disappointment. When your teen gets angry at you, there is a good chance that he will defect to the enemy camp. Keep your teen out of the middle!

## Teens and Divorce

Teens may have more difficulty reconciling themselves to a divorce than younger children. While little ones simply grieve, teenagers grieve, analyze, and philosophize. To have their parents' marriage dissolve at a time when young people are beginning to explore intimate relationships triggers doubts as to whether enduring love and fidelity are realistic goals. Parents' decision to break their vows to one another causes teenagers to question whether it is safe to trust anyone. They may become cynical about the whole idea of commitment. Pessimism about marriage as an institution often develops.

Help for marital misery is possible. Psychologists, marriage and family therapists, and pastoral counselors are a phone call away. And yes, you can afford the sessions! The cost is a drop in the bucket compared to that of maintaining a second household. Trying to keep the family together is worth the struggle.

After witnessing their divorcing parents' emotional devastation, teenagers may decide to protect themselves from similar hurt by avoiding intimate relationships altogether. Alternatively, they may solve the problem of losing their family by impulsively marrying in an effort to find a new one. After a parent leaves, many teenagers spend years trying to come to terms with their personal sense of betrayal and abandonment. A common pattern is for them to become romantically involved with people who abandon them and leave them feeling similarly betrayed.

## Teen Life after Divorce

Spouses often claim they have been emotionally divorced for years, but most partners require at least a year to recover after the physical break. During that time they are too self-absorbed to dedicate much energy to the children. Regardless of which parent moves out, teenagers typically feel that they have lost both of them. To further complicate matters, teenagers often try to fill the parental void by becoming surrogate parents to their siblings. While this can bring the children closer to one another, it can also lead to considerable resentment on the part of adolescents who feel their own childhood has been foreshortened. Because teenagers are old enough to comprehend and empathize with their parents' distress, it is easy for young people to end up serving as their parents' confidantes. At a time when they need to be developing an identity apart from the family and work on separating emotionally, they often find themselves more psychologically enmeshed.

A divorce notwithstanding, both parents should attend their teenager's special events. Remain civil so as not to usurp center stage and ruin your teenager's moments in the sun. Don't blame any scenes that develop on your ex. It takes two to argue, so don't!

## Caught in the Middle

Teens often find themselves caught in the middle of warring parents long after a divorce decree has been signed, sealed, and delivered. When younger children are asked to scout for information and relay messages between households, they artfully avoid becoming entangled in their parents' conflicts by saying, "I don't know" or "I forgot." Teens usually have strong opinions about what is going on and readily take sides. Selectively sharing information can enable them to covertly express anger toward whomever they feel mad with at the moment. This is not healthy for anyone.

FACT

One positive result of divorce is that the children frequently pull together. Siblings who have been lifelong enemies often become close. Another benefit is that single parents often assign more chores to their children and ask them to help care for one another. In the process, they become more responsible and giving.

Psychologists are belatedly recognizing the price everyone pays when one parent undermines their child's relationship with the other parent. Commiserating with your teen about your ex is more likely to escalate your child's upset than to help her resolve anything. Working with your ex to ensure your teen's best interests are served is hard under any circumstances; try to poison the relationship between your teen and the other parent, and it will become impossible. As the custodial parent, it is imperative that you encourage regular visits and phone calls. Forbid your teen to make disparaging comments about the other parent. If your teen needs a confidante to help resolve feelings about the divorce, find someone more objective for her to talk to. Your teen needs a positive relationship with both parents.

Hearing your teen disparage your ex can provide a much-needed boost to your sagging ego, but keep your pleasure to yourself. However much you enjoy having your teen in your court, encouraging disrespect toward the other parent has predictable consequences: When your teen is angry with you, you'll become the target.

## Post-Divorce Runaways

In an all-too-predictable post-divorce pattern, a teen gets mad at one parent, flees to the other parent for comfort, and tries to wrangle an invitation to stay. Hopefully your ex will provide some TLC and send your child back, because if your teen moves in eventually he will get mad at the other parent and return to you for comfort. If your child wants to move back in with you again, setting limits will be virtually impossible. The next time your teen gets angry at you he can simply take off again. The grass is always greener in the other household. Worse, the pattern of running from conflict instead of dealing with it and learning to settle disputes can easily be established during these formative years.

Teens can easily turn into chronic runaways if they are allowed to move back and forth between parents' homes. Once your teen moves out, insist that she stay put until the end of the school semester no matter how much you want her back. Listen when she tells you how unfairly her other parent treats her but don't help her avoid her problems. She needs to learn to solve conflicts, not run from them.

If teens aren't part of the solution, they may feel like part of the problem. If you are unemployed, having financial problems, or grieving the death of a parent, your teen is probably hurting for you. Suggest ways he can help to cheer you up.

## Part-time Parenting

Hanging around the house of a part-time parent on the weekends isn't fun when your teenager's friends and possessions are across town. Although you are accused of being a Disneyland dad or mom, you may need to woo a teen who is too hostile or busy to write you into his social calendar. You may need to dispense with discipline, too, since trying to tackle problematic behavior during weekend visits may bring them to a screeching halt. Although you are certain that your child needs you to serve as an authority figure, you may find yourself helpless to impose discipline. You may discover that serving as a confidante, guide, mentor, and trusted friend is more rewarding to you and equally beneficial for your teen. Unless you have joint custody or a very good relationship with your ex, you may need to let the custodial parent serve as disciplinarian.

Fifty percent of new marriages end in divorce; ninety percent of the children involved end up in sole custody of their mothers according to R.N. Atkins' article in a book entitled *Fathers and Their Families.* Father/child relationships sometimes improve but usually suffer.

Regardless of a child's age when a divorce takes place, teenagers almost always want to move in with their noncustodial parent and establish a full-fledged parent/child relationship before graduating from high school. Otherwise, they feel they would miss an important childhood experience. However, most are afraid to admit that they want to do this. They worry about hurting their custodial parent and may also fear being rejected by their other parent. A typical teenaged solution is to create enough havoc so that the parents reach an independent decision to change custody in hopes that a new environment and fresh start will help. While not all teens consciously set their parents up to trade custody, many do so on purpose. If your teen suddenly becomes unmanageable and ends up moving in with your ex, don't doubt your adequacy as a parent or your child's love for you. Teenagers really need the chance to try to form a relationship with each parent.

## Single Parenting

It seems logical that once your child is old enough to chauffeur himself about town and help with the cooking, laundry, cleaning, and other chores, single parenting wouldn't be quite so hectic and draining. Unfortunately, childrearing usually gets harder during adolescence. Teenagers require more supervision than younger children and are harder to discipline. Children of all ages need lots of hand-holding through a crisis, but since having a peer fail to say "hello" in the hallway at school is a major disaster to a teenager, the parent ends up having to do lots of hand-holding!

More than 3 percent of children under age eighteen have had a parent die. Even teens who put on happy faces may be grieving. Adults typically avoid the subject for fear of evoking a flood of tears, but talking helps teens to process their loss and recover.

Without another adult on the premises, maintaining discipline is likely to be much harder. An even bigger problem is not having a cooler head available to help the two of you resolve disputes and get a better perspective when you clash. And as a single parent of a teen, you're likely to have lots of clashes. Without a spouse on hand to usurp time and attention, separation issues will probably be harder for you and your teen. The closer two people are, the harder it is for them to handle losing one another. Having your teen become more independent can feel like a major loss.

## Teen Challenges

Teens growing up in single-parent households are usually more conflicted about leaving home than children from two-parent families. Because single-parent/teen relationships are closer, children are more aware of the emotional toll their departure will take. Teens worry that their parent will be completely alone when they are gone. Because single parents are more stressed and needy, and because children with only one parent feel more dependent and vulnerable, they tend to be more protective. This can be hard for single parents to believe since their teenagers often dish out larger-than-average helpings of verbal abuse and can be very noisy about their intention to never look back once they leave. However, the closer two people are, the harder it is for them to separate. When confiding in therapists and friends, teens from single-parent homes routinely express fears about whether their parent can survive without them and worry about their own ability to handle moving away.

## Getting a Life

If you are like most single parents, you have probably been focused on your children to the exclusion of most everything else, so that even while you are at work you think about what is happening at home. Between keeping your teen in Nikes and washing his gym socks, you probably haven't invested much time in outside activities or relationships. That can make losing your job as a full-time parent especially difficult. Teens are often so worried about leaving a single parent behind to fend for herself, growing up seems like a betrayal. Develop other interests and relationships so your teen won't need to feel so guilty about starting her own life.

It is especially important for single parents to establish some meaningful involvements outside the home in order to develop relationships and a new sense of purpose. That can seem impossible given the lack of time, money, and supervision for teenagers. Activities that you can do together now and continue on your own after your teen leaves home provide a way out of this morass. Consider possibilities like the following:

- Singing in the church or community choir.
- Joining a club in which members write poetry, bicycle, hike, or play African drums together.
- Attending a support group for parents and teens.
- Doing volunteer work at a hospital or shelter.
- Pursuing a hobby, which can be anything from ceramics to breeding and showing dogs.
- Starting a small home business doing woodworking, selling cosmetics, or organizing weddings.
- Becoming involved in local politics.
- Taking a continuing education course in quilting, carving arrowheads, or pottery at a local recreation center or community college.

Try to find an activity you can both enjoy. If that's not possible, your own need for satisfying involvements should take precedence. Addressing your teen's fears directly and giving her a concrete way to help can go a long way toward assuaging her guilt about leaving, so explain the situation to your teen: You need to "get a life" that isn't so totally focused on her in order to prepare for life without her. Ask for her help to get started by accompanying you for the first month or two. If she consents to go with you, she'll get an inside look at the world of adults, and you'll get to see her as others do. If your child is the only young person in a group of adults, so much the better. Seeing the adult world up close is an important educational experience; being treated as an equal by adults is affirming. But if your teen refuses to accompany you, go by yourself.

## Single Parents and Dating

Since most teenagers are very uncomfortable with the idea that their parents are sexual beings, having them date may seem repugnant. Moreover, your teenager may be too busy to spend time with you, but that doesn't mean she is willing to share you. She may view your date as a rival and treat him accordingly. While younger children may be glad for a new father or mother, adolescents rarely accept having a "total stranger" assume that role when they are trying to obliterate their need for parents altogether. Mom's boyfriend or dad's girlfriend are often the targets of unresolved feelings of abandonment by the noncustodial parent. They threaten any lingering teenaged fantasies of a parental reconciliation.

A family move that involves a change of schools can be overly challenging for teens. Rather than moving your child during senior year, it may work out better if he can live with a friend until graduation.

Teens can be sufficiently obnoxious toward their parents' dates as to kill potential relationships before they get off the ground. There is a saying among therapists that feelings that don't get talked out get acted out, so it is probably best to have some very straightforward conversations about your desire to date before you bring someone home to meet "the kid." Explain to your teen that soon he will be gone and you need to develop some other meaningful relationships so you won't be too lonely. If you hope to remarry some day, say so. Announce that you have decided to start dating and have made plans to go out. Empathize with the fact that this may be uncomfortable for both of you, but express the hope that your teen will try to be considerate of your friends just as you try to be considerate of his. When you are ready for your date to meet your teen, make sure your teen is amenable before arranging for introductions.

## Solving Family Problems

David was very upset about having to change high schools after his parents' divorce, and his mother felt badly that it was so hard on him. She talked to the school counselor, and they decided David would benefit from a counseling group at school. It would give him some much-needed emotional support and a way to make some friends. Although David couldn't play football because he missed the tryouts, his mother pointed out that in order for him to go to college he would have to get scholarships. She urged him to devote his extra time to his schoolwork.

If you are called out of town on business or to tend to a family emergency, don't leave your teen to fend for himself. Make arrangements for him to stay with a friend. Even if he is responsible enough not to require adult supervision, he will probably appreciate the company.

David rebuffed his father for a month, but he continued to call his son every day even though his son's curtness was painful. His dad finally bought David a new video game and used it to lure him out for pizza so he could give it to him. David's attitude softened, and they began making it a habit to go out once a week. An argument over David's rudeness toward a waiter turned into a major blow-up. Suddenly David was accusing his father of having ruined his life. David ended up sobbing, but the confrontation helped David get a lot of things off of his chest and cleared the air. David continued to wish that his parents hadn't divorced, but in time he was able to cope and move on.

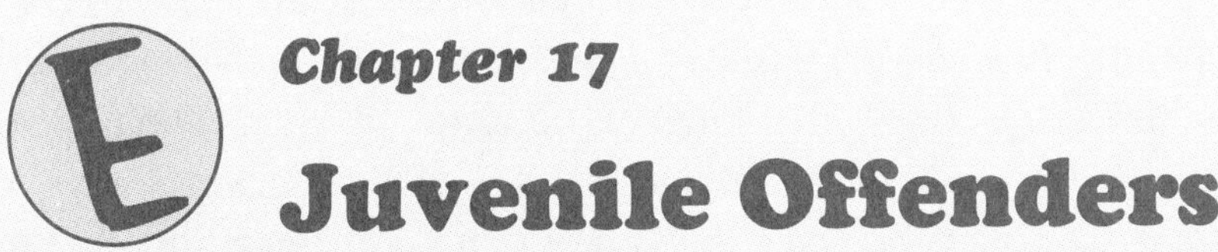

# Chapter 17
# Juvenile Offenders

Most crimes are committed by youth between the ages of sixteen and twenty-four. Your teen is at risk for criminal behavior if he has a history of lying, fighting, and poor school achievement, has poor family relationships, and spends a lot of time unsupervised. Factors that help teens stay on the straight-and-narrow path include doing well in school, having an extracurricular activity, someone to keep track of them, and warm relationships with parents.

## On the Wrong Path

Andrew had always been a slow reader. When he saw the huge history, science, and English textbooks on his first day of high school, he knew there was no way he could plow through so many words. He was supposed to get help from the special education teacher, but his friends saw him going in the resource classroom and called him a retard. He refused to return. He spent his days sitting in the back of each classroom feeling bored and miserable. He thought if he were athletic maybe people would like him, but as it was he felt like a misfit. His mom was always on his case about something, so home was no better. He couldn't wait to turn sixteen, drop out, get his own apartment, and never look back. The one guaranteed way to take his mind off of his troubles was partying. At least when he was high, his problems went away for a while. So more and more, he stayed high.

Parents and teachers routinely lecture underachieving students about the terrible fate that awaits them if they don't buckle down in school. Teens do get the message but to succeed, they need more than lectures. They need academic help as well as structure, supervision, help for personal problems, respect, and kindness.

Now that Andrew was almost sixteen, he was starting to realize that dropping out of school wasn't the life jacket that would save him from drowning in school and family problems and float him to safety. His mother kept telling him that unless he finished high school, the best he could hope for was a boring minimum wage job. He was already short on the credits he needed to graduate with his class, and having to spend an extra semester in high school felt like too much. When he looked into the future, he saw himself being sucked under giant waves of problems, which was pretty much how he felt now. Then he was asked to join a gang. The kids were into pretty rough stuff, but it was kind of exciting and at least he had friends. His mother continued to read him the riot act over every little thing, which dragged him down. Soon his gang felt more like family than his own family. Things were definitely looking up.

## Boys Will Be Boys

Some teenagers commit crimes quite by accident. Usually this is because an opportunity presents itself, and in their excitement they fail to consider that someone might be harmed by their actions or that there might be consequences. Accordingly, they spray paint street signs without realizing the danger to motorists or the cost to the county of cleaning up or replacing signs. Teenagers shoplift without realizing that other customers end up paying for the stolen merchandise by way of the higher prices. They drink and drive without realizing that their reaction time and judgment have been affected.

It is important to impress your teen with the seriousness of his mistake when he commits a crime due to poor judgment. Let him know that you are displeased and insist that he be held fully accountable for his error. Instead of simply demanding an apology and figuring out some sort of punishment, insist that he apologize and compensate whoever has been harmed by his actions. Accidents happen, boys will be boys, and yes, everyone makes a mistake now and then. That doesn't, however, absolve people of responsibility. They need to clean up their messes and do what they can to right any wrongs that have resulted from their actions.

## Delinquency Risk Factors

The risk factors for serious delinquency are well known. Parents need to be familiar with them and take steps to help their teen sooner rather than later to lessen the likelihood of having their child become involved in criminal activity. It's easier to prevent a stone from rolling off a cliff than to halt its fall once it's catapulted over the edge.

Here are a few of the warning signs:

- Parent/child relationships riddled by conflict
- Parents perceived as cold and rejecting
- Inadequate supervision
- A history of child abuse
- Hyperactivity

- Learning disabilities
- Poor academic achievement
- No extracurricular involvements
- Peer rejection
- Poverty

Impoverished families are generally more stressed and have more problems than families that aren't struggling to keep a roof over their heads and food on the table. In addition, poor families usually live in neighborhoods where so many people are involved in delinquent activities that some teenagers feel compelled to join in. The alternative is harassment and rejection. Hyperactive children are also at risk for committing crimes during adolescence. Approximately a fourth become delinquent.

## Thrill Seekers

Another major risk factor, "sensation seeking," or "thrill seeking" as it is sometimes called, appears to be physical, perhaps genetic. Adolescents with nervous systems that require extra stimulation in order to have an emotional or even a physical response are at especially high risk for committing delinquent acts. It is conjectured that they require extra doses of adrenaline to overcome boredom and feel the thrills that others can get from reading a good book, watching a lovely sunset, or shopping at a mall. Sensation-seekers' need for intensive stimulation to feel small twinges of excitement leads them to engage in risky behavior that other people would in no way consider fun. Sneaking about in the dark to vandalize cars knowing you would be put in detention if caught really gets the juices flowing. Alcohol relieves chronic feelings of emptiness for those who are bored and reduces the inhibitions of those who are shy. Hallucinogens provide an adrenaline rush, heroin anesthetizes emotional pain so the good feelings can roll, and cocaine and speed rev up the system to the point that everything feels more exciting.

Although a sensation-seeking personality may be inborn in some cases, it can apparently develop as a reaction to life experiences as well. This personality characteristic is common among abused and neglected children, youngsters who have grown up in homes fraught with domestic violence, and those who have been subjected to any sort of ongoing trauma. Extended periods of intense turmoil can apparently reset the nervous system, so people eventually require greater intensity to be able to feel emotions, physical pain, and even heat and cold. Abused and neglected children run an 80 percent risk of juvenile delinquency and adult criminality.

## Family Problems

Some adolescents have none of the risk factors but still become delinquent. When a teenager is mad at his parents, upsetting them by getting in trouble can be an effective way to punish them. Getting into trouble at school or in the community can also be an effective attention-getting device for young people who feel neglected. Lack of adequate supervision is definitely a risk factor for delinquency. The loneliness drives them to affiliate with other unsupervised peers. Feeling that their parents don't really care what happens to them makes it harder for young people to care about themselves enough to want to stay out of trouble.

Many warring couples pull together when one of their children is in serious trouble. Their teenagers often express the belief that by acting out and precipitating a carefully timed crisis, they can unite their parents and keep the family from dissolving. In addition, when faced with a child who has stolen a car or been picked up for underage drinking, problems with messy rooms and chores that didn't get done seem petty by comparison. Although the teenager understands that his parents are deeply distressed by his behavior, they may actually come across as much nicer. When parents are hiring lawyers and checking to see that their child is keeping up with the terms of his probation, their child sees that his parents care about his welfare.

## Behind the Mask

Some teenagers appear hard as nails when they thumb their noses at authority, break rules, violate the rights of others, and lash out at the world. However, the tough-guy mask is usually a front. Some sociopathic teenagers do, in fact, lack consciences, but although these "bad seeds" get lots of play in the media, conscienceless kids are rarities. The typical delinquent is an unhappy child who lacks a belief in his own worthiness and feels bored, lost, rejected, unloved, and very much alone. Although professionals readily diagnose delinquent teenagers as oppositional, defiant, conduct disordered, or as having substance abuse problems, deep down inside most are depressed.

The pattern for girls has been to respond to personal and family problems with classic signs of depression—weepiness, changes in appetite, and difficulty sleeping—but that has changed in recent years. Girls are starting to act out when they are troubled, too. Hence, crime among girls is on the rise.

As delinquent youths cling to their tough-guy masks to ward off feelings of hopelessness and helplessness, they come across as angry and overly quick to take offense. In fact, most are hypersensitive to rejection and believe that the best defense is a good offense. When they feel humiliated, they may work overtime to avenge the insult and punish the perpetrators by harassing them, fighting, or slashing their tires. To get back at a teacher or principal, teenagers with anger control problems may pull fire alarms, make bomb threats, or vandalize buildings. A youth who generally feels helpless is powerful and in control when committing random acts of violence and daredevil crimes. Indulging in dangerous and forbidden activities provides a heady adrenaline rush.

## Young Con Artists

When parents are upset because of their teenager's serious misdeed, it is understandable that they want to impress their child with the gravity of the problem. When he seems unconcerned, finds something humorous in his predicament, or flashes a nervous smile, some frustrated parents exclaim, "Wipe that smirk off your face!" Their intention might be to make their child suffer as much as they are suffering in hopes that he will comprehend the error of his ways. However, insisting that a child appear remorseful and contrite despite an absence of any feelings of guilt is destructive. It is a mistake to give lessons on how to deceive others!

Some teenagers are true sociopaths. Because they don't have a conscience, they don't see anything wrong with doing whatever gratifies their whim of the moment. Their sorrow when they get into trouble is over having been caught, not over having harmed someone or broken a law. Their lack of regard for others often reflects a core sense of their own worthlessness. It is important to get them into therapy; otherwise, they are candidates for the juvenile justice system, and eventually for the adult prison system. School counselors are free, and most communities have low-cost or even no-cost counseling clinics. If your teen goes before a juvenile court judge or is assigned to a probation officer, ask that your child be court-ordered to attend counseling sessions. Juvenile detention is likely to do more harm than good.

## The Parent Factor

Whether teens who commit crimes are helped or punished depends largely on the family's social and economic status. College-educated parents typically view antisocial behavior as a symptom of a deeper problem. Accordingly, they are likely to schedule their teen to see a psychologist, psychiatrist, social worker, or counselor. Psychological counseling can help troubled youth solve their problems, which reduces the chances that they will continue to act out in antisocial ways. Judges are less likely to send teenagers to detention or jail if they see that the family has taken action to fix whatever is wrong without the state having to step in.

A night in detention can convince your son that crime doesn't pay and that he needs to change his ways. But detention won't teach him how to do the things that do pay and how to change. In therapy he can learn to solve his problems and manage his life without hurting himself or others.

Less-educated parents are more likely to view lawbreakers as bad and believe that punishment is the best way to teach a lesson. Unfortunately, punishment makes teens who already feel worthless feel like complete failures and doesn't teach the skills they need to solve academic, social, family, and substance abuse problems and get along in society. While being in detention or jail does protect society, it also improves children's relationships with other delinquents who school them in the art of crime. Teenagers may leave lockup determined to stay out of trouble but without the skills necessary to follow-through. Hence, they are more likely to get into more serious kinds of trouble. Most juvenile probation officers agree that in most cases, locking up teens costs big dollars and makes little sense. Since poor parenting and delinquency so often go hand in hand, juvenile court officers and judges usually require parents to attend parenting classes and family counseling. If parents cooperate, the child can often be helped. If parents will seek help before judgment is passed, a sentence is often suspended.

## Solving Authority Problems

Adults often think that teens who can't get along with authority figures need to learn some respect. Although adults are offended when teens don't treat them respectfully, teens can impress adults as being exceptionally polite but have no respect for them whatsoever. Whether your teen accepts adult authority isn't based on respect but on her ability to trust. To be willing to compromise, cooperate, and sacrifice her own desires to do what people in authority tell her, she must feel that the adults with power over her care about her as a person. She must trust that their rules, limits, and consequences are designed to help and teach her even if she very much dislikes being disciplined. She needs to believe that their goals for her are in sync with her goals for herself and have a sense that the people who make the rules are intent on her well-being. Basic trust overrides teenagers' occasional irritation with rules they consider nonsensical or unfair.

Without a relationship based on trust, rules, explanations, alerts, warnings, reminders, limits, punishments, and consequences seem designed to ruin her fun. At best, she will see adults as simply out of touch. More likely, she will think they are on a power trip. At worst, she may see them as out to get her.

Issuing repeated warnings to try to protect teens can feel to them like harping. Some youngsters learn best by experience. Let your teen suffer the consequences of his actions, but remember that, "I told you so" is more likely to damage your relationship than teach a lesson. Instead, ask, "What can you do differently in the future?"

Teenagers' ability to trust adult authority usually reflects the quality of the parent/child relationship. From a harsh parent with a cold, rejecting attitude, teens learn that adults are not sources of support, affection, affirmation, or help. A poor relationship does not, however, mean that the mother and father are terrible people! Teens can see parents as cold when they are not. Youngsters with difficult personality types can be extremely challenging to deal with from the day they are born. Overly active, aggressive, cranky children with poor impulse control can quickly turn parents, teachers, and assorted caretakers with the patience of saints into critical beasts and raging maniacs.

If your relationship with your child is poor and she lacks a basic feeling that you love her, telling her that you care is not enough. If she has proven that you cannot control her, stop trying. Instead, focus your efforts on providing extra doses of positive attention. Share something you like about her every hour you are together. Bite your tongue to contain the urge to criticize, direct, admonish, control, and even teach. Say "please" and "thank-you" before and after each request. Apologize if you are cranky or critical. If your teenager doesn't respond, ask her for a list of things that you do and say that make her feel unappreciated or unloved. If your relationship doesn't improve, it's time to schedule an appointment for family therapy to find out how to reach her.

## Teaching Honesty

Adolescent egos being what they are, criticizing or punishing your child for breaking the law will probably do more to motivate him to justify himself or get even with you than to change his behavior. If a teen expects to be punished for misbehaving, he may lie, deceive, blame someone else, or do whatever else he can think of to avoid getting caught. If he is cornered, he may do or say whatever necessary to get his sentence reduced or suspended. Some parents are very gullible and easy to trick. Others are wise and hard to outfox. Either way, adolescents who expect to be punished for misbehaving can be very skilled at deception. You can lecture until you are blue in the face about the importance of honesty. But if your teen has learned from experience that an admission of guilt will result in punishment, confessing simply doesn't make good sense.

In saying, "I don't want my parents to find out what I'm doing," teenagers are in essence indicating that they feel compelled to protect themselves from their parents instead of from the dangers they have been warned about. The issue should be, "I should avoid something that might hurt me or get me into trouble." If your teen sneaks, lies, and tries to deceive you, he needs to know you are on his side. The way to start convincing him is to sell him on the idea that honesty really is the best policy because he doesn't need to fear the person who is there to help him. Tell your child you won't punish him as long as he tells the truth. Handle confessions by saying you are glad things didn't turn out worse than they did, then describe all of the problems that could have resulted. Next, discuss why his behavior was wrong or dangerous and brainstorm ways he can better handle similar situations in the future.

## Teaching Accountability

When parents do discover that their child has committed a crime, many blow up and pour on the guilt. Nevertheless, they leap to their youngster's defense when teachers, coaches, or the police try to hold the teenager responsible for his behavior. Such mixed messages are very confusing to teenagers. Communicating your displeasure over an antisocial act is fine if your child wants to please you. If your good opinion of him doesn't really count for much or if he considers you impossible to please, getting angry will only serve to alienate him further. If your teen lacks a conscience, a guilt trip won't give him one.

If a youngster has a good record of wriggling out of predicaments at home and school, during adolescence he may believe he can break laws in the community without getting caught. Some young con artists are quite successful, but sooner or later most end up in trouble with the law. Hold your child accountable for his actions.

The better strategy is to ensure that your child experiences some consequences for any criminal act he commits, no matter how petty or minor. Punishing your child yourself may not have an effect except to make him feel abused by you. Some teens need to experience the consequences of their behavior directly and resent parents serving as policemen intent on enforcing the law. Instead of passing judgment and a sentence, let the professionals do it. Tell your child that you will notify the school authorities about a crime he has committed on campus, the owner of the store he stole from, the neighbor whose car he vandalized, or the police about a crime he committed in the community. Then do it! Share what you know and state that you want your child to be held accountable so he can learn from his mistakes while he's still young and before he does something even more serious. When people realize that a parent cares enough to try to protect their child from more serious problems down the road, most comply. They dedicate their efforts toward helping the young person learn rather than simply looking for ways to see that he suffers. Provide emotional support and comfort to your child, but don't try to bail him out. Feelings are one thing; actions are quite another.

Gangs function like families, offering members protection from dangerous peers, opportunities to socialize, and a sense of belonging. To deter your child from joining a gang, notify the school and/or police if he is being threatened, pursue hobbies and activities that your teen can participate in, and solicit his input about issues that effect the family's welfare.

### Rebels Without a Cause

When youngsters use their fists to settle disputes, it's called fighting and they get in trouble at school. When teens do the same, it's called assault and battery and they get in trouble with the law. Your child may blame others for provoking a fight. In fact, he may have been seriously provoked. Still, you must not accept that his antagonists are to blame! At the very least, your child didn't leave when he should have. The questions to address are: What could your child have done differently? What can your child do if the same situation comes up again?

FACT

Fear is not enough to keep teenagers on a straight-and-narrow course; they need a conscience. Once they learn that their parents are powerless to control them, teens' fear dissolves and they realize they can do whatever they want. Teens without a conscience need intensive psychological help.

Whether your child fights, swears at his teachers, or uses other antisocial methods to best his enemies, he must learn healthier ways to settle disputes. His enemy may well be toting a gun, so his life could depend on his ability to diffuse struggles instead of escalating them. See Chapter 2 for ways to teach anger management or contact a public mental health clinic or juvenile probation office for information about anger management classes.

## A Potpourri of Solutions

When Andrew was caught breaking into a neighbor's house, his parents swung into action. They told him that they considered his actions a cry for help and that they were going to answer it. Instead of going into debt to pay an attorney, they went into debt to hire a tutor to work with him four days a week after school. That way, he got homework help and adult supervision until shortly before they returned from work. They told Andrew that as long as he lived at home he would be expected to attend school, and that included during the summer. He could make up the credits he lacked and graduate with his class.

Although Andrew denied having a drinking problem, he was drinking when he committed the crime. They took him to AA twice a week so he could learn about the consequences of drinking and how to deal with his emotions without alcohol. In addition, Andrew's probation officer required him to attend weekly group counseling sessions and weekly anger management classes to help him learn how to get along with peers and cope with his anger. His parents signed him up for karate lessons so he could have a hobby he enjoyed that would improve his self-esteem and provide a social outlet. They felt confident the judge would go easy on him since he was doing chores around the house to make money to pay for what he had stolen. They felt confident, too, that Andrew wouldn't get into any more trouble, if only because they were keeping him so busy. He simply didn't have time. E

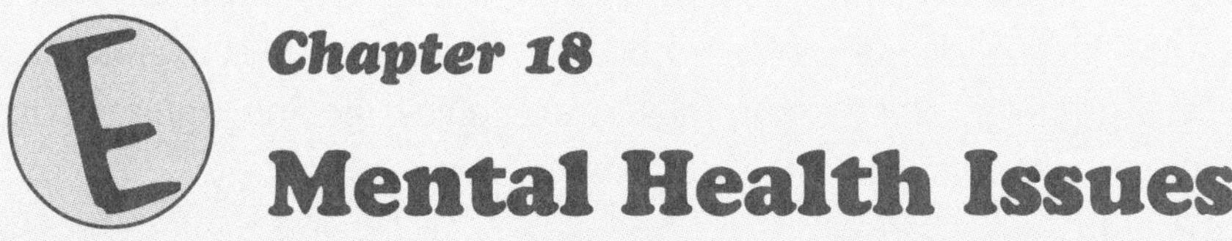

# Chapter 18
# Mental Health Issues

Psychological problems tend to worsen during adolescence. There is an epidemic of depression, and suicide is the second leading cause of death for teens. In addition, some major mental disorders such as schizophrenia and manic depression typically make their first appearance during the teenage years. Too often, people think teenagers are purposely acting out, so years go by before they are properly diagnosed and treated. Medication helps, but pills don't teach teens to cope with life. Therapy can be a long, arduous journey, but it is worth it.

## Teens and Depression

Marcia's parents didn't know what mysterious force had stolen their daughter's smiles and caused her to withdraw into herself. They supposed such moodiness was typical for teens. It made sense that Marcia spent so much time in her room with her door closed. She had a lot of studying to do. She was taking calculus and an honors English class, and was something of a perfectionist to boot. When the semester ended and the pressure let up, they assumed she would start getting together with her friends again. It didn't happen.

Girls are more likely to blame themselves when things go wrong, so they can end up feeling worthless about themselves and hopeless about improving their situation. The combination puts them at risk for depression. Meanwhile, unhappy boys typically lash out. Fighting, drinking, and delinquent behavior are more common.

### Parents in the Dark

Marcia's parents were completely caught off guard when her band director at school called to talk to them. He said that Marcia was failing several subjects and warned that unless her grades improved, she wouldn't be able to compete in the band state finals. Marcia burst into tears when her parents tried to talk to her to find out what was going on. She admitted that she was behind in several classes and didn't know how to catch up. Her parents promised to find a way to help, and were still trying to decide what to do when Marcia's school counselor called. The terrifying message was that a group of Marcia's friends had said they were worried that Marcia might be contemplating suicide! Her parents were sure it must be a mistake, but when they confronted Marcia, she admitted it was true. She felt worthless, she said. Hopeless. Her life was terrible and would never get better. The only way to end the pain of living was to die.

## Symptoms of Depression

Depressed teens don't necessarily appear despondent, although they often do. Sometimes they seem irritable and cranky. There are a number of clear-cut symptoms of depression:

- Loss of interest in previously enjoyed friends and activities
- Change in appetite
- Sleep disturbance
- Difficulty making decisions
- Difficulty concentrating
- Hopeless about the future
- Helpless to change things
- Feeling down or "blue"

Not all depressed teenagers report feeling sad or unhappy. Instead, they describe feeling drained of energy, so that even small tasks feel overwhelming. They may attribute this to being too busy or needing more sleep or exercise, but it is more than that. As they lose their ability to experience pleasure they withdraw from activities and friends they previously enjoyed. The loss of interest can extend to schoolwork even for a very dedicated student, and difficulties concentrating can precipitate a sudden decline in grades even though the student is really trying. Appetite changes are common and are often dramatic enough to cause depressed teenagers to pack on or shed pounds. Sleep patterns are disturbed, causing depressed teenagers to sleep too much or suffer serious bouts of insomnia. Many awaken in the wee hours of the morning and have difficulty falling back to sleep. They are likely to feel exhausted no matter how much rest they get, possibly because of their disturbed brain activity.

Depression can be difficult for parents to diagnose because it is often triggered by an upsetting event or trauma. When parents see their child reacting to a breakup with a girlfriend or an upset about not making the football team, they assume he will be back to normal in a week or two. They may try to pamper him for a bit, make greater efforts to cheer him, try to pry him out of the house to do something fun, then accuse him of wallowing in self-pity. Watching parents work overtime to try to help can cause depressed teenagers to feel guilty. Either way, they may make heroic efforts to conceal their distress. Unfortunately, that doesn't make it go away.

FACT

A diet rich in fatty fish (such as salmon), and regulated daily dosages of the dietary supplement SAM-e have been demonstrated to help relieve depressive symptoms at rates equivalent to anti-depressant medications such as Prozac. Food and pills can't solve your child's problems, however. To learn to do that, she needs to see a therapist for counseling. Ask your family doctor for a referral.

Teenagers with agitated depression may be more anxious than sad. Their minds race and they may worry so much that they wring their hands and pace. The anxiety makes it difficult for them to relax enough to fall sleep and keeps them from concentrating in school. If you aren't sure whether your child needs professional help and she resists seeing a therapist, follow the guidelines: If your child's grades worsen, if his weight changes by five pounds in a month (and he's not trying to diet or gain weight), or if he reports sleep problems for two weeks, get a professional evaluation. As many as a third of teenagers have been clinically depressed at some point in their lives, according to the results of the National Health and Nutrition Examination Survey. After one bout of depression, the risk of a second increases dramatically. That increases the risk of suicide, too.

## Teen Suicide

Depression is often accompanied by feelings of hopelessness about the future and helplessness to change whatever seems wrong. The combination is a dangerous brew. Add in the common teenaged trait of impulsiveness, which causes young people to act first and think later, and the result is a recipe for disaster. The teenaged suicide statistics are shocking.

## Suicide Statistics

Suicide is the second leading cause of death among teenagers. Although the leading cause is accidents, many deaths that are recorded as accidental are actually suicides. In a Gallup poll, 6 percent of teenagers reported having attempted suicide, and 15 percent said they had come close to trying. In addition, an estimated 8 percent of teens have purposely harmed themselves. Girls attempt suicide approximately six times more often than boys, but because girls use less effective methods, more boys actually succeed in killing themselves. Girls usually take pills, which increases the odds they can change their minds or be discovered in time to have their stomachs pumped. Disturbingly, boys gravitate toward more violent weapons of self-destruction, especially guns and hanging.

The firearms that teens use in suicides come from three major sources: their own home, their friends' homes, and their relatives' homes (*www.cdc.gov*). Parents who think their guns are safely locked away later learn that their child knew the combination or where the key was hidden. Forget trying to teenproof your firearms. Get rid of them!

## Suicide Warning Signs

Given that teenaged suicide has reached epidemic proportions, parents need to be on the lookout for warning signs. While it's not true that all suicidal young people first let someone know how desperate they are feeling, it is true that many people realize too late that their child was sending out distress signals they failed to heed. Mumbled comments about wishing never to have been born or wishing he were dead suggest that your child is in a lot of emotional pain. Teens who speak in punctuation marks often make innocent comments like, "If he doesn't notice me, I'll just die!" Comments on the order of, "If I don't get to go, I'll just die" can sound similarly innocent. Even if you are quite convinced that your young dramatist doesn't mean what she says, make it a policy to respond by saying, "Really? Is that how you feel? That worries me. Would it help to talk to a counselor?" Your child needs to know you take suicidal comments seriously and will get help for her if she needs it.

FACT

When one student at a high school commits suicide, it is common for several others to make attempts. Schools typically have counselors standing by to help teens cope in the aftermath. Any teenager who has lost a friend or relative to suicide immediately moves into the high-risk group for a suicide attempt, so take your child to a grief support group immediately.

## Helping Suicidal Teens

If you discover that your child has created any sort of suicide plan, however vague and unrealistic, you need to get her in to see a mental health professional that day. Take her to the nearest hospital emergency room if the plan is specific and doable or if she has started taking steps to implement it. Steps might include writing a note, giving away personal possessions, or arranging to get hold of a weapon (e.g., collecting pills). Teenaged suicide gestures overwhelm parents. They can't live in constant terror and their child rebels against being watched 24/7 and wants to put it behind her. They begin to tell themselves it wasn't so serious since their teenager wouldn't have actually tried to harm herself, or she didn't take enough pills to do any damage, or she timed things so she would be discovered. Denial that saves parents' sanity can be fatal for a child.

It is usually impossible for parents who have never been depressed or suicidal to understand what their child is experiencing. Pat phrases such as, "Look on the bright side," "Don't be so glum," or "Think of all your blessings" don't help. Such wisdom can add to your teen's feelings of worthlessness by implying that she is choosing to feel miserable and is ungrateful. Depression is not a choice teens make.

## Schizophrenia

Hallucinations, delusions, paranoia, bizarre behavior, being out of touch with reality—these are common features of schizophrenia. Nevertheless, not all schizophrenics display such extreme behavior. Instead, some show other symptoms of disturbed thought processes, which seem less bizarre but are actually harder to treat. Teenagers' thinking may be convoluted or irrational so that their conversation is disjointed, irrelevant, incoherent, or nonsensical. They cannot easily make or follow-through with even very simple plans. Hygiene, appearance, and diet often deteriorate as schizophrenics lose their ability to care for themselves in basic ways.

Approximately 1 percent of the population suffers from schizophrenia. The first schizophrenic episode typically occurs during adolescence or early adulthood. When the onset is sudden and the symptoms include hallucinations and delusions, the chances of recovery are better than for symptoms that appear more gradually and are less dramatic.

The early symptoms of schizophrenia are often subtle. The teenager's functioning deteriorates over time until the child who was always shy cannot look a stranger in the eye and won't leave the house for fear of running into an acquaintance. The aggressive child begins to perceive insults when absolutely nothing was intended. The happy child commits increasingly major social blunders, rising to dance in the classroom or laughing when everyone else is sad. Mood is likely to be disturbed, too, with severe bouts of depression and anxiety. When the change is gradual, it is often harder for parents to recognize because they adjust.

### Parental Confusion

Because the personality changes can be so gradual, many parents do not recognize what is happening. Even when the teenager puts on every piece of clothing she owns before going outside on a hot summer day or smears lipstick over the bottom third of her face before going to school, her parents may not react. Over time they have become accustomed to increasingly bizarre behavior. Some compliant teenagers will change their clothes and wash their faces if told. Trying to get other teenagers to follow normal social rules is like trying to push a boulder up a mountain. Parents learn there is no point in trying.

Many schizophrenics turn to alcohol and drugs to try to control their careening emotions, and parents often assume they have a normal teenager with an abnormally severe substance abuse problem. The truth may remain obscured until a child sobers up. Then, instead of getting himself together, the teenager becomes more dysfunctional.

## Treatment for Schizophrenia

Most schizophrenics require long-term treatment. They may need to go into a psychiatric institution when they are suicidal, violent, or deteriorate to the point that their family cannot care for them properly. Schizophrenics used to live most of their lives in hospitals, but now the stays are brief. Psychiatrists dedicate the little time insurance companies allow to stabilizing patients on medications. Medicines can lessen the patient's emotional intensity and help control the hallucinations and delusions. Day treatment programs offer opportunities to socialize and learn personal and vocational skills in a protected setting while parents work. However, many schizophrenics are too difficult for families to maintain. Sometimes schizophrenics can live in group homes where staff members supervise, guide, and teach basic self-care and social skills. Unfortunately, the lack of group homes for ongoing care and hospitals for emergencies means that many patients end up on the street. In fact, many homeless people are schizophrenic.

Some notable individuals have in fact learned to thrive despite their illness. John Nash, who won the Nobel prize in 1994 for economics and whose life story was made into a popular movie, is a notable example. Some schizophrenics improve after periods of months or years and never have a second psychotic episode. Although parents tend to be more concerned about their teen's hallucinations and bizarre behavior, patients can often learn to manage them through therapy or control them with medication. Schizophrenics who are emotionally numb, apathetic, and very socially withdrawn are less likely to find their way back into the mainstream and may require continued care or supervision. Ironically, the prospects for recovery are a bit better in some undeveloped countries, although the reasons are unclear. U.S. professionals view schizophrenia as a neurological disorder, emphasize medication, and strive to keep patients functional to prevent further deterioration. In traditional societies, extended family networks are less upset by the inability to work and contribute to the household. They focus on TLC, prayers, and willingly scale back demands.

Schizophrenic children need to be seen by a psychiatrist, but don't pin all of your hopes on pills. The side effects are so difficult, many teens refuse to take them. Furthermore, your child needs intensive therapy, not just medication management, and you need to take parenting classes to learn how to help your child at home.

## Bipolar Disorder

The actress Patty Duke brought national attention to the problem of manic depressive illness, or "bipolar disorder" as it is now called. Her book helped hundreds of thousands of parents realize their child wasn't spinning out of control on purpose. Still, parents are likely to assume their darling child has become a delinquent teenaged substance abuser. Although the first clear-cut symptoms typically appear before age eighteen, it is typically diagnosed several heartbreaking years later.

Even professionals often have difficulty distinguishing borderline personality disorder from bipolar disorder. The acting out and bouts of black depression are similar, as are the long periods when the child gets along wonderfully and seems to be completely fine. A full psychological evaluation is likely to be required for an accurate diagnosis.

The defining features of bipolar disorder are dramatic swings from the darkest depression to at least one episode of mania during which the child may have inflated self-esteem, decreased need for sleep, increased talkativeness, racing thoughts, and agitation. Often there is a madcap pursuit of fun without thought of the consequences. Some of the fun may be relatively harmless, such as scaling the town's water tower to moon passersby. Some may be definitely dangerous, such as breaking into a business to steal. There may be delusions, and wild alcohol and cocaine binges are common, though in the manic phase teens may act like they are on cocaine when sober.

A psychological or psychiatric evaluation is required for an accurate diagnosis and medication. Some general practitioners are comfortable writing the prescriptions, but it is better to have a psychiatrist involved until the child is stabilized. Lithium salts are the standard first attempt at treatment.

Many of the world's greatest poets, artists, and writers were diagnosed with manic depression. The acute sensitivity and massive intelligence so typical of this illness combined in such greats as Picasso, Edgar Allan Poe, Virginia Woolf, and Sylvia Plath, who suffered mightily as they created their masterpieces. Genius inspiration and phenomenal productivity often occur in the manic phase, and many manic-depressives refuse medication so as not to lose these precious moments. However, often the inspiration and frenetic behavior is simply crazed, and many kill themselves to find relief from the nightmarish depressive phases that follow.

## Self-Mutilation

Many psychologists are distressed by the large number of teen clients who self-mutilate. They slash themselves with knives or broken glass or burn themselves with cigarettes. This is not life-threatening, although the wounds can become infected and often leave scars, but many "cutters," as they are sometimes called, make suicide attempts and end up killing themselves.

Tattooing and body piercing are the height of teen fashion, and many parents don't realize that some youngsters undergo these procedures not in the interest of beauty but for the "rush." They are addicted to the pain.

If your teen has turned her body into an artist's canvas or is a walking jewelry display, ask her what it's like to get a tattoo or have her tongue pierced. Listen closely to her answer and consider it carefully. Normal young people dislike the pain but enjoy the results enough to endure it. Others compulsively undergo these painful procedures and feel like addicts.

Most people cringe at the very idea of inflicting pain on themselves and are at a loss to comprehend why anyone would purposely do it. While it's hard for the average person to relate to, when emotional pain is especially intense and long-standing, physical pain can actually provide a respite. It's like the old joke that a way to get temporary relief from a sore thumb is to stub your toe, though purposely clawing, cutting, and burning oneself is not funny.

Another reason that teenagers self-mutilate is because they cannot stand feeling emotionally numb. Numbness often sets in after a trauma or period of intense emotional pain, but instead of providing relief, numbness can be equally excruciating. People often say, "I had to pinch myself to know it was really happening," and physical pain can in fact eclipse emotional numbness and restore the feeling of being in touch with reality, if only briefly. Teens who feel emotionally numb often say that the terrible pain is a relief—that nothing is worse than feeling unreal or dead. People who self-mutilate need intensive psychotherapy. In addition, those living in metropolitan areas may be able to join a self-help group for cutters. Contact your local mental health clinic for information.

Estimates of teenagers who self-mutilate run as high as 1 percent. The pain provides a release for tension and psychological pain on the one hand. It can also penetrate emotional numbness and restore a sense of reality. These children need intensive therapy and may benefit from self-help groups.

# Attention Deficit Disorder

For many of the estimated 3 to 5 percent of teens diagnosed with ADD, childhood was not a happy time, especially if they are also hyperactive and have learning disabilities, as is often the case. Many took methamphetamines to help control their difficult behavior and received special education, but few receive much assistance to conquer their emotional and social challenges. During early adolescence, many stop taking their medication and refuse academic help because of the social stigma. Put it all together, and many ADD teenagers struggle with a core sense of worthlessness. They arrive at the door of adolescence poorly equipped to handle the stress of this age. It's tragic if not surprising that many gravitate toward similarly troubled peers, begin self-medicating by taking amphetamines or "speed," drop out of school, and become involved in delinquent activities.

## Helping the ADD Teen

It is unfortunate that so many adults focus on what teens with ADD don't do well instead of concentrating on their many strengths. Doing so can build their self-confidence and help them to build on their personal assets to compensate for their challenges. When the exceptional creativity, physicality, spontaneity, daring-do, kindness, energy, and independent spirit of the typical attention-deficit-disordered child are considered, everyone else seems deficient and disordered by comparison. In fact, ADD teens may not be deficient or disordered but merely have a different personality type. But because they march to the beat of a different drummer, and because that drummer doesn't play well indoors, they are likely to be continually assailed with news of their flaws and failing as adults struggle to get them to join the rest of the band.

If you have fallen into that common parental trap, it's time to stop telling your child to stop fidgeting, sit still, settle down, think ahead, pay attention, concentrate, be considerate, and watch out. If your well-intentioned reminders haven't taught your teen how to regulate his own behavior by now, it is safe to assume that more of the same won't help. Most teens resist being told what to do. Most ADD children begin resisting shortly after age two.

| Instead of . . . | Try . . . |
|---|---|
| "You left your coat in the living room again. How many times do I have to tell you . . .?" | "Would you mind hanging up your coat? I was trying to get the house straightened up . . ." *(And, after five more reminders . . .)* "I really appreciate your hanging up your coat. Thanks." |
| "What do you mean you don't have any homework again? Unless you bring up your grades and go to college, you're never going to make anything of yourself." | "Have you thought about what you might like to do after high school if you don't go to college?" |
| "Now look what you've done! Why can't you watch where you're going?" | "Accidents happen. After you sweep up, you can take the broken pieces to the trash." |
| "When are you going to get started on your homework?" | "It's homework time!" |
| "All you do is play computer games!" | "Pack your gym bag. We're going to the spa." |

## Hope Restored

When Marcia admitted to her parents that she had given away some of her possessions to her friends because she was planning to kill herself, they took her to the emergency room. The ER doctor prescribed some medication to calm her down and provided a referral to a therapist. In her therapy sessions Marcia learned stress management and relaxation techniques. She learned how to express her anger instead of turning it back on herself. She also learned some special techniques to control her thoughts so that instead of viciously berating herself for being less than perfect, she was able to forgive herself for being fallible. On her therapist's recommendation, her parents had her drop a class so she wouldn't be under so much pressure. They met with her other teachers, who gladly worked out ways for Marcia to make up some of her schoolwork in a way that wouldn't put too much pressure on her. Two months later Marcia began to return to her bubbly old self. She never could understand where the dark cloud had come from or exactly what made it go away. But her family was very relieved that it was gone.

## Chapter 19

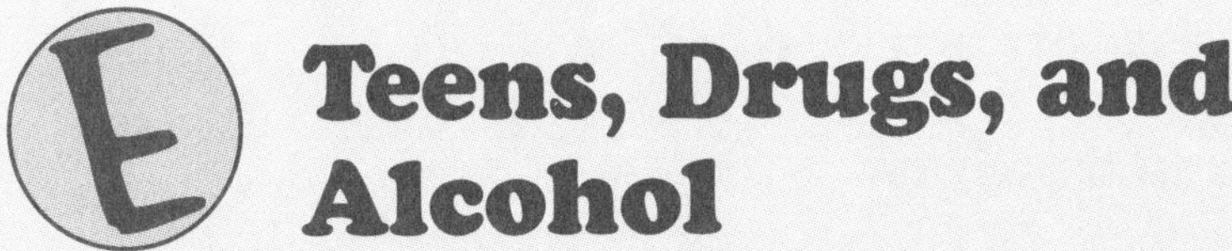

# Teens, Drugs, and Alcohol

When caught with marijuana in her bedroom or beer in her backpack, the average teenager can't imagine how it got there. Alternatively, young people insist that the contraband belongs to a friend. Even those with serious drug and alcohol problems may only admit to moderate recreational use. They aren't necessarily lying; many substance abusers and addicts are truly in denial. You need to know the warning signs, but don't try to diagnose and treat your child by yourself. Get a professional involved.

## From Experimentation to Addiction

Hindsight is often twenty-twenty, and when Wesley's parents looked back, they could clearly see the many warning signs that their son was abusing drugs. Because the problems developed gradually, it was hard for them to realize what was going on. Taken individually, it was easy to explain his behavior problems in other ways. What they should have been looking at, they realized now, was the pattern.

### Early Warning Signs

Wesley's parents knew that their son felt *rejected by peers* as far back as junior high when he complained about not having any friends. They also knew he had *low self-esteem* because once he said that he felt like "a total loser." His parents' friends had been reassuring. "Everybody feels that way in junior high!" they told Wesley's worried parents. "Nobody likes being thirteen!" Wesley made some friends before high school started, but his parents were concerned that he was *involved with antisocial peers.* Wesley came home the first day of high school smelling of cigarette smoke because, he said, "Some kids were smoking on the school bus." Soon after, his dad found cigarette butts in the flowerbed outside his son's bedroom window. "You act like it's the end of the world!" Wesley yelled when confronted. "It's not like I'm hooked! And anyway, whatever happened to 'live and let live'?" He was quoting his dad's favorite line. His parents were shocked that he was *smoking cigarettes before age fourteen.*

**I am an ex-addict. How can I tell my son that drugs are bad?**
You know from first-hand experience about the dangers, the damage, and the incredible waste of using drugs. Be honest in the hopes that your teen can learn from your experience instead of having to find out the hard way.

Wesley's *grades began to drop*, but his parents couldn't convince him to study. "Live for today and the future will take care of itself," he said. That was his mother's solution for worrying, and she couldn't think of a comeback. His parents' concern increased when Wesley *became very withdrawn.* He stayed in his room, and when he did come out *he was hostile and aggressive* to the point that once they actually felt afraid of him. But lots of other parents said their teens stayed in their rooms and were hostile, so Wesley's parents supposed this miserable adolescent stage would pass.

## Signs of Substance Abuse

Wesley's parents were livid when they found an empty beer can in their car. After a lengthy interrogation Wesley admitted that his friends had been drinking. "I was the designated driver," he said proudly. That didn't reassure them. "Okay!" Wesley yelled. "So I'm not a saint! I've sampled the devil's brew. Once I got rip-roaring drunk and ended up sick as a dog. I learned my lesson the hard way. It's not like I can undo it! It's no big deal, anyway." Wesley's parents argued with the small voice inside telling them this was in fact a big deal, but their son's words made perfect sense.

Wesley's *moods became erratic.* He might walk through the door, hug his parents, and talk a blue streak, or he might arrive sullen and argumentative. They expressed concern about his mood swings, and the next day he tossed a pamphlet entitled *You and Your Emotions: A Guide for Teens* at them. It was a handout from Wesley's child development class explaining how stress and hormones affected adolescents' moods.

## Signs of Addiction

Wesley had always been a clothes hound but now *neglected his appearance.* Sometimes he didn't even bathe or comb his hair. "Beauty is skin deep," he said. "Clothes don't make the man. Don't judge a book by its cover." Then he added, "Earth to Mom! I did the dishes! Don't I get any credit for that?" To make amends, his mother apologized and added, "I'm glad you've been keeping up with your homework, Wesley," she said. Wesley had led her to believe his grades were better and he had stopped *skipping classes*, but a call from the school informed her that Wesley was *lying* on both counts.

When Wesley's mother couldn't find her pearl earrings a month later, she was upset about her *missing valuables*. Her husband promised to pull the bureau away from the wall so she could look but never got around to it. Soon after he went out to lunch with his colleagues and discovered that he was *missing money* from his wallet, a twenty-dollar bill. His first thought was, "Wesley took it!" Then he felt guilty. Wesley said he got blamed for everything, and what child would steal from his father? But that evening his wife said she had to borrow money from a colleague at lunch because money was missing from her wallet.

## Substance Use, Abuse, and Addiction

When is a teenager's substance use serious enough to warrant more than a lecture about the dangers of drugs and alcohol? Everyone expects teenagers to experiment, most people consider marijuana basically harmless, and many families debate how much someone has to drink to be a true alcoholic. A high school junior comes home with alcohol on his breath, but was he intoxicated? ("I wasn't drunk or even tipsy, Mom! I just had half a beer to relax!"). A senior comes home stumbling and slurring, but is he abusing alcohol? ("Get real, Mom! Teenagers drink at parties! That's just the way it is!") A college student doesn't drink everyday, so how could he be in the grips of a full-blown addiction? ("I don't drink everyday. At most I party twice a month. I can quit whenever I want!"). Many parents' terror and confusion lead them to overreact or go into denial.

Mental health professionals don't get confused, because the fourth edition of the *Diagnostic and Statistical Manual of Mental Disorders* ("DSM-IV") published by the American Psychiatric Association (Washington, DC, 1994) clearly spells out the definitions of alcohol-related problems. Substitute the word "drug" for "alcohol," and you've got the rest of the substance abuse definitions:

- **Alcohol intoxication** involves physical and psychological changes after drinking. Alcohol is a poison, and the liver can only metabolize it at the rate of about one drink per hour. The rest builds up in the blood stream, causing intoxication. The psychological changes include rapidly changing moods, impaired judgment, or behavioral problems, such as sexual acting out or fighting. Or, the changes cause problems in a major area of life, for example, work, school, or significant relationships.

- **Alcohol abuse** involves having some work, school, or home responsibilities fall by the wayside due to drinking. Alternatively, alcohol consumption during a twelve-month period that results in multiple legal problems or social problems classifies as abuse. Examples include drunk driving or arguing enough to alienate family and friends.
- **Alcohol addiction** (a.k.a., "alcoholism") is diagnosed if three of seven major problems are present during a twelve-month time frame: Having to drink more to achieve the same high; experiencing withdrawal from not drinking; ingesting more alcohol than planned; wanting to quit drinking but continuing to drink anyway; dedicating a significant amount of time to getting and consuming alcohol and recovering from alcohol's effects; dropping out of some significant activities; continuing to drink after realizing that it is causing problems.

The above definition answers the question as to how someone who only drinks excessively once or twice a month could possibly be considered an alcoholic. Psychologists have long known that lots of teenagers (and adults!) with poor coping skills manage to hold themselves together through life's ups and downs for brief periods. However, they feel compelled to get rip-roaring drunk every couple of weeks to relax, release pent-up tensions, and get a break from the trials and tribulations of everyday life. It is a critical psychological crutch. A study by the National Household Survey on Drug Abuse indicated that 28 percent of children ages twelve to twenty had used alcohol and 19 percent had binged on it within the previous month. A "binge" means they consumed five or more drinks on a single occasion.

A twice-a-month bender might be harmless if people didn't create so much havoc while blowing off steam, but havoc is exactly what they create. They crash cars while driving under the influence, fall and sustain concussions when they pass out, beat others to a pulp in drunken brawls, hurt and alienate family members by being argumentative, spend more money than they can afford, and can't function afterwards because of hangovers. Although the physical symptoms of intoxication differ, the definitions of intoxication, abuse, and addiction are the same for all mind-altering or "psychoactive" substances. People tend to think of addiction in physical terms, but the psychological addiction is much harder to break.

## Nicotine

Most drug abusers and addicts begin with cigarettes. The average teenaged smoker first dabbles before age fourteen. Thirteen percent of eleven- to fifteen-year-olds smoke regularly, according to research reported in *Understanding Children and Adolescents.* Adolescents seriously underestimate how addictive nicotine actually is and believe they will be able to quit whenever they wish. Seventy percent of teen smokers find out the hard way, indicating in surveys that if they had it to do over again, they never would have started. New smokers may enjoy the high, but tolerance develops rapidly. Soon, the primary reason for smoking is to fend off nicotine cravings.

## Alcohol and Teens

Drinking alcohol creates a feeling of warmth and relaxation. It decreases inhibitions and increases sexual interest. As inebriation increases, people begin to show exaggerated emotional responses, becoming more talkative, cheerful, glum, or angry. Next, coordination and speech suffer as people lose muscular control and disorientation and confusion set in. At the next stage of inebriation, people typically pass out, but if they don't and they continue drinking, they can overdose. Every year, many young people pass out during drinking games and never regain consciousness. Be sure that your teenager understands that alcohol is a poison. A blood alcohol level of .55 is usually lethal.

Experimentation with alcohol typically begins during junior high school, but don't assume that what is typical is okay. Starting to drink prior to age fifteen rather than waiting until twenty-one increases the risk of alcoholism by four-fold. Early starters have the hardest time quitting and staying sober; they missed too many critical developmental years. Eighty-seven percent of high school seniors have drunk alcohol, according to *Understanding Children and Adolescents, Fourth Edition* by Schickedanz and Forsyth (Allyn and Bacon, 2001).

Alcohol, marijuana, and cocaine increase sexual feelings and are a factor in 70 percent of teen pregnancies. A popular date rape drug, Rohypnol, called "ruffies," "roche," "R-2," "rib," and "rope," is often slipped into a female's drink to render her unconscious so she can be taken advantage of sexually. That's a good reason for your daughter to avoid drinking at parties.

Teens at higher risk for alcoholism also include those with below-average school achievement, poor self-esteem, impaired family relationships, and antisocial friends. Although the debate remains as to whether alcoholism is or is not hereditary, having alcoholic relatives dramatically increases a child's risk, and studies of identical twins suggest a genetic link. Whether the tendency toward alcoholism is inborn or a learned pattern of coping, it definitely runs in families. Children with an alcoholic parent are at special risk.

## The Marijuana Conundrum

How upset should parents be about finding drug paraphernalia in their child's bedroom? Many adults still remember the "reefer madness" movie that was popular with teen audiences back in the 1950s and 1960s. The phony documentary followed clean-cut teenagers from their first innocent puff through their inevitable descent into the gutter, where they wallowed as full-blown heroin addicts. The controversy continues as to whether the government should legalize marijuana or toss users in jail. Given the problems associated with moderate to heavy use, tossing them into a treatment center would make more sense.

## Teens' Drug of Choice

To add to parents' conundrum about how to respond to teen marijuana use, a study cited by Riera in *Uncommon Sense for Parents with Teenagers* indicated that adolescents who smoked it once a month actually had *better* social adjustment than youths who didn't smoke it at all! A follow-up study showed that the once-a-month users also enjoyed *better* mental health in adult life than those who abstained! It turns out that marijuana use is so widespread among adolescents, abstaining from marijuana use may signal the kind of social alienation that either reflects psychological problems or creates them. Overall, its use by adolescents doubled in the past few years.

"Typical" and "normal" don't mean harmless. Research indicates that when compared to light marijuana users (once a month or less), heavier pot smokers are significantly more disturbed. It is unclear whether marijuana use causes emotional problems or whether troubled students turn to marijuana for relief. Either way, using more than once a month signals serious trouble.

Heavy users listed a variety of withdrawal symptoms when they tried to stop. Marijuana was the primary substance being abused by about 15 percent of people admitted to drug and alcohol treatment facilities. Don't assume marijuana is harmless!

As compared to nonusers, teenagers that smoke marijuana more than once a month report having more social problems (difficulties getting along with others), more thought problems (obsessive and strange thoughts), more attention problems (difficulty concentrating), more emotional problems (anxiety and depression), and more physical problems (dizziness, tiredness, or nausea). Delinquent behavior is prevalent among more-than-once-a-month users, too. Surveys show that as many as a quarter had run away from home (versus only 4 percent of nonusers), 60 percent had cut classes (versus 11 percent of nonusers), and a third admitted to theft outside the home (as compared to 6 percent of nonusers). Users are much more likely to lie, cheat, verbally abuse others, fight, disobey school rules, and even destroy their own possessions.

Students with D's and F's on their report cards were four times as likely to have used marijuana in the last year as were students who were making A's. Students are more likely to end up with a heavy-duty drug addiction if they smoke marijuana before the age of fourteen. One study on *www.druglibrary.org* indicated that the risk of a car accident increases by 30 percent for high school seniors who smoke marijuana daily. Contrary to the prevailing stereotype, the National Household Survey on Drug Abuse found that white youths are more likely to use marijuana than young minority group members.

QUESTION?

**Is marijuana addictive?**
Whenever drugs or alcohol are used as a psychological crutch, they can quickly lead to addiction. Many adolescents use marijuana to lessen the intensity of depression and anxiety. Although there is no indication of physical addiction, heavy users often require regular "fixes" to be able to function.

## Marijuana Facts and Effects

Marijuana and hashish, a stronger drug derived from the same plant, are usually smoked but can also be drunk as tea or even eaten. Marijuana's nicknames include "pot," "grass," "reefer," "dope," "buds," "Mary Jane," "Mary J," "weed," "ganja," "herb," "smoke," "hemp," "chronic," and "leaf"—to name a few. THC, the psychoactive ingredient, can have the effect of either a stimulant or a depressant. Because marijuana and hashish can distort sensory perceptions, causing colors and sounds to seem more vivid, they are classified as hallucinogens. Most often smokers begin to feel relaxed, drowsy, mildly euphoric, or withdrawn about twenty minutes after ingestion. Negative effects include anxiety, depression, paranoia, delusions, and hallucinations, lethargy, and passivity. Memory impairment, difficulties recalling words, slowed thinking, and clouded consciousness are common problems for chronic users ("potheads"). The psychological addiction can be extremely difficult to break.

## Heavy Hitting Drugs

Problems such as overdoses, addiction, homelessness, and crime aren't just for the poor and uneducated. Even clean-cut teenagers from educated, upper-class families can end up destroying their lives. Be sure your child knows the facts about the heavy-hitters of the drug world.

### Cocaine

Out of nearly a million new cocaine users in 2000, one-third were teenagers aged twelve to seventeen! Surveys indicate that 9 percent of high school seniors have tried cocaine. Derived from the coca leaf, this stimulant that was an ingredient in the original Coca-Cola can be sniffed, swallowed, or injected to increase alertness, energy, endurance, self-confidence, and sex drive. The depressive crash as the drug wears off strongly motivates users to ingest more. When the money runs out, the depression can be so severe that some people respond by committing suicide. It's not just the desire for a high but the need to escape the ensuing low that makes cocaine so very addictive. Chronic abuse can lead to concentration and memory problems, and hallucinations that mimic schizophrenia. Keeping up with once-every-four-to-six-hour doses can easily cost $1,000 per day, which accounts for the criminality so common among addicts. Cocaine is sufficiently dangerous to unborn babies that pregnant addicts are often charged with child abuse.

### Hallucinogens

LSD (or simply "L") is a popular odorless, tasteless drug. Like marijuana and hashish, it is classified as a hallucinogen, but alterations in sensory perceptions are much stronger and last much longer—a typical "trip" may involve hallucinations ranging from mild to wild and lasts about eight hours. Back in the 1960s, many people hoped that the novel experiences would spark their creative impulses, but to date there are no documented cases of any artistic achievements that originated during a trip. However, there are many documented cases of users leaping from buildings, setting themselves on fire, and committing other atrocities during bad trips. Although there is little risk of physical addiction, the psychological addiction can be difficult to overcome. Another serious problem is flashbacks, wherein people re-experience some of the sensory distortions they had while under the influence. If their mind conjured horrific scenes, re-experiencing one or more of their bad trips can be very traumatic.

A second, even more dangerous hallucinogen is PCP, also referred to as "angel dust," "rocket fuel," "crystal," and "superweed." Besides reactions ranging from sensory distortions to hallucinations, confusion, euphoria, and nausea, the delusions of invincibility can lead to recklessness, while the paranoia can cause violent psychotic behavior. Personality changes are often very dramatic.

## Ecstasy

Approximately one in eleven American teens have tried Methylenedioxymethamphetamine ("MDMA"), according to the Partnership for a Drug-Free America. Users call it Ecstasy or simply "X" or "smurf." The high creates an exceptionally affectionate, almost trance-like state, but side effects are not for the faint of heart. They include profuse sweating or chills, dehydration or exceptional thirst, rapid eye movement or blurred vision, and paranoia or anxiety. Ecstasy also produces clenching of the jaw or grinding of the teeth, and regular users develop sore jaws. The DEA (U.S. Drug Enforcement Administration) has now determined that chronic use leads to brain damage, which may explain ex-users' continuing problems with depression. Paraphernalia include water bottles (due to the intense thirst) and pacifiers or hard candy (used to mask jaw clenching).

## Heroin

Heroin's many nicknames include "junk," "smack," "dope," and "brown sugar." This narcotic is derived from morphine, which comes from opium poppies. Whether smoked, injected, inhaled, or snorted, heroin provides a very quick and intense euphoria that is highly addictive because tolerance develops rapidly. When under the influence, users have slowed and slurred speech, constricted pupils, and droopy eyelids. They may nod off midsentence, appear to be asleep, and then suddenly come to and finish it. Because heroin provides the ultimate escape for those in emotional pain, even addicts who manage to achieve sobriety are at high risk for relapse.

### Amphetamines

Known as "speed," "meth," "crystal," "chalk," "ice," and "glass," amphetamines are stimulants like those prescribed for most hyperactive children. Amphetamines increase alertness and concentration, produce a feeling of well-being, and curb appetite. Amphetamines were popular as diet pills in the 1950s until doctors realized that the side effects from prolonged use outweighed the benefits: anxiety, psychosis, and serious addiction that builds rapidly. Prescriptions for Ritalin are in tremendous demand, and many hyperactive children make fortunes by selling their pills instead of taking them.

## The Family Medicine Chest

When it comes to the recreational use of pain relievers, tranquilizers, sedatives, and stimulants, all of which are highly addictive, teenagers are the fastest growing segment of the population.

Commonly abused prescription medications are those prescribed for anxiety and pain, such as codeine, Valium, Xanax, Vicodin, and Percocet. Keep track of your prescription drugs! Over-the-counter medications that induce sleepiness or contain alcohol are also abused, so finding lots of empty containers in your teen's trash should be cause for alarm.

More teenagers have begun inhaling everyday household chemicals such as spray paint, gasoline, lighter fluid, furniture polish, fingernail polish remover, glue, rubber cement, cleaning fluids, or other chemicals to get a rush. Some teens sniff "whippets," which contain nitrous oxide and are used for making whipped cream. The low cost and ready availability of inhalants hold special appeal for the twelve- to seventeen-year-old set. Sixteen percent of adolescents have tried inhalants. The brain extends to the top of the nasal cavity, and when sniffed, the fumes go directly to the brain. Teenagers may enjoy the high, but the side effects include brain damage and death. And it isn't just chronic use that takes a toll. Of the hundreds of people who die each year from inhalants, about 30 percent are first-time users! Keep track of any products with a strong chemical smell. If an unusual item turns up in your teen's backpack or bedroom, take him to the doctor.

Get all the latest information about drug abuse, prevention, treatment, slang, signs of current use, side effects, results of long-term use, technical research studies, and most everything else you need to know from the Partnership for a Drug Free America at *www.drugfreeamerica.org*.

## The Long Road Back

Wesley's parents placed him in a drug/alcohol treatment center. He returned from his two-month stay committed to staying clean but was picked up for driving while intoxicated a month later. His parents sent him back for more in-patient treatment. A month later he was released and felt more determined than ever to get his life together but was back on drugs within two weeks. He refused to go in a third time, writing off treatment as a useless hoax and secretly feeling hopeless. His probation officer helped his parents out and convinced Wesley to again get help by offering him a choice between jail and treatment. This time, his parents took the doctor's recommendations seriously about getting him to an Alcoholic's Anonymous or Narcotic's Anonymous meeting every single day. Wesley insisted that was too much, but it seemed obvious to his parents that he needed daily help. They hoped that help would come from an AA or NA meeting instead of from drugs. After a month they allowed him to cut back to three meetings per week, and six months later he was down to one. He realized he might need to continue for years. The road into drugs had been a long one, and so was the road back.

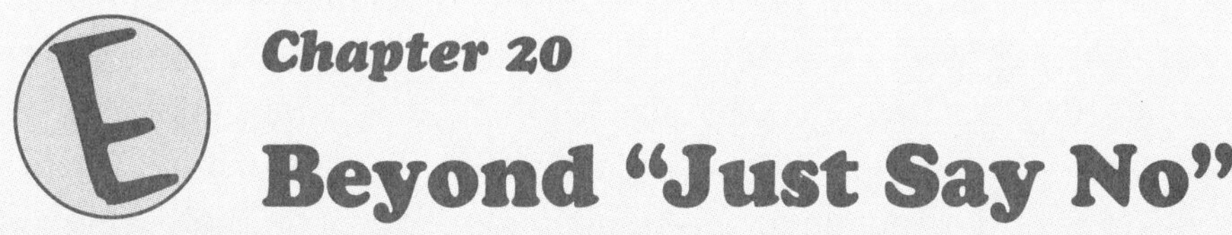

# Chapter 20
# Beyond "Just Say No"

Underage drinking is illegal, dangerous, and can be lethal, yet so many high school students consume alcohol that "normal" teens occasionally indulge. Similarly, using any kind of drug without a prescription is illegal, dangerous, and often lethal, yet most teenagers smoke marijuana, and a majority has experimented with harder drugs. There is no such thing as safe sex, yet many teenagers consider virginity a social handicap and are anxious to take the sexual plunge. The "Just say no" campaign isn't working. Your child needs better tools.

## Peer Pressure

Cassandra tried to please her parents but recently that seemed impossible. They complained about how she did her hair, dressed, wore her makeup, and were generally clueless about what it was like to be thirteen. Cassandra knew that they strongly disapproved of teenagers having sex, so she had held back. But now virginity had become a burden. When her girlfriends talked, Cassandra felt like an outsider, as if everyone was in on a secret but her. She kept quiet during conversations about sex because once when she put her two cents in, her friends burst out laughing. They kidded her about being too young and innocent to know what she was talking about.

Cassandra's best friend asked her why she didn't just hook up with a guy, do it, and get it over with. Cassandra said she wanted to wait until she found the right person, but her friend pointed out that it was better to get some experience first. That way, when she met Mr. Wonderful, she wouldn't blow it. That made a lot of sense to Cassandra. Her parents would be horrendously upset, but what they didn't know wouldn't hurt them. And so her decision was made.

## Help from Parents

It would seem that teenagers would be deluged with information about drugs, alcohol, and sex. Not so. It turns out that few get more than the same tired warnings to, "Just say no." The question on many teens' minds is how to say no without alienating their peers. It may help to inform your child that most people feel a bit guilty about drinking, using drugs, looking at pornography, having sex, skipping school, or doing something illegal. Like gobbling bags of potato chips while others nibble on salads, those who do things they know are wrong prefer to have everyone participate. By joining in, your teenager not only risks harming himself but enables others to harm themselves, too.

If your teenager needs an excuse for abstaining from drugs and alcohol, some work better than others. "My Mom and Dad disapprove" is not acceptable in most teenaged circles. Sadly, "I've got six months sober and am going for six months and one day" may draw nods of understanding. Peers also back off when they are told that someone has to take random UAs (urinalyses) and can't risk turning in a dirty sample. (Contact your family physician for help arranging spot checks.) Physical "excuses" may draw sympathetic understanding from peers, so "I can't; I'm allergic," can play well. Athletes may also be excused. Most teenagers are concerned about getting caught, so by saying, "I was intending to keep you dudes out of trouble by being your designated driver," teens can sometimes pass themselves off as participants without fully participating. Humor is always effective for diffusing tensions, so simply saying, "I'm going for the contact high. Give me five," may eliminate the pressure. Explaining that, "Sex outside of marriage is against my religious convictions" can work. Ensuing challenges may need to be followed up with an assertive statement like, "I don't judge others for their beliefs and don't expect people to judge me for mine."

## Help from Teachers

On surveys, the majority of teenagers say that they wish they could talk to their parents about drugs, liquor, and sex. Teenagers also say that their peers serve as their primary sources of information. More experienced friends may not have many facts, but that doesn't stop them from tutoring novices. Older and not much wiser teens often insist that even very dangerous drugs are harmless if taken properly. Many don't even know that it is possible to overdose and die from alcohol poisoning. Self-proclaimed sexual experts spread myths that pregnancy can be avoided by standing up during sex or by having the boy pull out in time. To avoid AIDS, they recommend douching afterwards. Your teenager needs adults to supply her with information! If she won't listen to you, she may be receptive to a teacher or someone a few years older that your daughter considers hip.

Many parents fear that if their child is exposed to information about drugs and alcohol in a teen issue's class or learns about birth control and sexually transmitted diseases in a sex education course, she will be more likely to act out. Yet drugs, alcohol, and sex are favorite topics of conversation among teenagers. Drugs and sex are central themes in movies and television programs. Countries that have put more effort into sex education programs have succeeded at reducing teen pregnancies and disease. While most American youth think that there is nothing wrong with having premarital sex, recipients of comprehensive sex education programs are less likely to endorse it. Via teacher-led classroom discussions, young people are helped to ponder the physical, emotional, and moral risks.

QUESTION?

**Isn't it normal for teens to drink occasionally?**
If your child insists that *all* teenagers drink and smoke pot, he is so enmeshed with peers that are using that he doesn't realize there's another world. It's best to assume that your child drinks, too, quite possibly to the point of needing treatment.

## Thoughts Versus Actions

By age thirteen, your child's thinking should have become much deeper and more complex than during elementary school. If he's like most teenagers, he no longer expects everyone to mean exactly what they say and say what they mean. He doesn't accept everything that people say and doesn't believe everything he reads. He can use his own mind to weigh and evaluate information, separate facts from opinions, and draw his own conclusions. Dealing with an intellectual equal can make conversations more interesting and enjoyable. However, for your teen to enjoy talking to you, you must acknowledge his right to his opinions even when you disagree with them.

Because teens can think abstractly, their sense of humor broadens beyond the puns and knock-knock jokes that delighted them in elementary school. They can appreciate subtle turns of phrase and find humor in statements and stories that have meanings on several levels. They can mentally develop and analyze hypotheses instead of having to struggle through problems with a trial-and-error approach. Hence, they can work through abstract algebra and geometry problems. Just as toddlers experience a heady surge when they discover they can use their own legs to explore the house's nooks and crannies, teens discover they can use their own minds to explore the ideas and experiences of the larger world.

And like toddlers, they may end up poking about in areas their parents consider too dangerous. When discussing touchy subjects, remember that it is not wrong for your teen to *want* to have sex, to be *tempted* to try drugs, to *think* that the drinking age should be lowered to sixteen, to *talk* about hitchhiking to Florida during spring break. It's only a problem when he *does* these things.

Expect to have lots of clashes with your teen if you try to control your child's thoughts. Teens have minds of their own and want to use them. You may be older and wiser, but the world needs new ideas, too. Don't criticize your teen for having opinions that differ from yours. Being an independent thinker will help her resist peer pressure.

As teens' thinking matures, they are able to consider different ideas and draw their own conclusions. As they contemplate other peoples' beliefs, they learn to consider what others tell them instead of automatically accepting whatever anyone says. Their tendency to question every pearl of parental wisdom is important, if sometimes trying.

Teenagers' expanded intellect enables them to comprehend that there are few absolutes in life and many shades of gray. In fifth grade, your child was probably convinced that sex before marriage translates to disease and a baby. Most elementary school students believe that drinking and driving guarantee a car accident, cigarette smoking inevitably leads to cancer, and a puff of marijuana means a life of addiction and crime. Not realizing it was their own black-and-white thinking that led them to these conclusions, many teenagers feel that their parents exaggerated the dangers and write off adults as credible sources of information. Parents who trusted that their upright child would never stray sometimes worry that he is out of control. Remember that questioning, pondering, and talking are different than acting.

Accuse your teen of being an out-of-control troublemaker when he's not, and he may decide to enact the role you've given him. On the other hand, to close your eyes to your teen's out-of-control behavior is to ignore what could well be desperate pleas for limits and consequences that will help him control himself. Defend him when he's done something terribly wrong and he'll lose respect for you for being so easy to manipulate and unable to face what's really going on. Try to tighten up limits, enforce consequences, and impose punishments, and your teen may rebel. It's not easy being a parent. Deciding how to respond is difficult, and there are no guarantees that you can help your teen. But before calling in the professionals, there are some other things to try.

Because you were on the wild side during adolescence doesn't mean your teen is. You are two different people! You can't help your teen find her path if you've already made up your mind that she's trudging doggedly down the wrong one. Help her live up to your expectations, not down to them!

## Responding to Teen Wildness

If you are like most parents, memories of your own teenaged years are probably very vivid. If so, you undoubtedly have a feel for the temptations your child will likely face and the peer pressure he will experience. While a bit of wildness during the teen years may be distressing, some experimentation is par for the course. Your teen isn't necessarily headed for a lifetime of trouble because he makes some mistakes. What matters most is that he learns from them.

### Talking It Out

How do you respond if you discover that your child has been drinking, using drugs, having sex, looking at pornography, hanging out with a gang, or doing something illegal? None of the options may seem very appealing:

- **Say, "Kids will be kids" and look the other way.** By responding this way, you are tacitly condoning dangerous behavior. Worse, you may ignore the fact that your child has a serious problem.

- **Say, "I disapprove."** In this way, you communicate your values and let your child know where you stand. If your approval matters to your teen, he may change his behavior. Unfortunately, the other possibility is that instead of changing, he will work harder to conceal his activities from you so you won't be unhappy. Once your teen knows where you stand, continuing to respond to misbehavior with anger and disapproval may just be spinning your wheels.

- **Say, "If you're going to do that, do it at home."** Many parents hope that by supervising they can keep their teen safe. Unfortunately, they are suggesting that the behavior in question is acceptable under controlled circumstances. Depending on the activity, you are at risk for being charged with contributing to the delinquency of a minor. Whether or not you like the laws, aiding and abetting underage drinking and drug use are crimes. Letting your child share his bed with his girlfriend enables him to indulge in sex without having to assume any responsibility for his partner.

- **Say, "Tell me about what happened."** This opens the way to a discussion so you can begin collecting information. Before deciding how to react, ask the critical question, "How did you feel about what happened?" You may not need to do anything if you are comfortable with how your teen answers. If he feels badly about having violated his own moral standards or about having placed himself in harm's way, ask, "If the same situation comes up again, would you do anything differently?" You may not need to take further action if your teen learned from his experience and doesn't seem likely to repeat it.

Things get tricky when your child admits to having participated in an illegal or dangerous activity and clearly enjoyed it. You can let him know that's exactly why forbidden activities can be such a problem: They can be so much fun that people forget about the danger. Admit your fears: "I tremble to think that somebody could have slipped a date rape drug into your drink, that you could have had a bad trip when you took LSD, that you could have ended up in jail if you had been caught spray painting graffiti around town," and so on. Compliment your child on anything she did that was positive, "I'm glad you had a designated driver, didn't hang out in the bedroom with a guy, didn't mix drugs and alcohol." Conclude the conversation with, "I'm glad that we can talk about these things. So many kids can't talk to their parents." Hopefully, you planted the seeds of doubt that will motivate your child to take better care of herself and avoid dangerous activities in the future.

To help your teen become autonomous, you need to allow him to express his own thoughts and feelings while continuing to place kind, consistent limits on his behavior. That means the next time he wants to go to a party, you may need to just say no. If he heads out without your permission, tell him the truth: He doesn't seem able to take care of himself and won't let you take care of him, either. Tell him you are very afraid for him. Then, try to help him learn by other people's bad experiences.

## When Logic Fails

Teenagers' tendency to disregard parental warnings is partly because they feel invincible during this stage of youthful vigor. In addition, most teenagers' exposure to life's harsher realities comes from television, where every hour-long show has a happy ending. Talks and lectures may fail to convince teenagers to buckle their seat belt, observe the speed limit, and say no to cigarettes, alcohol, drugs, and sex. Fortunately, appeals to emotion can succeed and leave an enduring impression even when logic fails to penetrate.

Arrange for your child to meet some real-life victims so he can learn about the repercussions of other people's unfortunate decisions. Visit an open Alcoholic's Anonymous meeting. Take a field trip to the hospital emergency room or physical rehabilitation center and ask a nurse, doctor, or physical therapist to describe open head injuries and mention how wearing helmets can help prevent them.

## Vicarious Learning Experiences

Many teens aren't moved by statistical dangers—they are sure they can beat the odds. Meeting someone who has become a statistic, on the other hand, can leave a lasting impression. Instead of family outings to the zoo or museum, drive through a red-light district or ghetto where the havoc wrought by drugs is readily apparent.

Offer to help your child's health or P.E. teacher put together a program of speakers to address your child's class. Most teachers would appreciate help organizing some presentations. Contact first responders to accident scenes, such as police officers, emergency medical technicians and physicians, and fire fighters. Professionals in public health and safety, including nurses, social workers, and drug and alcohol counselors, can give great talks. If the speakers will bring a real criminal, accident victim, or addict for show-and-tell, that is definitely better! Personal testimonials tend to be especially moving. Lots of community organizations and governmental agencies have designated speakers or will gladly choose someone to address a high school class. Check the yellow pages to find appropriate organizations:

- Alcoholic's Anonymous
- Narcotic's Anonymous
- Smoker's Anonymous
- Local or state police
- Probation or parole officer
- Hospital cancer support group
- Mothers Against Drunk Driving
- Emergency room nurse or doctor
- Physical therapist
- Battered women's shelter social worker
- Rape crisis center advocate
- Planned Parenthood nurse
- Drug and alcohol rehabilitation center social worker
- Hospital emergency room nurse or doctor
- Emergency medical technician (ambulance driver)

- Victim's advocate from the District Attorney's office
- Social worker for an ex-offender's program

Social workers from the Children, Youth, and Family Services Department give powerful talks about America's youngest victims: Fetal Alcohol Syndrome and crack babies. Pregnant teens may not know that their babies ingest drugs and alcohol along with the mother. The state can take newborns who test positive for drugs or alcohol and place them in foster care.

Do not condone your teenager's substance use. Do not condemn your child for using drugs. Keep the lines of communication open as you share your fears, give advice, and gently nudge your child to make safe decisions. Millions of college students make the wrong ones because their parents aren't there to "just say no" to them.

## Spiritual Solutions

Active religious involvements protect teenagers from a wide range of adolescent dangers. Unfortunately, teenagers' ability to weigh and ponder thoughts and ideas typically causes them to reconsider many of the teachings of their church or synagogue. Instead of wondering "what"—as in "What does God look like?" or "What happens to people after they die?"—they can consider the "what ifs." They wonder, "What if there is no God?" "What if there isn't an after-life?" Getting answers to the questions people have asked across the globe and throughout the millennia can pave the way to a deeper understanding of religious and spiritual matters. If you can't answer your child's questions about religion and spiritual matters or find conversations with a doubting Thomas upsetting, bring in a professional. Religious leaders have lots of experience addressing these issues with skeptics. Schedule an appointment for your teen to consult with a clergy member.

## Parents in Charge!

As the parent of a teenager, the biggest mistake you can make is thinking that you can control your child. The fact is, the only way to do that is to get a judge to declare him incorrigible and commit him to a locked detention center. Some desperate parents do just that. That very extreme solution may keep your teen from harm in the short run but puts him at greater risk for more serious problems down the road. Many teens thrive in military or boarding school, and clearly benefit from being in such a highly structured, intensely supervised environment, but there are no guarantees. Some teens manage to stir up enough trouble to get themselves expelled.

All other forms of discipline require your teen's consent, however grudging, and his cooperation, however half-hearted. That is why maintaining a positive relationship with your teen is so critical. Without it, you may find that when you tell your child not to leave the house, he walks out the door anyway and doesn't bother to look back. When you insist that he help with the dishes, he may simply refuse and not even consider an argument worth the trouble. Threaten to throw him out of the house if he doesn't show some respect and follow some minimal household rules, and he may take to the streets while you remain liable for his actions. You'll be in a worse fix than you are now: having all of the responsibility and no control. As long as he is living at home, you may have all of the responsibility and no control, but at least you might be able to have an influence.

## Teen Rebels

Eventually, teenagers stop being afraid of their parents. That day may not come until children are living on their own, but when it arrives, many show little regard for their safety. Amazing numbers of teens who are on their own for the first time don't take care of themselves in very basic ways. They don't get enough sleep, eat properly, drive safely, and aren't responsible about work and school. Strong-arm methods to control teens that work by making them afraid of what will happen if their parents find out can postpone problems until teens are on their own but don't solve anything. Teens need to fear what they would be doing to themselves by failing to respect and care for themselves.

When teens are rebelling, they are not just doing what they want or doing what feels best to them at the moment. Rather, they are in a covert struggle with their parents. Rebellious teens consider what their parents would want them to do and then proceed to do the opposite. This can happen long after children have moved away from home. They continue the battles in their minds. Some young people are aware of what they are doing. Many don't realize until later what caused them to violate their own values and jeopardize their health and welfare.

| Issue | What Rebellious Teens Say Now . . . | What Rebellious Teens Later Realize . . . |
|---|---|---|
| Drugs and alcohol | "Partying is a blast!" | "I was trying to make the pain go away." |
| Sex | "Everybody's doing it." | "If my parents said 'don't,' I did." |
| Dangerous/risky behavior | "It's a rush." | "I was on self-destruct and didn't care what happened to me." |
| School failure | "School's boring; the stuff they teach is worthless." | "I flunked/dropped out to hurt my parents." |
| Marriage | "This is true love." | "I was desperate for a way out of the house." |
| Pregnancy | "I want a baby." | "I wanted someone to love who would love me back." |

Fortunately, even when children pretend not to care what their parents think, most very much want their approval. Teenagers are as distressed by conflict as their parents and are willing to do much more than most adults imagine to get along with them, or at least get their attention. Parenting experts continue to emphasize the importance of maintaining a good relationship with your child. If your child will try to please you or can realize that she is hurting herself, half the battle is won.

## Back on Track

Cassandra didn't much enjoy having sex with a boy she hardly knew. He made up a bunch of stories about what they had done and told the world. Cassandra felt humiliated. Guys started propositioning her left and right. She soon found herself on a sexual merry-go-round and couldn't seem to get off of it. Her parents found out and made her feel "like scum," to use Cassandra's words. She experimented with drugs, and although she sometimes had fun she mostly felt desperate, as though her life was out of control. Drinking helped ease her guilt about sleeping around. Cassandra credits her teen issues class with having saved her. There she learned that every day is a new beginning. Her parents might not forgive her but she could forgive herself. Even if some guys didn't respect her for saying no, by saying no she could respect herself.

Cassandra also learned that there are two kinds of virginity. Most people only talked about the physical kind, but her teacher said there was something called psychological virginity, too, which was a state of mind. It meant realizing that whether or not you had consented to let someone violate your body, it was still sacred because it housed your spirit. You could reclaim them both whenever you wanted. Cassandra decided to do just that! The very first time she said no to a guy, he acted disgusted and asked, "What are you, a virgin or something?" She didn't mean to insult him, but she couldn't help herself. She was so delighted, she laughed.

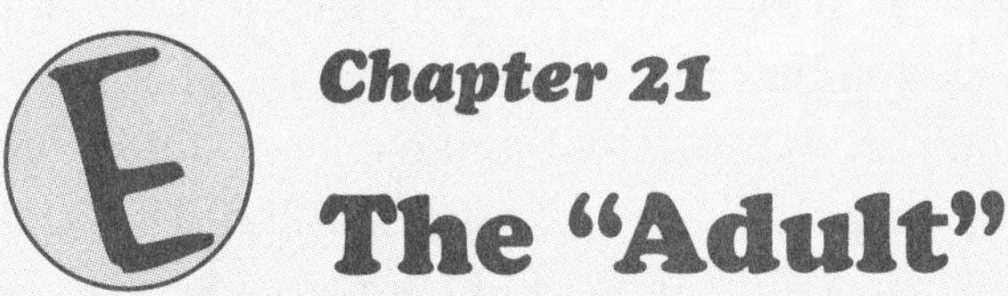

## Chapter 21

# The "Adult"

If your teenager has a baby, gets married, drops out of high school, or moves away from home prematurely, financial problems are likely to necessitate a return to the family nest at some point. Even college graduates may need to return to save on rent until they can accumulate enough cash for an apartment. Dealing with an adult child can be a challenge whether he lives under your roof, visits during college vacations, or keeps his distance except for an occasional phone call.

## Home for the Holidays

Lucas had been so busy during his senior year of high school, his parents didn't expect their lives to change much after he moved out of the house. But a week after they helped him move into his college dorm, they realized how much their lives had revolved around their son. Lucas's younger sister missed her big brother so much that she took to marking off the days on the calendar until he arrived home for Thanksgiving vacation. Although the family members talked and e-mailed one another regularly, the contacts left Lucas's parents feeling unsatisfied. They didn't know the new players in their son's life and could barely follow his conversations, which were filled with unfamiliar abbreviations and slang. Moreover, Lucas was so self-involved, he wasn't interested in hearing news from home. Too often, they ended up feeling that the only reason he called or e-mailed was to ask for money.

You can encourage a homesick college student to continue with school by inviting her home for a weekend visit. Enforce rules and assign chores so she remembers the price of dependency. Finding that her friends have moved on or away can free your child to focus on the future instead of clinging to the past.

## Neglected Parents

Lucas's family looked forward to spending some quality time with their college boy. But when he arrived home, he barely acknowledged his sister, immediately hit his parents up for money, and took off to visit his friends who were also home from college for Thanksgiving. The next morning Lucas announced plans to have Thanksgiving dinner with his girlfriend's family.

His dad had to lay down the law before Lucas grudgingly agreed to eat at home. That turned out to be a mixed blessing.

During Thanksgiving dinner, Lucas pontificated about the toxic chemicals lurking in the turkey his mother had prepared—apparently enlightened individuals only bought free-range poultry. Although Lucas ate second helpings of everything, he criticized the side dishes his mother had cooked especially for him. He claimed that the supermarkets were destroying traditional cultures by encouraging the peasants to grow cash crops. Lucas's dad enjoyed political talks and was happy to discuss the globalization problem. But since Lucas was such an expert, all his father could do was contain his irritation while Lucas delivered a long-winded political science lecture.

FACT

A central challenge for adolescents is to establish a personal identity, but research suggests that few teenagers get very far. At age twenty-one, only 40 percent know what they want to do with their lives—or whom they want to spend them with. The median age for first marriages has crept up to twenty-five for women and twenty-seven for men according to research reported in Wayne Weiten's *Psychology: Themes and Variations*.

A few hours before the end of a most unsatisfying visit, Lucas put his arm around his mother and said, "You're the best mom in the world." Tears of relief sprang to her eyes, but they turned into tears of frustration when Lucas added, "I told my girlfriend I'd stop over before I leave town, and I won't be back until late. Could you do my laundry while I'm out? It's such a hassle using the machines at the dorm."

## Worldly-Wise Teens

Not all older teenagers are inconsiderate of their families and work overtime to impress their parents, but these behaviors are common and understandable. If young adults have been on their own for a time, they have had many new experiences and learned a tremendous amount in a very short period. Whether living in apartments near home or in far-off student dormitories, they are exposed to diverse opinions and lifestyles. Conversing with roommates, colleagues, and classmates broadens their perspective and causes them to question much of what their parents taught them. This is especially true for college students, who are exposed to new ideas and information via their textbooks and professors while learning about other people's habits and lifestyles in crowded dormitories. It's not surprising that young people are eager to share what they have learned with their parents. It's understandable, too, that teenagers are so focused on themselves as they try to process their many new experiences that they often do more talking than listening.

Trying to convince young know-it-alls to listen or admit that they are wrong isn't likely to get very far. A better strategy is to let them show off how grown up they are while demonstrating by your words and deeds that you accept them as adults. When they truly feel grown up, they may turn into delightful human beings.

The somewhat pompous attitude that many older teenagers display as they talk to their parents doesn't usually extend to other adults. That alone suggests that these children have another agenda besides wanting to share what they have learned with their parents. In fact, many young people work hard to impress their parents by trying to sound like experts on subjects they know little or nothing about. The need to impress reflects their personal insecurity. By showing off, they hope to mask how young and vulnerable they feel while trying to convince themselves that they are grown up enough to handle being independent.

Research indicates that after children leave home, conflicts between parents and children typically decrease and they develop warmer relationships. When children continue to live at home, parent/child discord and resentment tend to increase. Struggling to make it on their own helps teenagers appreciate their parents. Sometimes absence really does make the heart grow fonder!

Adjusting to independence is not easy. Newly liberated teenagers typically suffer bouts of homesickness, long for the security of home and family, and feel a bit lost without their parents' rules and structure. The minor family irritations and conflicts children couldn't wait to escape seem insignificant once they have struggled to manage their own finances, run their own households, and live outside the circle of their parents' protection and love.

FACT

Like the toddler who insists he can put on his own socks and staunchly denies his need for help, many older teenagers fight their feelings of helplessness and wish to remain dependent to keep themselves moving forward with their lives. They pretend more confidence than they feel.

The urge to return home can be intense once young people discover the realities of living independently. There is no reason for them to struggle with adult challenges out in the big, scary world when they could toss in the towel and return to their parents' care—unless, of course, their parents know virtually nothing about anything, do everything wrong, and have nothing (but money) to offer. Perceiving their parents that way strengthens children's resolve to move forward with their own lives and reassures them that if their poor parents managed to survive, they can do the same.

## Boomerang Kids

Parental divorce prompts many boys to drop out of high school and set out on their own at an early age, while a family move during adolescence often causes girls to leave home prematurely, according to research reported in *Leaving Home: Understanding the Transition to Adulthood* by Julia Graber and Judith Dubas, Editors. Such early departures virtually ensure that children will return home for several months or years. That's because they typically end up in low paying hourly-wage jobs and cannot survive financially. The first time they are laid off, miss work due to illness or unreliable transportation, or have an unexpected expense, they cannot pay their rent and are forced to turn to their parents for support.

Pregnancy interferes with many girls' ability to work, and the expense of a baby may force them back home. Even after college graduation, many students must live at home until they can accumulate enough cash for a car and an apartment. At age twenty-three, 40 percent of children were still living at home in 2002. Lots of parents find themselves arguing about loud music and messy bedrooms long after the teenaged years.

Communicate your expectations before your adult child moves in. Even if you try to respect her boundaries and treat her like a regular roommate, she may not understand the etiquette of informing you of her whereabouts and calling when she's going to be late coming home. By detailing your rules in advance, you may be able to head off problems.

Many teenagers act like responsible adults outside of the house but revert to acting like youngsters around their parents even as they insist they are all grown up. Changing the rules of any long-standing relationship is extremely difficult because patterns of interacting are well established. Don't be surprised if your adult child expects you to provide maid service, spending money, and the keys to your car like in the good old days before she left home. More than four in ten young women become pregnant at least once before they reach the age of twenty, and teen mothers and fathers often expect their parents to tend to their babies' needs and to be on-call babysitters. At the same time, these teenagers may be outraged when their parents impose rules, assign chores, and fail to honor their wishes regarding the baby. The key to getting along is open communication and flexibility on both sides. Unfortunately, teenagers may be happy to say what is on their minds but may not be very flexible. For your grandchild's sake, it may be important to accommodate your child so she'll continue to live at home. Teenagers are often less responsive and patient with their offspring than is required for their babies' well-being. As long as your grandchild lives with you, you can provide much needed support and hopefully demonstrate the art of good parenting.

## Tough Love

Members of some American minority groups are more enthusiastic about having adult children and grandchildren live at home indefinitely than is typical for Anglo families. Traditional Hispanic and Native American parents may consider themselves fortunate because their fifty-year-old never married and still resides with them. Many African-American parents are also content to have their grown children at home with them and view raising their grandchildren as a privilege. Teenagers raised in these traditional families may be more accepting of parental authority and are accustomed to being involved in the upkeep of the household. As young adults, they may feel that the family home is as much theirs as their parents' and be more committed to participating in family life.

QUESTION?

**My teenager won't work, go to school, or help with housework. What can I do?**
Charging a small amount of rent can motivate your child to get a job, teach him responsibility, and build confidence in his ability to manage his personal affairs.

Anglo parents, on the other hand, may feel unhappy when their eighteen-year-old doesn't show signs of moving toward independence. They may feel that her continued presence at home is an imposition and worry that something is wrong. The situation is ripe for conflict because most Anglo children are taught to value independence early on. Accordingly, they may view living at home as a personal failure, resent having to contribute to the upkeep of their parents' house, and resist rules and limits that remind them of their dependent status. "As long as you're under my roof, I make the rules," many Anglo parents say, thereby reminding their children that they are guests rather than full-fledged family members.

One recommended tough-love parenting strategy is to charge your adult child a small amount of rent and follow-through with an eviction if she doesn't pay on time as you would any other tenant. You can soften the blow by letting her know that you will put the rent money into savings and return it when there is enough for a down payment on a car or apartment. Another strategy is to insist that your child pay for her room and board by honoring your wishes that she further her education so that she can eventually get a good job. Accordingly, make living at home contingent on attending school. Although many parents fear that their child will refuse to cooperate and end up on the street, it rarely works out that way unless drugs are involved. Resentful children may avoid paying rent by staying at a friend's house for a few days or weeks before deciding that the price to live at home isn't so exorbitant after all. Although some teenagers complain bitterly about having to pay rent or attend school, many later thank their parents for holding firm.

Your young adult may seem to have it made when he watches television all night, sleeps all day, and has you waiting on him hand and foot. However, children in this situation are unhappy and feel paralyzed. If your child won't go to school or get a job, make his room and board contingent on going for counseling.

## Education for Independence

The best way for your adult child to achieve independence is to get an education. Lots of self-taught computer wizards have all the skills they need to handle complex high-tech work, and self-taught automobile mechanics may be as qualified to do automobile repair as trained professionals. Nevertheless, without a degree or certificate, finding a decent job is virtually impossible. Entry-level workers with college degrees make about 80 percent more than those with only a high school diploma. They are more likely to land good positions even if their major is completely unrelated to the actual work. The bias toward hiring and promoting employees with college diplomas or technical certificates may not be logical but is nevertheless very real. To encourage your teenager to continue her education, provide as much moral and financial support as you can. People will come and go from your child's life, money will be made and lost, but an education once acquired is hers forever. A degree or certificate *in anything* will open doors for the rest of her life.

## Earning a GED

If your child dropped out of high school before graduating, the first step to employability is to obtain a General Education Diploma (GED). Many teenagers view this high school equivalency diploma as a lesser accomplishment than graduating from high school, but employers and college admissions departments regard the GED to be the same. In fact, for the purposes of employment (hiring, salary, and promotion) and college (admission and financial aid), 95 percent of employers and institutions of higher learning don't differentiate between a GED and a traditional high school diploma. They recognize that preparing for a seven-hour test takes considerable motivation and accept passing the GED test as proof of having mastered the core high school subjects: reading, writing, language arts, social studies, mathematics, and science. The 860,000 students who pass the GED test each year outperform more than 40 percent of high school seniors academically, so the GED is nothing to sneer at!

FACT

**If your high school dropout takes and passes some community college courses, he can forever put a checkmark in the box that says "some college" on employment applications. Having gone to college despite not having finished high school will strike many employers as especially impressive.**

GED classes and tests are offered through community colleges, libraries, and local literacy programs across the country and around the world. GED classes are also offered on a public television program called The GED Connection. Working students can buy the textbooks, videotape the lectures, and study at their convenience. For help locating GED classes and test sites, call (800) 62-MY-GED or see *www.acenet.edu*. Be sure to request brochures with practice tests and study tip lists, or have your child view the information online.

## Earning a Diploma or Certificate

Many parents urge their teenager to attend college or a post-secondary training program immediately after high school. Getting teenagers to enroll is often a battle. Many insist they would be better served by taking some time off from school, insisting that they will be more motivated once they've sorted out what they want to study and have a career goal. Many college instructors agree, noting that older students are usually more motivated to learn and conscientious about their studies.

The Job Corps is a good alternative for many young adults who lack job skills and training. Participants typically live in a dorm and receive a small stipend while learning a trade. Check with your state's Department of Labor to learn about government work/study opportunities and apprenticeship programs sponsored by private businesses.

A research study on post-secondary students published in 1998 concluded that students were more likely to earn an advanced diploma if they enrolled in an educational program immediately after high school, attended full time, and remained continuously enrolled instead of taking a semester off (visit *http://nces.ed.gov* for more information). This study tracked the progress of 9,000 students from more than 800 institutions of higher learning for half a decade. Over the course of the five years of the study, the researcher uncovered some interesting facts:

- 58 percent of the students received financial aid.
- Recipients of financial aid were more likely to finish their degree programs.
- 92 percent of students held a job at some time while enrolled.
- Working less than twenty hours a week did not lower the rate of degree completion.
- Half of the students completed a degree or certificate in the five-year period.
- 37 percent dropped out of school without completing a degree within five years.

- 13 percent remained enrolled after five years and had not yet completed a degree.
- 29 percent of students transferred schools at some point during their studies.
- Transferring schools didn't interfere with completing a degree program.

You can't force your child to enroll or stay in school, but since young people give much more weight to parents' advice than most realize, it is advisable to take a firm stance. Let your child know that you consider post-secondary education critical for his current and future well-being. Provide as much financial help as you can and discourage your student from working more than twenty hours per week. Don't discourage a college student from switching schools but do urge him to settle on what he wants to study. A study reported by *www.careeradvantage101.com* found that the biggest risk factor for dropping out is failing to declare a major.

## A New Relationship

Lucas's semester break visit home was not unlike his Thanksgiving vacation. He spent most of the time with his friends, treated his parents as if they knew nothing, didn't help around the house, and was constantly in need of money. After he returned to school, they had a number of worrisome conversations with their son. First, Lucas was sure he was flunking Spanish, which would jeopardize his scholarship. Because he switched majors twice, he would require an extra semester to graduate. Then he decided he couldn't stand his roommate and would rather drop out than spend another week in the same dorm room. His typical pattern was to call home with a desperate problem, reject his parents' advice, and sound surprised when they called a few days later to check on him. They finally realized he called because he needed a shoulder to cry on, things were never as bad as they sounded, and no news meant he was doing well.

Lucas spent the entire summer at home after his freshman year. The job he lined up fell through, and instead of finding another one he stayed out until all hours of the night with his friends, slept all day, and wouldn't lift a finger to help around the house. However, his parents noted a definite change shortly before his twentieth birthday. Lucas appeared more self-assured and confident, seemed to appreciate their advice, called home just to talk, and not only asked how they were doing but seemed genuinely interested. The second summer vacation from college went much better than the first. Lucas and his old high school buddies had drifted apart, and when he wasn't at work he helped his dad renovate the house. His mother knew the teenaged years were over when she overheard Lucas talking to his younger sister. "I know Mom and Dad can seem hopelessly old-fashioned, and some of their rules can seem unfair," he told her. "But someday you'll look back and realize they only want what is best for you. Believe me, when that day comes, you'll be grateful."

Many teenagers remain close to their parents throughout their young adult years, but many need to pull away until they are confident of their ability to make it on their own. At that point they are likely to return to the family fold and strive to develop a real friendship with their parents.

All the doubt and insecurity of the last seven years was wiped away in an instant. Lucas's parents agreed that they had made plenty of mistakes during their son's teenaged years. But since they now got along well and viewed him as such a fine young man, they had obviously done many things right.

*Appendix A*

# Resources for Parents

Arnett, Jeffrey Jensen. "Emerging Adulthood: A Theory of Development from the Late Teens Through the Twenties." American Psychologist (Vol. 55 (5) May 2000, pp. 469–480).

Bach, George. *The Intimate Enemy: How to Fight Fair in Love and Marriage* (William Morrow, 1968). All the same do's and don'ts for handling arguments with a spouse can do wonders for reducing parent/child conflict. This classic remains the best book on the subject of how to solve problems by turning arguments into constructive disagreements.

Ben-Zur, Hasida. "Happy adolescents: The link between subjective well-being, internal resources, and parental factors." *Journal of Youth and Adolescence*, April 2003 v32 i2.

Biddulph, Steve. *Secrets of Happy Children.* (Marlowe & Company, 2003). Learn about "softlove," "firmlove," and how to develop a more flexible parenting style.

Duke, Patty. *A Brilliant Madness: Living with Manic Depressive Illness.* (Bantam Books, 1993). This famous actress describes her personal battle with mental illness and how she was able to get her life on track after a belated diagnosis.

Elkind, David. *The Hurried Child: Growing Up Too Fast Too Soon.* (Addison-Wesley Publishing Company, Inc., 1988). This classic describes how family and societal pressures and expectations blur the lines between children and adults and induce teens to try to grow up before they are ready.

Free Spirit Publishing, Minneapolis, MN. 866-703-7322, *www.freespirit.com.* Good books make great teen gifts; good authors make great teen mentors. This company has tons of each. After checking out the titles on everything from stress relief to making A's in school, you might want to glance through their titles for parents.

Gibran, Kahlil. *The Prophet.* (Knopf, 1923). This inspirational poetry is profound yet easy to read. Parents and teens alike can enjoy pondering the wisdom and beauty of this classic literary masterpiece.

Jamison, Kay Redfield. *Touched with Fire: Manic Depressive Illness and the Artistic Temperament.* (Touchstone Books, 1996). The author describes the suffering and genius of brilliant manic-depressives. Her research points to a hereditary component of a mental disorder that has afflicted many of the world's greatest geniuses.

Jones, Stanton L. and Brenna B. *How and When to Tell Your Kids About Sex: A Lifelong Approach to Shaping Your Child's Sexual Character.* (Navpress, 1993). While acknowledging that most kids do have sex, the authors suggest ways to discourage premature sexual involvements.

Kaplan, Louise J. *Adolescence: The Farewell to Childhood.* (Touchstone Books, 1995). Designed for a sophisticated audience, this book approaches adolescence from a psychoanalytic perspective. Nevertheless, many of her astute observations elucidate the conflicts of this stressful life stage.

Maine, Margo. *Father Hunger: Fathers, Daughters and Food.* (Gurze Books, 1991). This book discusses girls' father hunger, that is, their need to have a loving, involved father in order to develop a healthy self-concept.

McDowell, Josh. *How to Help Your Child Say "No" to Sexual Pressure.* (Word Publishing, 1987). Readers are taught to combine Christian principals with basic psychology to help to strengthen children to withstand sexual pressure.

Nelsen, Jane and Lott, Lynn. *Positive Discipline for Teenagers: Empowering Your Teen and Yourself Through Kind and Firm Parenting.* (Prima Publishing, 2000). How to set limits with teens who just say "no" to your every rule or say "yes" to your face and proceed to do as they please? This book gives readers the magic keys to garnering teen cooperation—one conversation at a time.

Opperman, Jeff. "The Secret Killer of Parent-Child Relationships." *Counseling Today.* (April 2003). This article alerts mental health professionals to Parent Alienation Syndrome, which damages children by forcing them to side with one parent against the other in a divorce.

Phelan, Thomas W. *All About Attention Deficit Disorder: Symptoms, Diagnosis and Treatment: Children and Adults.* (Child Management Incorporated, 2000). Despite the emphasis on medication, the suggestions for helping ADD and ADHD teens to improve their behavior are excellent.

Phelan, Thomas W. *Surviving Your Adolescents: How to Manage and Let Go of Your 13–18 Year Olds.* (Child Management, Inc. 1998). This parenting guide provides a wealth of practical advice for dealing with this difficult life stage.

Riera, Michael. *Uncommon Sense for Parents with Teenagers.* (Celestial Arts, 1995). This author tackles all of the hard questions, from whether to let a slacker teen get a driver's license to how to comfort a grief-stricken child after a divorce.

Riera, Michael. *Staying Connected to Your Teenager: How to Keep Them Talking to You And How to Hear What They're Really Saying.* (Perseus Publishing, 2003). Your child may greet your pleasantries with surliness and sarcasm, but don't give up hope of having a decent conversation. This author shows you how.

Snyderman, Nancy L. and Streep, Peg. *Girl in the Mirror.* (Hyperion, 2002). Myths about teenagers abound, and these authors maintain that teen girls don't need to separate emotionally from their mothers as many experts claim. This book is full of facts about teen girls and suggests ways that mothers can shore up their relationships with their daughters.

Sonna, Linda. *The Homework Solution: Getting Kids to Do Their Homework.* (Williamson Publishing, 1990). You can motivate even the most resistant student to bring his books home and actually do his homework. The solution is to teach study skills and set up a study hall. This book teaches parents how to motivate their child to buckle down.

Sonna, Linda. *The Homework Plan: A Parent's Guide to Helping Kids Excel in School.* (Berkley Publishing Group, 1994). Learn to read between the whines to diagnose your child's academic problems, apply a quick fix, or follow the advice for affecting a real cure for especially tough cases.

Sonna, Linda. *The Everything® Tween Book: A Parent's Guide to Surviving the Turbulent Preteen Years.* (Adams Media, 2003). By the time your child is a teenager, her basic values and attitudes are already formed. Before your next child enters the teen scene, lay the kind of solid foundation to help carry her through.

Taffel, Ron. *The Second Family.* (St. Martin's Press, 2001). Pop culture is now teens' second family, and many adolescents are more loyal to it than to their parents. Learn how to enter Planet Teen and meet the stranger who lives in your house.

White, Emily. *Fast Girls: Teenage Tribes and the Myth of the Slut.* (Scribner, 2002). Junior high and high school can be brutal for girls who have the misfortune to be more physically developed than their peers. This book explores the plight of some young females who become the object of their peers' obsessive scorn.

Wiseman, Rosalind. *Queen Bees Wannabes: Helping Your Daughter Survive Cliques, Gossip, Boyfriends, and Other Realities of Adolescence.* (Crown Publishers, 2002). The social world at school is brutal enough to destroy the confidence of even very self-possessed girls. Learn how to minimize the effects on your daughter.

Wolf, Anthony E. *Get Out of My Life: But First Could You Drive Me and Cheryl to the Mall?* (Noonday Press, 1991). This author provides common sense advice for dealing with what he calls "the new teenager," that is, a youth who is often as angry and uncooperative as a toddler.

*Appendix B*

# Resources for Teens

Canfield, Jack, Hansen, Mark, and Kirberger, Kimberly (editors). Chicken Soup for the Teen Soul. (Health Communications, 2001). A gift book of short essays designed to cheer and inspire teenagers.

Covey, Sean. *The 7 Habits of Highly Effective Teens.* (Simon & Schuster, 1998). Your teenager hates to read and would never pick up a book unless forced. Buy this one anyway and put it in his room. Sooner or later he'll thumb through it, study a cartoon, or read a quote, and realize that a book can teach him what he most wants to learn: how to do life.

Daldry, Jeremy. *The Teenage Guy's Survival Guide: The Real Deal on Girls, Growing Up, and Other Guy Stuff.* (Little Brown & Co., 1999). Everything your son needs to know, from how to ask a girl out to how to cope with criticism, is in this simple, engaging book.

Desetta, Al and Wolin, Sybil (editors). *The Struggle to Be Strong: True Stories by Teens about Overcoming Tough Times.* (Free Spirit Publishing, 2000). These real-life stories may make more of an impression than all your warnings about risky choices and dangerous pursuits. Reading about teenagers who strayed and straightened out can inspire your child to do the same.

Galbraith, Judy and Delisle, Jim. *The Gifted Kids' Survival Guide: A Teen Handbook.* (Free Spirit Publishing, 1996). It's not easy being different, but your gifted teenager can come to appreciate his talents. This book will show him how.

Huegel, Kelly. *GLBTQ: The Survival Guide for Queer & Questioning Teens.* (Free Spirit Publishing, 2003). The straight scoop for teenagers who are questioning their sexual orientation or have decided they are homosexual.

Mayall, Beth. *Get Over It!* (Scholastic, Inc., 2000). Written in language teens can relate to, this book, filled with sage advice, shows them how to handle the heartbreaks of bad hair days, big time breakups, mind-boggling betrayals, and everything else. The style is so upbeat and engaging, some teenagers will laugh even before their tears are dry.

Schneider, Meg. *Help! My Teacher Hates Me.* (Workman Publishing, 1994). This one small book contains everything you want to tell your child about coping with the teacher he thinks is picking on him, the kids who reject him, and the coach who keeps him benched during games. If you can only buy one book for your teenager, this is it!

Zager, Karen and Rubenstein, Alice. *The Inside Story on Teen Girls: Experts Answer Teens' Questions AND Experts Answer Parents' Questions.* (American Psychological Association, 2002). Written in question and answer format, one half addresses the concerns of parents, the other half is for teens. If your teen isn't turning to you for advice about problems, this book will tell her what you'd want her to hear.

*Appendix C*

# Getting Teens to Do Chores in Seven Easy Steps

In households across the country, conflicts over messy bedrooms and chores erode parent/teen relationships and sour family life. Here is a typical parental complaint:

*I have to nag and ground my teenager to get him to clean his room, or to help me with the dishes and other chores. I work, and I really need him to do more. How can I motivate him?*

Getting your teen to handle chores responsibly involves some effort on your part. However, you will be well compensated for the time and energy you invest once your child does them without being nagged. Your teen will reap even bigger benefits. In learning to manage chores, he will have made important strides toward independence.

## Step 1: Adopt a New Mindset

It is a mistake to ask your teen to "help" with chores, since that suggests that housework is your job. Your child may consider requests to do "your" work an imposition and resent being forced to do "favors." Meanwhile, having your own flesh and blood deny your request for assistance probably hurts and causes you to view him as callous and self-centered. Accordingly, when you are stressed, you may react personally to your teen's failure to complete chores as promised. When you are in a good mood, you may be inclined to overlook his lapses in hopes of maintaining family harmony. Responding inconsistently will convince your teen that your upsets stem from your mood-of-the-moment rather than from his behavior.

To achieve the correct mindset, remember that your child needs to be able to care for his personal space and possessions, pick up after himself, and participate in the upkeep of the household regardless of how he feels at the moment. These skills are required for independence. Rather than getting him to help you, your challenge—and your parental duty—is to help him grow up.

## Step 2: Communicate Clearly

Set the stage for a new beginning by telling your teen that you are concerned about her difficulty in handling chores responsibly. Explain that you are committed to helping her develop the skills she needs to function independently and get along with future roommates. Emphasize that your goal isn't just to teach her to dust, do dishes, or clean her room; it is to help her develop self-discipline. Point out that being able to follow-through with tasks she dislikes or doesn't feel like doing at the moment are crucial for job and school success. Learning to fit chores into a busy schedule will strengthen her time management skills. If you have nagged your teen about chores in the past, apologize and commit to teaching her to handle household responsibilities.

## Step 3: Create a List of Chores and Tasks

Daily chores develop self-discipline; weekly chores are more effective for teaching responsibility. Assign some of each. Take your teen's preferences into account. If she doesn't mind doing dishes but can't stand yardwork, assign the one she prefers or rotate them.

List the specific tasks for each chore on a calendar so your teen understands exactly what to do. When straightening her room, is it enough to put her dirty clothes in the laundry, or must she also clear her desk of papers and return dirty dishes to the kitchen? If her job is vacuuming, the tasks might be to give the living room and hall carpets a quick once-over each day, to vacuum along the walls and in the corners each week, and to vacuum beneath and behind the furniture once a month. Write the tasks on the calendar and note the deadlines: "before breakfast," "before watching TV after school," "immediately after dinner," "before going out with friends."

## Step 4: Teach and Supervise

If your teen has a poor track record with a particular chore, assume that it is hard for her. Even if you suspect the real issue is laziness, dedicate yourself to teaching and supervising. Use the same techniques you used to teach your toddler to wash his hands before meals years ago. Break the chore into a series of small tasks and demonstrate each one, just as you showed your toddler by helping him turn on the faucet, check the temperature, wet his hands, rub on soap, rinse, dry his hands, and straighten the towel. Later you were on hand to supervise your tot ("That's enough soap," "Don't forget to turn off the water"). Similarly, you may need to join your teen for the first few weeks to supervise while she cleans her room. Chat about other things and provide input if she gets sidetracked or appears overwhelmed. Be patient, avoid criticizing, and do what you can to keep the atmosphere cheerful and light. Gradually reduce your hands-on help and supervision.

## Step 5: Prompt and Monitor

Provide prompts as needed to help your child start on chores. Just as you prompted your toddler by saying, "It's time to eat; go wash your hands," remind the teen who is heading off to play video games to check his chore list. Just as you monitored your toddler by asking if he had washed his hands and by inspecting them, ask your teen if he did his chore and inspect his work when he finishes. Learning takes time! A decade after your toddler learned to wash his hands, you still conducted occasional spot checks, heard occasional grumbles, and sometimes had to set limits. Don't expect perfection from your teen.

## Step 6: Acknowledge Successes

If hanging up his towel after bathing is on your teen's chore list, ask whether he hung it up as soon as he emerges from a bath. If he forgot, tell him to hang it up and then call you so you can check. Praise compliance by saying, "Great! You're growing up!" If he says he'll hang up his towel later, say, "No, I promised to prepare you for independence. You'll be eighteen in just twenty-two months. You need to learn to hang up your wet towels. Do it now." When he complies, provide positive acknowledgment even if you are irritated about having to devote so much energy to this project. Always acknowledge what your teen did well or correctly before commenting about what he did wrong or left unfinished.

## Step 7: Provide Consequences

Hold to the "work before pleasure" principle. If you allow your teen to postpone a chore, insist that he first devise a plan telling when he will do it and how he will help himself to remember. Determine in advance what the consequence will be if he doesn't follow his plan. When problems arise, inform your teen that if you use all of your energy teaching self-discipline and responsibility, you won't have any left for driving him to the mall. Calmly announce that you will cancel your child's cell service so talking on the phone doesn't prevent him from handling his responsibilities, but that you will reactivate the service after he does chores consistently for a month. Should you move the TV to the attic and make the whole family suffer because your teen watches it instead of doing required chores? You bet! Everyone would sacrifice to help a handicapped sibling. Being irresponsible is a serious handicap that will have lifelong consequences!

If your child fusses and storms about having to do chores, be empathetic! There are undoubtedly times when you consider chores a pain. Don't make yourself a target of her anger by trying dictate how she feels about them. Your child needs to do chores; she doesn't need to like them.

Some teens do an about-face as soon as their parents explain the true importance of learning to manage chores. Most children require some hands-on teaching and a lot of supervision at the outset, and continued monitoring. Even parents who are sure their teen would never comply commonly see dramatic improvements in attitude and behavior after a week or two of noisy protests. The secret is to contain your personal irritation and frustration and remain a patient but firm teacher. It may help to imagine your teen as a toddler—which may in fact be much easier than imagining him as an adult! By structuring your teen's chores as you would for a tot, you really can help your teen mature.

# Index


## A

Accomplishments, hidden, 2
Accountability, 201, 208–9
Acne, 172–73
Acting out, 64. *See also* Alcohol; Anger; Drugs; Juvenile offenders
ACTs, 176, 181, 182
ADD (attention deficit disorder), 224–25
Addiction, defined, 231
Adult activities (for teens), 130–32
Adulthood, 255–66
 boomerang kids and, 259–60
 case studies, 26, 34–35, 256–57, 265–66
 emerging into, 34–35
 Job Corps alternative, 264
 leaving home and, 33–34
 living with parents, 261–62
 neglected parents and, 256
 planning for, 31–32, 41–42
 tough love and, 261–62
 visits home, 256–57
 worldly wisdom and, 257–59
Advanced placement (AP) classes, 180, 181
Affording college, 182–84
Alcohol, 230–32
 abuse defined, 231
 addiction defined, 231
 breathalyzer tests, 106–7
 case studies, 211, 239
 death from, 243
 delinquency and, 202, 203
 drinking, prevalence, 244
 driving and, 97, 101, 102, 106–7
 effects of, 231–33
 exaggerated use claims, 3
 help abstaining from, 242–43, 244
 intoxication defined, 230
 peer pressure and, 242–43, 244
 poisoning, 243
 responses to using, 246–50
 schizophrenia and, 220
 sex, pregnancy and, 233
 spiritual solutions, 250
 statistics, 231
 tests, 106–7, 243
 thoughts vs. actions and, 244–46
 thrill seeking and, 202
 urine tests, 243
 vicarious learning opportunities, 249–50
Alcoholic's Anonymous (AA), 239, 248, 249
American Camping Association, 134
American Institute for Foreign Study, 135
Amphetamines, 238. *See also* Drugs
Anger
 boys and, 56
 calming tactics, 20–21
 cause of, 19–20
 controlling, for discipline, 80
 fighting and, 210
 righting past wrongs, 23
 role models for, 21–23
 value of, 19
Anorexia. *See* Eating disorders
AP (advanced placement) classes, 180, 181
Attention deficit disorder (ADD), 224–25
Authority
 control and, 7, 74, 251–52
 of parents, 7, 8–9, 251
 rebellion against, 7, 251–52
 respect for, 206–7
 righting past wrongs, 23
 rules rationale and, 7
 *See also* Discipline
Auto insurance, 103–5, 106, 107, 109. *See also* Driving

## B

Babies. *See* Pregnancy
Bedtimes. *See* Sleep
Big Brothers/Sisters, 114
Bipolar disorder, 221–22
Blame game, 78
Bodily changes, 26–27
Body piercing, 222–23
Boomerang kids, 259–60
Boredom
 extracurricular activities and, 26, 126
 grades and, 29, 30
 junior year and, 30–32
 sophomore year and, 29
Boys
 anger management and, 56
 being boys, 201
 dads and, 60
 dating. *See* Dating
 early puberty, 89–90
 establishing identity, 10, 56–57
 first crushes, 88–89
 gaining weight, 163
 hygiene for, 172–73
 makeup for, 138, 146
 moms and, 55–57
 sexual impulses, 56
 as studs, 89–90
Breaking up, 92
Bulimia. *See* Eating disorders
Bullying, 78–79
Burnout signs, 135–36
Buying cars, 107–9

## C

Calming tactics
 anger management, 20–21
 exuberance, 16–17
Cancer self-exams, 170–71
Cars. *See* Driving
Change
 in bodies, 26–27
 of friends, 27
 resistance to, 14
 stress of, 14
 *See also* Development stages
Cheering up teens, 16–18
Chores
 easy steps for, 278–81
 money for, 155
 motivating completion of, 30, 81, 278–81
 refusing, discipline, 30, 81, 281
 supportive instruction for, 77
 teaching life skills, 42–44
 *See also* Job(s)
Church youth groups, 130
Cigarettes. *See* Tobacco
Cliques, 86
Clothing. *See* Fashion
Cocaine, 236. *See also* Drugs
College, 175–86
 affording, 182–84
 after dropping out, 263
 case study, 176, 185–86
 choosing appropriate, 184–86

College *(continued)*
credit, in high school, 180–81
diplomas/certificates, 264–65
entrance tests, 176, 181–82
extracurricular activities and, 182
financial aid, 183
honors classes for, 178–80
overview, 175
planning for, 32, 176–81
preparatory classes, 177–78
requirements, 177–78
scholarships, 181, 183
statistics, 264–65
time off before, 264
two-year, 177
vocational training and, 178, 179
Communication, 63–72
acting out vs. talking out, 64
calming exuberance, 18–19
case study, 64, 71–72
cheering up teens, 16–18
confession responses, 71–72
conversation starters, 66–67
daily talk time, 65–66
do's/don'ts, 70–71
drama responses, 67–69
electronic barriers, 65
of expectations, 74, 279
with friends, 8, 67, 70
listening skills, 69–70
reading between lines, 64
time for, 64–66
trust and, 68
weekly "date" for, 65
Community clubs/organizations, 129–32
Complaints, 28–29
Con artists, 204–5, 209
Confession responses, 71–72
Conflict resolution
anger and. *See* Anger
family conflicts, 47–48, 61
parent mediation, 46–47
teaching, 45–48
Control. *See* Authority
Conversation starters, 66–67. *See also* Communication
Cooking, 42–43
Corporal punishment, 76
Crime. *See* Juvenile offenders
Crushes, 88–89
Culture
finer aspects, 6
pop culture, 4–6
Cursing. *See* Obscenities

# D

Dads
boys and, 60
family triangles and, 54–55
girls and, 58–60
mom/daughter relationship and, 54–55, 59
respect for, 57–58
teens and, 57–61
*See also* Parents
Daily talk time, 65–66
Date rape, 233
Dating, 85–95
age limits, 91
assessing readiness, 93–94
breaking up and, 92
case study, 86–87, 95
choosing winners, 95
between cultures, 86–87, 95
dilemmas, 86–89
double dates, 91
early puberty and, 89–91
first crushes and, 88–89
flirting and, 87–88
in junior high, 89, 91
love connections, 92–93
risks, 89
sex and, 85, 89, 90–91, 92
for single parents, 196–97
stages, 91
Daughters. *See* Girls
Deception, protecting parents, 7
Defensive driving course, 102
Delinquency. *See* Juvenile offenders
Depression, 214–16
bipolar disorder, 221–22
case study, 214, 225–26
diagnosing, 29, 213, 215–16
diet and, 216
family problems and, 204
schizophrenia and, 219–21
statistics, 29, 216
suicide and, 216–18
symptoms, 215–16
treating, 29, 213, 216
Development stages, 25–35
body changes, 26–27
case study, 26, 34–35
changing interests, 26
dating and. *See* Dating
freshman year, 27–28
junior high years, 26–27
junior year, 30–32
senior year, 32–33
sophomore year, 6, 28–30
*See also* Adulthood
Diet, 162–67
depression and, 216
dieting and, 162, 163
eating disorders and, 160, 162, 164–66, 174
fast food and, 164
gaining weight and, 163
growth spurts and, 163
healthy habits, 164
obesity and, 163, 164
prepackaged food and, 164
supplements and, 166–67, 216
vitamins, minerals and, 166–67
Dietary supplements, 166–67, 216
Discipline, 73–83
adults dictating, 7
anger control before, 80
appraising strictness/lenience, 79
blaming others and, 78
bullying teens and, 78–79
case study, 74, 83
for chores, 30, 81, 281
communicating expectations, 74, 279
control and, 7, 74, 251–52
corporal punishment and, 76
creative solutions, 83
disallowing slang/obscenities, 4
driving and, 75, 100, 101, 109
examples, 79–81, 82, 83
homework motivation, 30, 75–76
individuality and, 74–76
logical consequences for, 79–81
mom-to-daughter, 53
moral problems and, 77
for poor grades, 42, 79–80
protecting teens and, 82–83
punishment and, 76–77
respect and, 81–82
for sarcasm, 82
for school tardiness, 80
for sexual activity, 246–50, 251–53
for substance abuse, 246–50, 251–53
support and, 27
supportive instruction and, 77
for swearing at parents, 81

tailored approach, 74-76
*See also* Authority
Divorce
case study, 188–89, 197–98
effect on teens, 188–89, 190–93
part-time parents after, 193–94
respecting ex after, 191–92
runaways, 192
single parenting and, 194–97
statistics, 193
Double dates, 91
Drama responses, 67–69
Dreams, 9
Driving, 97–109
accidents, 104, 105–6
alcohol and, 97, 101, 102, 106–7
as bargaining chip, 97, 101, 109
buying cars and, 107–9
carefully, 101, 109
car insurance and, 103–5, 106, 107, 109
case study, 98, 109
defensive, course, 102
denying access to, 99, 100
discipline and, 75, 100, 101, 109
driver education class, 102–3
drugs and, 97, 102
excessive caution toward, 98, 99–100
expenses, 104–9
fatalities, 104, 105, 106
freedom and, 98, 99
GDLs, 105–6
grades and, 103
irresponsibly, consequences, 100
licenses, 105–6
motorcycles, 106
practice, training, 101–2, 103
prerequisites, 100
restricted licenses, 105–6
as right of passage, 98–100
safety factors, 101–4
setting limits, 100
unrestricted licenses, 106
vehicle safety features, 102–3
youth group membership and, 103
Dropping out
case studies, 148–49, 158–59, 200, 210–11
college after, 263
Drugs
abuse defined, 230, 231
addiction, 229-30, 231
amphetamines, 238
case study, 228–30, 239
of choice, 234–35
cocaine, 236
date rape and, 233
delinquency and, 202
driving and, 97, 102
ecstasy, 237
exaggerated use claims, 3
fashion and, 139, 142
grades and, 228–29, 235
hallucinogens, 236–37
heavy hitters, 236–38
help abstaining from, 242–44
heroin, 237–38
information resource, 239
LSD, 236–37
marijuana, 233–35
from medicine cabinet, 238–39
nicknames, 233, 235, 236, 237, 238
PCP, 237
peer pressure and, 242, 253
pervasiveness of, 3
responses to using, 246–50
Rohypnol, 233
schizophrenia and, 220
sex, pregnancy and, 233
signs of use, 229
spiritual solutions, 250
statistics, 235
thoughts vs. actions and, 244–46
thrill seeking and, 202
TV influence, 11
urinalyses for, 243
vicarious learning opportunities, 249–50


# E


Eating disorders, 60, 162, 164–66, 174
Ecstasy, 237. *See also* Drugs
Education. *See* College; High school
Electronics, 65
Emotions, 13–24
basic understanding, 16
calming exuberance, 16–17
case study, 14, 23–24
divorce and, 188–89, 190–92, 193–97
gripping, 15
hormones and, 14–15
humor and, 18
junior high and, 26–27
melodramatic responses, 67–69
mom/daughter bonds and, 52, 59
mood swings, 14–15
overcoming negative, 16–18
reality of, 15
working with, 16
*See also* Anger; Depression; Mental health
Estrogen, 14
Expectations, communicating, 74, 279
Extracurricular activities, 125–36
adult activities (for teens), 130–32
benefits of, 26, 121, 126–27
boredom and, 26, 126
case study, 126, 136
choosing, 132–33
church youth groups, 130
college and, 182
community clubs/organizations, 129–32
hobbies, 9, 26, 29, 30, 136
park/rec departments, 129–30
private lessons, 132
in senior year, 32–33
sports, 127–28
in summer, 133–35
types of, 32–33, 127–29
youth clubs, 103, 130
Exuberance, 16–17


# F


Families, 49-61
activity participation, 8–9
alienation from, 4–5
boys, dads and, 60
boys, moms and, 55–57
dads, teens and, 57–61
girls, dads and, 58–60
girls, moms and, 51–55
moms, teens and, 51–57, 59
pop culture and, 4–6
problems. *See* Family problems
resolving conflicts, 47–48, 61
siblings, 9, 50–51, 61, 191
time together, 66
triangles within, 54–55
visiting relatives, 49
Family problems, 187–98
case study, 188–89, 197–98
delinquency and, 203
parental arguments, 189
post-divorce runaways, 192
professional help for, 190
single parenting, 194–97
solving, example, 197–98
*See also* Divorce
Fashion, 137–46
case study, 138, 146

Fashion (continued)
choosing battles, 139
drugs and, 139, 142
gang clothes/colors and, 144
identity issues and, 140–41, 142–44, 146
male makeup and, 138, 146
media influence, 139, 142
music and, 139, 140
offenses, 138–40
opinions, 141, 142
peer pressure and, 144–45
school uniforms, 145
separation issues and, 141–42
setting limits, 59, 144, 145–46
sexual attention with, 145
tattoos and, 138, 139, 222–23
wars, 138–40
winning war of, 140
Fathers. *See* Dads; Parents
Fighting, 210. *See also* Anger
Financial aid, 183
Financial management, 43–44
First crushes, 88–89
First Eagle insurance services, 106
Flirting, 87–88
Floaters, 86
Freedom
driving and, 98, 99
new morality and, 6–7
Freshman year, 27–28
Friends
changing, 27
communication with, 8, 67, 70
influence of, 9–10
losing, 15
parents as, 9, 40, 266
parents criticizing, 10
*See also* Peers

## G

Gangs, 2, 144, 200, 209. *See also* Juvenile offenders
GDLs (Graduated Drivers Licenses), 105–6
General Education Diploma (GED), 263
Gibran, Kahil, 61
Girls
academic slide of, 118
appreciating moms, 53-54
dads and, 58–60
dating. *See* Dating
delinquency and, 204
disciplining, 53
early puberty, 90–91
eating disorders and, 60, 162, 164–66, 174
family triangles and, 54–55
first crushes, 88–89
hygiene, 171–73
maternal bonds, 52, 59
moms and, 51–55
respecting sexuality of, 59, 60
saying "no" to sex, 92
thoughts about moms, 54
understanding, 51–53
Goals
family together time, 66
of parent mediation, 46
parents defining own, 39–41
Grades
boredom and, 29, 30
case study, 200, 210–11
diagnosing problems, 112–14
driving and, 103
honors classes and, 179
as indicators, 29-30
motivating improvement of, 39, 42, 79–80
slipping, 29–30
substance abuse and, 228–29, 235
*See also* High school; Homework motivation
Graduated Drivers Licenses (GDLs), 105–6
Growth spurts, 163
Guns
in school, 121
suicide and, 217

## H

Hallucinogens, 236–37. *See also* Drugs
Happiness, 174
Harassment, 88, 90, 121
Hazing, 28
Health, 161–74
acne and, 172–73
cancer self-exams, 170–71
case study, 162, 174
diet and. *See* Diet
happiness and, 174
hygiene and, 171–73
immune system safeguards, 173–74
immunizations and, 173
medical exams, 169–70
mental. *See* Mental health
mono symptoms, 174
safe sex myths, 170, 171, 243
scoliosis detection, 172
sexual health, 169–71
sleep and, 167–69
Heroin, 237–38. *See also* Drugs
High school, 111–23
AP classes, 180, 181
balancing work with, 148-49, 153–54
case study, 112, 122–23
college credit in, 180–81
college entrance tests, 176, 181-82
college prep classes, 177–78
conferences, 114–15
contacting teachers, 113–14
freshman year, 27–28
GEDs and, 263
grades. *See* Grades
guns in, 121
harassment, 88, 90, 121
hazing, 28
honors classes, 178-80
junior year, 30–32
meeting principal in, 28
overachievers and, 118–20
post-high school plans, 31
problems, diagnosing, 112–14
segregated classrooms, 118
selecting classes, 120
senior year, 32-33
sex education, 243–44
social problems/solutions, 120–23
sophomore year, 6, 28–30
sports, 127–28
studying shortfalls, 112–18
summer school, 133–34
tardiness discipline, 80
uniforms, 145–46
vocational training, 158–59, 178, 179
*See also* Extracurricular activities; Homework motivation
Historical perspective, xi–xii
Hobbies, 136
adjusting attitudes, 29, 30
motivating teens, 30
quitting, 26
uniting parents/teens, 9
*See also* Extracurricular activities
Home office management, 44
Home study halls, 115–17
Homework motivation
contacting teachers, 113–14
home study halls, 115–17
individual approaches, 75-76
mentors, 114

perspective for, 117–18
reverse psychology, 117–18
setting limits elsewhere, 30, 112
Homosexual play, 88
Honesty, 207–8
Honors classes, 178–80
Hormones, 14–15
Humor, 18
Hygiene, 171–73


# I


Identity
creating, 10, 56–57
delayed development, 257
fashion issues and, 140–41, 142–44, 146
separation issues and, 141–42
Immune system safeguards, 173–74
Immunizations, 173
Independence
education for, 262–65
preparing teens for, 41–42
Individuality, 74–76
Insecurity
junior high years, 26–27
saying "no" and, 6
Insomnia cures, 168
Insults, 4
Insurance, auto, 103–5, 106, 107, 109. *See also* Driving
Insurance Information Institute, 105
Interpersonal problem-solving, 44–45
Intoxication, 230. *See also* Alcohol; Drugs


# J


Job Corps, 264
Job(s), 147–59
auto-related, 157
balancing school with, 148–49, 153–54
benefits, 149–50
case study, 148–49, 158–59
connections for, 154
construction, 157
demanding employers and, 152
discrimination, 150–51
education and, 150, 152–53, 154, 262–65
first real, 149, 152–53
flexibility and, 151
future of, 151
GEDs and, 263
inexperience and, 151–52
internship programs, 156
losing, 151, 153
motivation, 154–56
negative experiences in, 152–53, 154
networking for, 154, 157–58
parents consulting on, 153–54, 157–58
reluctant teens and, 155–56
search seminars, 156
setting limits, 154
summer, 156–58
types available, 149–50, 157, 158
undue blame in, 151
vocational training for, 158–59
volunteering, 159
Journals, reading, 2
Junior high years, 26–27
dating and, 89, 91
first crushes, 88
*See also* Extracurricular activities; Grades; Homework motivation
Juvenile offenders, 199–211
accountability, 201, 208–9
alcohol and, 202, 203, 211
authority problems and, 206–7
boys being boys, 201
case study, 200, 210–11
con artists, 204–5, 209
delinquency risk factors, 201–5
drugs and, 202
family problems and, 203
fighting by, 210
gangs and, 2, 144, 200, 209
honesty and, 207–8
parent education and, 205–6
rehabilitating, 205–6, 207–11
socioeconomic status and, 205–6
sociopaths, 203–4, 205
thrill seekers, 202–3
underlying problems, 203–4


# L


Language, 4. *See also* Obscenities
Leaving home, 33–34
Lessons, 132
Letting go, case study, 38–39, 47
Life skills
cooking, 42–43
financial management, 43–44
home office management, 44
jobs providing, 154–56, 157, 158, 159
parents teaching, 42–44
Listening skills, 69–70
Love, tough, 261–62
LSD ("L"), 236–37. *See also* Drugs


# M


Makeup, on boys, 138, 146
Manic depression. *See* Bipolar disorder
Marijuana, 233–35. *See also* Drugs
Media
fashion and, 139, 142
influence of, 5–6
music influence, 139
*See also* Television
Mediating conflicts, 46–47
Medicine cabinet drugs, 238–39
Melodrama responses, 67–69
Mental health issues, 213–26
ADD, 224–25
bipolar disorder, 221–22
case study, 214, 225–26
depression. *See* Depression
schizophrenia, 219–21
self-mutilation, 222–23
suicide, 216–18
Mentors, 114
Midlife crisis, 39
Minerals, 166–67
Moms
boys and, 55–57
family triangles and, 54–55
girls and, 51–55, 59
respect for, 58
*See also* Parents
Mono symptoms, 174
Morality, new concepts, 6–7
Moral problems, 77
Mothering vs. smothering, 41
Mothers. *See* Moms; Parents
Motorcycles, 106
Music influence, 139


# N, O


Narcotic's Anonymous, 239, 249
Nicotine, 232

Obesity, 163, 164
Obscenities
case study, 2–3, 10–11
common use, 4
dealing with, 4, 10–11
disallowing at home, 4
disciplining for, 81

Obscenities *(continued)*
toward parents, 81
unexpected use, 2–3, 10–11
Overachievers, 118–20

**P**

Parents, 37–48
arguments between, 189
authority of, 7, 8–9, 251
bullying teens, 78–79
defining goals, 39–41
divided loyalty to, 8–9
divorced. *See* Divorce
family activities and, 8–9
as friends, 9, 40, 266
as job consultants, 153–54, 157–58
letting go case study, 38–39, 47
life skills from, 42–44
as mediators, 46–47
midlife crises of, 39
mothering vs. smothering, 41
neglected, 256
overreacting, 39
part-time, 193–94
preparing teen independence, 41–42
resolving family conflicts, 47–48, 61
as role models, 21–24, 39, 42–48
separation issues, 141–42
single parenting, 194–97
teaching conflict resolution, 45–48
teaching interpersonal problem-solving, 44–45
tough love, 261–62
*See also* Dads; Moms
Park/recreation activities, 129–30
PCP, 237. *See also* Drugs
Peers
academic performance and, 112–13
alcohol use and, 242–43, 244
drug use and, 242, 253
fashion and, 144–45
friendship importance, 9–10
power/influence of, 8–10
respecting saying "no", 6
sex and, 3, 242, 253
teen identity and, 10
withstanding pressure from, x, 242–44
Pop culture
alienating families, 4–5
influence of, 4–6
power of, 5
Post-divorce runaways, 192
Practice Scholastic Achievement Test (PSAT), 181
Pregnancy
alcohol, drugs and, 233, 243–44
babies, meaning and, 31
birth-control myths, 243
Privacy, 2
Private lessons, 132
Problem-solving, 44–45
Professional help
for bipolar disorder, 222
for depression, 216
for family problems, 190
local organizations, 249–50
for schizophrenia, 220–21
for self-destructive tendencies, 33
for substance abuse, 227
for vicarious learning, 249–50
Protecting teens, 82–83
PSAT (Practice Scholastic Achievement Test), 181
Punishment, 76–77. *See also* Authority; Discipline

**R**

Rebels, 210, 251–52. *See also* Authority; Discipline
Relationships
dads/daughters, 58–60
dads/sons, 60
junior high years, 27
moms/daughters, 51–55
moms/sons, 55–57
*See also* Dating
Relatives, visiting, 49
Resources
local organizations, 249–50
for parents, 268–71
for teens, 272–75
Web sites. *See* Web sites
Respect, 81–82
adults, discipline and, 7
for authority, 206–7
for dads, 57–58
for divorced parents, 191–92
for sexuality, 59, 60
for wife, 58
words vs. action and, 58
Rights of passage, 98–100
Ritalin, 238
Rohypnol, 233
Role models
for anger management, 21–23
for conflict resolution, 45–48
for interpersonal problem-solving, 45–48
for life skills, 42–44
parents as, 21–24, 39, 42–48
Rules
ignoring, 73
reasons for, 7
*See also* Authority; Discipline
Runaways, 192

**S**

Sarcasm, 4, 51, 53, 64, 82
SAT (Scholastic Achievement Test), 176, 181
Schizophrenia, 219–21
alcohol, drugs and, 220
recognizing, 219–20
statistics, 219
symptoms, 219
treating, 220–21
Scholarships, 181, 183
Scholastic Achievement Test (SAT), 176, 181
School. *See* College; Extracurricular activities; High school; Homework motivation
Scoliosis, 172
Secret lives, 2–3
Self-mutilation, 222–23
Senior year, 32–33
Separation issues, 141–42
Sex
abstaining from, 92, 243–44
case study, 242, 253
counseling, 89
dating and, 85, 89, 90–91, 92
education, 243–44
girls, dads and, 58–59
homosexual play, 88
love connections and, 92–93
new morality and, 3, 6–7
peer pressure and, 3, 242, 253
pregnancy and. *See* Pregnancy
public displays and, 3
reputations and, 90
responses to having, 246–50
risks, 89, 92
safe sex myths, 170, 171, 243
setting limits, 89
spiritual solutions, 250
thoughts vs. actions and, 244–46
TV influence, 5, 11

vicarious learning opportunities, 249–50
virginity and, 3, 242, 253
Sexual abuse, 89
Sexual health, 169–71
cancer self-exams, 170–71
medical exams, 169–70
safe sex myths, 170, 171, 243
STDs, 170, 171
Sexuality
adolescent boys and, 27, 56
clothing selection and, 145
respect for, 59, 60
sexual abuse and, 89
Sexually transmitted diseases (STDs), 170, 171
Sexual orientation, 88, 146
Sibling(s)
divorce uniting, 191
relationships, 50–51
rivalries, 9, 50, 51, 61
Single parenting, 194–97
dating and, 196–97
outside involvements, 195–96
teen challenges, 195
Slang, 4
Sleep, 167–69
controlling bedtimes, 169
depression and, 215
insomnia cures, 168
recommended amount, 168
Social problems
conflict resolution, 45–48
interpersonal problem-solving, 44–45
at school, 120–23
*See also* Juvenile offenders
Socioeconomic status, 205–6
Sons. *See* Boys
Sophomore year, 6, 28–30
boredom, 29
complaining, 28–29
dangers, 29–30
depression, 29
Spiritual solutions, 250
Sports, 127–28
Stages. *See* Development stages
Stress
burnout signs, 135–36
calming, 20–21, 51
change as, 14
mood swings, 14–15
Studying. *See* High school; Homework motivation
Substance abuse
addiction signs, 229–30
case studies, 228–30, 239, 253
definitions, 230–31
grades and, 228–29, 235
professional help, 227
responses to, 246–50
signs of, 229
spiritual solutions, 250
tobacco, nicotine, 3, 228, 232
use, addiction and, 230–32
vicarious learning opportunities, 249–50
*See also* Alcohol; Drugs
Suicide, 216–18
case study, 214, 225–26
following others, 218
guns and, 217
preventing, 218
statistics, 217
warning signs, 217–18
Summer school, 133–34
Summertime activities, 133–35
jobs, 156–58
learning camps, 134–35
summer school, 133–34
Support
for decisions, 34
discipline and, 27, 77
Swearing. *See* Obscenities

## T, V

Tattoos, 138, 139, 222–23
Television
as communication barrier, 65
influence of, 5, 10–11, 56, 139
prohibiting, 11
sex and, 5, 11
violence, 5, 139
Thinking process, 244–46
Thrill seekers, 202–3
Tobacco, 3, 228, 232
Tough love, 261–62
Travel
studying abroad, 135
visiting relatives, 49
Trust
breaking, 2
communication and, 68
Two-year colleges, 177
Violence, on TV, 5, 139
Virginity, 3, 242, 253
Vitamins, 166–67
Vocational training, 158–59, 178, 179
Volunteering, 159

## W–Y

Web sites
cancer information, 171
college entrance tests, 181
college selection, 185
college statistics, 264
driving/car insurance, 105, 106
drug use information, 239
financial aid, 183
GED information, 263
immunizations, 173
mentoring programs, 114
summer learning camps, 134, 135
volunteering, 159
*See also* Resources
Weekly talking "date", 65
Weight
eating disorders and, 60, 162, 164–66, 174
gaining, 163
watching, 162, 163
*See also* Diet
Wildness, responses to, 246–50
Work. *See* Job(s)

Youth group membership, 103, 130.
*See also* Extracurricular activities

# THE EVERYTHING® SERIES!

## BUSINESS

Everything® **Business Planning Book**
Everything® **Coaching and Mentoring Book**
Everything® **Fundraising Book**
Everything® **Home-Based Business Book**
Everything® **Leadership Book**
Everything® **Managing People Book**
Everything® **Network Marketing Book**
Everything® **Online Business Book**
Everything® **Project Management Book**
Everything® **Selling Book**
Everything® **Start Your Own Business Book**
Everything® **Time Management Book**

## COMPUTERS

Everything® **Build Your Own Home Page Book**
Everything® **Computer Book**
Everything® **Internet Book**
Everything® **Microsoft® Word 2000 Book**

## COOKBOOKS

Everything® **Barbecue Cookbook**
Everything® **Bartender's Book, $9.95**
Everything® **Chinese Cookbook**
Everything® **Chocolate Cookbook**
Everything® **Cookbook**
Everything® **Dessert Cookbook**
Everything® **Diabetes Cookbook**
Everything® **Indian Cookbook**
Everything® **Low-Carb Cookbook**
Everything® **Low-Fat High-Flavor Cookbook**
Everything® **Low-Salt Cookbook**
Everything® **Mediterranean Cookbook**
Everything® **Mexican Cookbook**
Everything® **One-Pot Cookbook**
Everything® **Pasta Book**
Everything® **Quick Meals Cookbook**
Everything® **Slow Cooker Cookbook**
Everything® **Soup Cookbook**
Everything® **Thai Cookbook**
Everything® **Vegetarian Cookbook**
Everything® **Wine Book**

## HEALTH

Everything® **Alzheimer's Book**
Everything® **Anti-Aging Book**
Everything® **Diabetes Book**
Everything® **Dieting Book**
Everything® **Herbal Remedies Book**
Everything® **Hypnosis Book**
Everything® **Massage Book**
Everything® **Menopause Book**
Everything® **Nutrition Book**
Everything® **Reflexology Book**
Everything® **Reiki Book**
Everything® **Stress Management Book**
Everything® **Vitamins, Minerals, and Nutritional Supplements Book**

## HISTORY

Everything® **American Government Book**
Everything® **American History Book**
Everything® **Civil War Book**
Everything® **Irish History & Heritage Book**
Everything® **Mafia Book**
Everything® **Middle East Book**
Everything® **World War II Book**

## HOBBIES & GAMES

Everything® **Bridge Book**
Everything® **Candlemaking Book**
Everything® **Casino Gambling Book**
Everything® **Chess Basics Book**
Everything® **Collectibles Book**
Everything® **Crossword and Puzzle Book**
Everything® **Digital Photography Book**
Everything® **Easy Crosswords Book**
Everything® **Family Tree Book**
Everything® **Games Book**
Everything® **Knitting Book**
Everything® **Magic Book**
Everything® **Motorcycle Book**
Everything® **Online Genealogy Book**
Everything® **Photography Book**
Everything® **Pool & Billiards Book**
Everything® **Quilting Book**
Everything® **Scrapbooking Book**
Everything® **Sewing Book**
Everything® **Soapmaking Book**

## HOME IMPROVEMENT

Everything® **Feng Shui Book**
Everything® **Feng Shui Decluttering Book, $9.95 ($15.95 CAN)**
Everything® **Fix-It Book**
Everything® **Gardening Book**
Everything® **Homebuilding Book**

All Everything® books are priced at $12.95 or $14.95, unless otherwise stated. Prices subject to change without notice.
Canadian prices range from $11.95–$31.95, and are subject to change without notice.

Everything® **Home Decorating Book**
Everything® **Landscaping Book**
Everything® **Lawn Care Book**
Everything® **Organize Your Home Book**

## *EVERYTHING® KIDS'* BOOKS

All titles are $6.95

Everything® **Kids' Baseball Book, 3rd Ed.** **($10.95 CAN)**
Everything® **Kids' Bible Trivia Book** **($10.95 CAN)**
Everything® **Kids' Bugs Book** **($10.95 CAN)**
Everything® **Kids' Christmas Puzzle & Activity Book** **($10.95 CAN)**
Everything® **Kids' Cookbook** **($10.95 CAN)**
Everything® **Kids' Halloween Puzzle & Activity Book** **($10.95 CAN)**
Everything® **Kids' Joke Book** **($10.95 CAN)**
Everything® **Kids' Math Puzzles Book** **($10.95 CAN)**
Everything® **Kids' Mazes Book** **($10.95 CAN)**
Everything® **Kids' Money Book** **($11.95 CAN)**
Everything® **Kids' Monsters Book** **($10.95 CAN)**
Everything® **Kids' Nature Book** **($11.95 CAN)**
Everything® **Kids' Puzzle Book** **($10.95 CAN)**
Everything® **Kids' Riddles & Brain Teasers Book** **($10.95 CAN)**
Everything® **Kids' Science Experiments Book** **($10.95 CAN)**
Everything® **Kids' Soccer Book** **($10.95 CAN)**
Everything® **Kids' Travel Activity Book** **($10.95 CAN)**

## KIDS' STORY BOOKS

Everything® **Bedtime Story Book**
Everything® **Bible Stories Book**
Everything® **Fairy Tales Book**
Everything® **Mother Goose Book**

## LANGUAGE

Everything® **Inglés Book**
Everything® **Learning French Book**
Everything® **Learning German Book**
Everything® **Learning Italian Book**
Everything® **Learning Latin Book**
Everything® **Learning Spanish Book**
Everything® **Sign Language Book**
Everything® **Spanish Phrase Book, $9.95 ($15.95 CAN)**

## MUSIC

Everything® **Drums Book (with CD), $19.95 ($31.95 CAN)**
Everything® **Guitar Book**
Everything® **Playing Piano and Keyboards Book**
Everything® **Rock & Blues Guitar Book (with CD), $19.95 ($31.95 CAN)**
Everything® **Songwriting Book**

## NEW AGE

Everything® **Astrology Book**
Everything® **Divining the Future Book**
Everything® **Dreams Book**
Everything® **Ghost Book**
Everything® **Love Signs Book, $9.95 ($15.95 CAN)**
Everything® **Meditation Book**
Everything® **Numerology Book**
Everything® **Palmistry Book**
Everything® **Psychic Book**
Everything® **Spells & Charms Book**
Everything® **Tarot Book**
Everything® **Wicca and Witchcraft Book**

## PARENTING

Everything® **Baby Names Book**
Everything® **Baby Shower Book**
Everything® **Baby's First Food Book**
Everything® **Baby's First Year Book**
Everything® **Breastfeeding Book**
Everything® **Father-to-Be Book**
Everything® **Get Ready for Baby Book**
Everything® **Getting Pregnant Book**
Everything® **Homeschooling Book**
Everything® **Parent's Guide to Children with Autism**
Everything® **Parent's Guide to Positive Discipline**
Everything® **Parent's Guide to Raising a Successful Child**
Everything® **Parenting a Teenager Book**
Everything® **Potty Training Book, $9.95 ($15.95 CAN)**
Everything® **Pregnancy Book, 2nd Ed.**
Everything® **Pregnancy Fitness Book**
Everything® **Pregnancy Organizer, $15.00 ($22.95 CAN)**
Everything® **Toddler Book**
Everything® **Tween Book**

## PERSONAL FINANCE

Everything® **Budgeting Book**
Everything® **Get Out of Debt Book**
Everything® **Get Rich Book**
Everything® **Homebuying Book, 2nd Ed.**
Everything® **Homeselling Book**
Everything® **Investing Book**
Everything® **Money Book**
Everything® **Mutual Funds Book**
Everything® **Online Investing Book**
Everything® **Personal Finance Book**
Everything® **Personal Finance in Your 20s & 30s Book**
Everything® **Wills & Estate Planning Book**

## PETS

Everything® **Cat Book**
Everything® **Dog Book**
Everything® **Dog Training and Tricks Book**
Everything® **Golden Retriever Book**
Everything® **Horse Book**
Everything® **Labrador Retriever Book**
Everything® **Puppy Book**
Everything® **Tropical Fish Book**

All Everything® books are priced at $12.95 or $14.95, unless otherwise stated. Prices subject to change without notice.
Canadian prices range from $11.95–$31.95, and are subject to change without notice.